971.00497 B157
Baillargeon, Morgan.
Legends of our times

ᴺᴮ
5-99
38.95

MID-CONTINENT PUBLIC LIBRARY

North Independence Branch
Highway 24 & Spring
Independence, MO 64050

NI

WITHDRAWN
FROM THE RECORDS OF THE
MID-CONTINENT PUBLIC LIBRARY

D1285971

LEGENDS OF OUR TIMES

Morgan Baillargeon and Leslie Tepper

LEGENDS OF OUR TIMES: NATIVE COWBOY LIFE

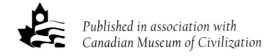

Published in association with
Canadian Museum of Civilization

UBC PRESS / VANCOUVER

UNIVERSITY OF WASHINGTON PRESS / SEATTLE

MID-CONTINENT PUBLIC LIBRARY

North Independence Branch
Highway 24 & Spring
Independence, MO 64050

NI

MID-CONTINENT PUBLIC LIBRARY

3 0001 00460093 0

© Canadian Museum of Civilization 1998

All rights reserved. No part of this publication may be reproduced, stored in a retrieval system, or transmitted, in any form or
by any means, without prior written permission of the publisher,
or, in Canada, in the case of photocopying or other reprographic
copying, a licence from CANCOPY (Canadian Copyright Licensing
Agency), 900-6 Adelaide Street East, Toronto, ON M5C 1H6.

Printed in Canada on acid-free paper

ISBN 0-7748-0656-7 (bound)
ISBN 0-7748-0657-5 (paperback)

Canadian Cataloguing in Publication Data

Main entry under title:

Legends of our times

    Includes bibliographical references and index.
    Published in association with: Canadian Museum of Civilization
    ISBN 0-7748-0656-7 (bound); ISBN 0-7748-0657-5 (pbk.)

    1. Native peoples – Prairie Provinces – Folklore. 2. Indians of
North America – Great Plains – Folklore. 3. Indian cowboys –
Literary collections. 4. Rodeos – Literary collections. 5. Ranch
life – Literary collections. I. Baillargeon, Morgan, 1956- II. Tepper,
Leslie Heyman, 1947- III. Canadian Museum of Civilization.

E78.C2L43 1998   971.2'00497   c98-910122-3

UBC Press gratefully acknowledges the ongoing support to its
publishing program from the Canada Council for the Arts, the
British Columbia Arts Council, and the Department of Canadian
Heritage of the Government of Canada.

Set in Californian and Foundry Sans
Printed and bound in Canada by Friesens
Canadian Museum of Civilization co-ordinator: Anne Malépart
Cartographer: Eric Leinberger
Designer: George Vaitkunas
Editor: Camilla Jenkins
Indexer: Annette Lorek
Proofreader: Gail Copeland

UBC Press
University of British Columbia
6344 Memorial Road
Vancouver, BC V6T 1Z2
(604) 822-5959
Fax: 1-800-668-0821
E-mail: orders@ubcpress.ubc.ca
http://www.ubcpress.ubc.ca

Published in Canada by UBC Press and in the United States by
the University of Washington Press.

Library of Congress Cataloging-in-Publication Data

Tepper, Leslie Heyman. 1947-
    Legends of our times : native cowboy life / Morgan Baillargeon
and Leslie Tepper.
       p. cm.
    Includes bibliographical references and index.
    ISBN 0-295-97728-0 (alk. paper)
    1. Indian cowboys – Prairie Provinces – History. 2. Indian cow-
boys – Great Plains – History. 3. Ranches – Prairie Provinces –
History. 4. Ranches – Great Plains – History. 5. Rodeos – Prairie
Provinces – History. 6. Rodeos – Great Plains – History. 7. Prairie
Provinces – Social life and customs. 8. Great Plains –Social life
and customs.
I. Baillargeon, Morgan. II. Title.
E78.P7T46 1998
971.2 – dc21   98-3001
                                              CIP

University of Washington Press
P.O. Box 50096
Seattle, WA 98145

This book is dedicated to the Native cowboys and cowgirls of the Plains and Plateau.

CONTENTS

PREFACE

This book is based on research for the Canadian Museum of Civilization exhibition *Legends of Our Times: Native Ranching and Rodeo Life on the Plains and Plateau.* Museum exhibitions can take a surprisingly large portion of a curator's working lifetime, and this one has been no exception. From its conception in 1992 to the exhibition opening and book publication in 1998, and beyond to the development of a travelling show in 2000, this project will be almost a decade in the making.

Along the way the curators have been fortunate to have had extraordinary support. The themes, content, and presentation have been shaped by the Native ranchers and rodeo participants whose story is being told. The idea for the exhibition itself came from a discussion between Morgan Baillargeon and ten Native cowboys from Hobbema, Alberta, in 1992. A consultative team of Charlie Bear, Caen Bly, Carol Gottfriedson, Fred Heathershaw, Dutch Lunak, and Tyrone Potts met the curators to begin to define the key themes and to suggest sources of information and support. Over the next few years some of these committee members left the project, while new members were added. Mike Bruised Head, Fred Holmes, Pat and Jenny Provost, Marlowe Kenny, and Charles and the late Verna Heathershaw not only brought their personal experiences to the discussion but also shared cultural perspectives from their diverse communities. As the project moved to the design stage new voices were added to the committee: David Pratt, Nathan Spinks, Stan and Tracey Waddell, Marvin Yellowbird, Martin Cross, Phil Baird, and Pete Standing Alone.

Not all contributors were able to come to the meetings. Barb Stewart, Mandy Jimmie, Rose Alexis, Mandy Brown, George Saddleman, Art Adolph, Dan Gravel, Caroline Basil, Phil Baird, the late Cecil Currie, Dan Old Elk, Gordon Raine, the late Brian Pratt, and many others 'spread the word' in their communities and arranged introductions to ranching and rodeo families. Over 300 people talked with the curators in their homes, at rodeos, at poetry gatherings, in cultural centres, at ceremonial gatherings, at Indian Days celebrations, and in band offices. They offered to lend personal memorabilia and family photograph collections and allowed us to videotape interviews with them. Many of their comments and stories appear in *Legends of Our Times* and in the exhibition. Lack of space prevents the publication of all the special contributions of these people. The curators wish to thank everyone who shared with us their insights, family history, and daily life. To the storytellers, essayists, and poets who have contributed to this volume, it's been a pleasure. Thank you.

A number of individuals from other cultural centres and museums joined forces with the project. Three institutions prepared material that will be shown as part of the museum exhibition. The Lakota of Wood Mountain Saskatchewan told of their arrival in Canada with Chief Sitting Bull and their transformation into a modern ranching and rodeo community. An essay based on their research is included in the book. The Three Affiliated Tribes Museum from Fort Berthold, North Dakota, told of the destructive impact that the Garrison Dam Project had on the Nuptadi/Nueta (Mandan), Hidatsa, and Sahnish (Arikara) community's ranching economy. We would like to thank Leonard Lethbridge, Mary Lethbridge, and Leonard Lethbridge Jr, Harold and Betty Thomson, Thelma Poirier, Gail Baker, Rose Marie Mandan, Marilyn and Kent Hudson, Phyllis Old Dog Cross, Tilly Walker, Martin Cross, and Emerson Chase. Madeleine Gregoire from the En'owkin Centre, Penticton, BC, and Gloria Trahan and Verna Lefthand from the People's Center in Pablo, Montana, provided input from the Okanagan and Kutenai-Salish communities respectively. The En'owkin Centre also lent material to the museum exhibition. All these people contributed to the ideas and concepts that developed into this book.

We would also like to thank our colleagues in other museums, archives and photographic collections who allowed us to work in their artifact and photographic collections. With their help we have compiled a rich resource of historical and contemporary images and a working knowledge of objects comparable to those in the Canadian Museum of Civilization collection. Our thanks go the staff of the American Museum of Natural History, the Buffalo Bill Historical Center, the Cheney Cowles Museum, the Cowboy Hall of Fame, the Glenbow Museum, the Royal British Columbia Museum, the O'Keefe Ranch and Interior Heritage Society, the Appaloosa Horse Museum, the Okanogan Historical Society, the Penticton Museum, the Idaho, North Dakota, and Montana State Archives, the St Albert Museum, the National Archives of Canada, the British Columbia Provincial Archives and Record Service, the Fort Benton Museum, the Omak Stampede Archives, the Medicine Hat Museum, the Carbon County Museum, the Calgary Stampede Board, and the Nicola Valley Museum and Archives.

A number of students and volunteers have donated hours of their time to transcribe tapes, catalogue information, and make photocopies. We are grateful to Lawson Greenberg, Marie Garbutt, Libby Kirby, Marcia Mordfield, Gwyneth Parry, Miranda Holbrook, Dan Rutherford, James Poulson, Sharon Brodo-Smith, Nadine Belize, Melanie Takahski, Vanessa Goggin, Robin Rockwell, Tasha Kravchenko, Brock Rochus, Emily Eacertt, Ed Walter, Tracy Prentice, Nancy Coleman, Cameron Patterson, and Chris Barr. We would like to thank Constables Jeff Ellis, Joann Sokolowski, Dennis Fraser, and Greg Peters and Corporals Bruce Willans and Jerry McCarty from the RCMP for their time and assistance.

We would like to thank our colleagues at the Canadian Museum of Civilization who have supported this project over its long life: from the Exhibition

Division, designer Amber Walpole and coordinator Hélène Arsenault-Désfossés; from Collections Management, Kelly Cameron, Ann Rae, and Marilyn Boyd; from the Native Student Intern Program, Clara Wildcat; from Photo Archives, Margery Toner and Greg Money; from the Audio-Visual Department, Dennis Fletcher; from the Publishing Group, Anne Malépart. We would also like to express our appreciation to the many members of the Conservation Department and Design and Technical Services. A special thanks to our division chief, Andrea Laforet, for her support.

The authors would also like to thank the staff at UBC Press and in particular the editor, Camilla Jenkins, and the designer, George Vaitkunas, for seeing this book through to production and for being so generous and supportive.

As well we wish to thank friends and family who have been of tremendous support during this project. Morgan Baillargeon would like to thank Larry Hodgeson, from the Ermineskin Reserve, for a great year at the Panee Memorial Agri-plex, Racetrack and Rodeo Facility back in 1980. The fond memories of that year inspired the creation of *Legends of Our Times* – both the exhibition and the book. Thanks for the help in getting this project off the ground in 1992. To Victor and Rema Buffalo from Samson Reserve, thank you for help and support, encouragement, food and lodging, and care over the past twenty years. To Pete Standing Alone from Stand Off, for your support, prayers, and friendship over the past six years and to you and Betty Bastien for taking the time to read the drafts of this manuscript to make sure I wasn't crossing the line by revealing things that should not be said, thank you. Thank you to Madeleine Dion Stout and family from Ottawa for your encouragement and home-cooked meals. To Denise and Tyrone Potts from Brocket I give thanks for your support, great BBQs, and for being such good friends. To the staff of Circle R, thanks for your help. I wish to give a special thank you to my family, Rose, Leo, Greg, Annette, and Mary Anne, for being there, and for understanding why I was not able to make it home for every holiday and celebration over the past six years. And finally, to 'the People' of the northern Plains, who so graciously shared your homes and great food, your tragedies and triumphs, and the many hours of laughter, thank you!

Leslie Tepper would like to thank the many people on the Plateau and Plains who welcomed her into their homes and gave their support to this project. Over the years, they shared their memories, their ideas about what was important, what needed to be shown, and how to show it. This has been an exciting project, one that has opened new worlds and new friendships. I am grateful to my family for their support.

The years invested in *Legends of Our Times* have been a pleasure. We hope that the final product is reflective of the great ranching and rodeo individuals and families we have met and who have contributed so generously to this project.

LEGENDS OF OUR TIMES

Native Cowboy Life

In the spring of 1992, a Western store in downtown Ottawa was asked if it would be interested in sponsoring an exhibition showing the involvement of Native people in ranching, rodeo, and related industries. The response was one of puzzlement and a question: 'Well, couldn't you do an exhibit on real cowboys? ... I mean if they're Indians, they can't be cowboys.'

Legends of Our Times began with two clear goals. The first was to help break the stereotype of 'the Indian versus the cowboy' and through remaking that image to bring to people's attention an entire field of western history and Native culture that remains largely unknown. The second was to acknowledge the contributions Native people have made to the ranching and rodeo industry. As the work progressed, the authors were frequently asked what makes Native cowboys and their rodeos different from their non-Native counterparts. This volume tries to answer that question through the words and artistry of Native people themselves.

The stories, local history, art, artifacts, and poetry offered in the following pages reflect how Aboriginal people have combined two cultures – that of the cowboy and that of the Native peoples of the North American Plains and Plateau. Cowboy culture, which includes women ranchers and 'cowgirls,' involves working on the land, working with animals, and having a freedom of choice and action rarely found in other forms of employment. As a group, cowboys have a characteristic apparel of boots and hats, jeans, chinks and chaps developed from the clothing of the Spanish *vaqueros* some 500 years ago. The tools of their trade – ropes, horse gear, and clothing – are distinctive. Working cowboys also share a common body of knowledge about horses and cattle, livestock markets and hay prices, and a set of expectations about themselves, their work, and how to get things done. For Native cowboys throughout the Americas their traditional beliefs, practices, and especially their history impart an additional dimension to cowboy culture. For many there exists a special relationship with the animals with which they work.

For thousands of years the Indigenous people of North America have lived in close relation to the natural and supernatural beings who occupy the sky, earth, and underworld. These beings shared their knowledge with humans, teaching them a means of livelihood, the proper respect for oneself and for the spirit world, and the ceremonies needed to sustain present and

Running Rabbit Robe, shown here in 1909, lived in the South Camp on the Siksika Reserve in Alberta, where he worked as a cowboy.

2

future generations. The story of ranching and rodeo life on the northern Plains and Plateau of North America begins with such natural and supernatural beings, especially the buffalo and the horse. Species of buffalo have occupied North American grasslands and forests for thousands of years. Daily life and seasonal activities in many Native cultures revolved around the buffalo and its yearly migrations. Skeletal remains of a miniature horse dating back some 26,000 years suggests that this animal also once roamed the North American continent and then died out. While Native stories recount the arrival of the horse from the sky or from the water, historians record its reintroduction almost 500 years ago, when the Spanish brought it to the Americas. Thus began a very special relationship between Native people and the horse. Used for transportation, in hunting, and in warfare, the horse was quickly incorporated into the social, spiritual, and economic life of Aboriginal people on the Plains and Plateau.

These two animal figures loom largest in the conventional concept of traditional Native life. Early explorers and missionaries wrote stories or drew pictures portraying the dangerous buffalo hunts. Some images showed men and women on horseback racing alongside the stampeding buffalo; others recorded winter scenes of hunters on snowshoes stalking small herds. The accounts also told of hunters driving herds of buffalo into stone or wooden corrals or over cliffs, where men waited with their bows and arrows while women waited to prepare the meat, hide, and bones. The drawings also showed horses beautifully decorated with quilled or beaded saddles, halters, blankets, and saddlebags. European observers wrote of the skill of the riders, both men and women. Clothing, tipis, containers, hunting equipment, and ceremonial objects were decorated with marvellous images of horses or buffalo. The quality of the craftsmanship reflected the respect and honour accorded these animals.

The role of the deer, coyote, and dog as creators and sustainers of the Native world is less generally known, yet these physically smaller beings were also central to everyday life and religious beliefs. For Plateau and some Plains communities Coyote, as trickster and transformer, created certain aspects of the physical landscape and of animal behaviour. The deer was the northern Plateau equivalent to the buffalo that roamed the more distant prairies. It, too, was herded into corrals and fenced enclosures or hunted on snowshoes and on horseback. The dog was important as a pack animal and as a symbol of wealth, and was used as payment for membership in societies and for the transfer of medicine bundles – which included songs, paintings, and sacred objects. Like the coyote, the dog was also a supernatural being, often acting as an intermediary with the spirit world to heal the sick. Its usefulness in carrying burdens and as a unit of payment was diminished with the arrival of the horse. Still, the dog continued to play a central role as hunting companion, guardian of the home, and loyal friend.

Buffalo Hunt on Snowshoes,
46.9 x 61.6 cm, hand-coloured
lithograph, by George Catlin
(1796-1872). Hunting buffalo on
the Plains on snowshoes was a
dangerous yet effective way of
acquiring meat in the winter when
the snow was too deep for hunting
either on foot or on horseback.

These animals – horse, dog, coyote, buffalo, and deer – intersected with every element of daily life and religious belief. They were admired for their strength, grace, and loyalty. They offered their bodies as food, clothing, and tools. They appeared in people's dreams and visions and were the focus of rituals. Their images appeared in paint, quillwork, and beadwork to decorate secular objects as well as items reserved for ceremony.

The relationship between the people and these special beings was altered forever by the rapid occupation of the North American West by European settlers. The arrival of the fur traders created a new market for meat, hides, and horses. Buffalo and deer were extensively hunted and the meat dried and stored to feed fur traders during the long winter months. Métis communities became involved in following the buffalo migrations, with major hunts taking place twice a year. The meat, hides, and tallow were then prepared for sale to fur trading posts. The Métis were also among the first ranchers in the western United States and Canada, raising the oxen needed to pull carts up and down the Red River trading routes. Other Native communities adapted their knowledge of running buffalo and deer herds into pounds to the driving and pasturing of cattle brought to the West by the fur trade companies. Their expertise with horse breeding and training was already well established before Europeans arrived. The fur brigades and later Canadian and American cavalry troops provided new markets for breeding and selling horses.

By the late nineteenth century Aboriginal people in the western United States and Canada had been forced onto reserve lands. The disappearance of the huge herds of buffalo and decline in the number of other large animals such as deer, elk, moose, and antelope removed traditional sources of food and clothing. Restricted access to extensive tracts of grazing land forced the reduction of their large herds of horses. Under pressure to adopt new ways of living, some Native people established their own ranches and farms, hoping that their new communities would become self-sufficient. European ranchers began to employ as cowboys the local Aboriginal men who had the knowledge, experience, and skill to breed horses and drive herds of cattle. Aboriginal women often became camp cooks, and children helped where they could with daily chores and at branding and haying season. A new economy of wage labour and small farming emerged.

From this history of frontier settlement came new forms of entertainment and sport. In the early 1880s, American impresario Buffalo Bill Cody and other entrepreneurs recognized that the ways of the old West were quickly vanishing. East of the prairies few Americans and Canadians knew about the great buffalo hunts, the culture of the Plains and Plateau people, or the unique way of life on the frontier. These showmen devised circuses and exhibitions to educate easterners and new immigrants to the West about frontier history – to show and preserve the 'Wild West.' Cowboys, ex-military men, and Aboriginal people found employment as actors and

At times there were several hundred carts to the Métis brigades that transported buffalo hides to the fur trade forts. Women often accompanied the brigades to assist with the work. As many Métis hunters were still nomadic and seminomadic, the entire family might follow a brigade.

stunt performers. Among the acts were demonstrations of trick roping, fancy riding, and the type of friendly competitions that cowboys enjoyed at the end of long round-ups or cattle drives. Wild West shows were the first time that bronc riding and roping events had been brought into a public arena. They sometimes also included mock battle scenes and Native religious ceremonies – ironically, often the same ones that missionaries and government agents were trying to prohibit.

Today Plains and Plateau people proudly continue a long tradition of 'cowboying.' As ranchers, stock contractors, and rodeo participants, they maintain the unique relationship that their ancestors had with horses. As entrepreneurs, artisans, poets, and artists, they contribute to the richness of North American economic and cultural life. As entertainers and athletes on the rodeo circuit, they provide enjoyment for millions.

The initial concept for this book was to include all Native ranching and rodeo communities in Canada and the United States. The surprisingly large number of communities involved, however, required limiting the study to only the northern Plains and Plateau. Even within this narrowed field, space has allowed the inclusion of just fifteen of the thirty-two Plains and five of the nineteen Plateau cultures. Thus it must be considered not as a definitive study of Native ranching and rodeo history but as a starting point for the exploration and expression of a complex and fascinating aspect of North American cultural history.

The ranchers and rodeo people whose history and lives are presented here live in the northwestern United States and west-central and southwestern Canada. In today's geographical boundaries the area includes central and southern Alberta, Saskatchewan, Manitoba, and southwestern British Columbia within Canada, and western Minnesota, North and South Dakota, Nebraska, Montana, Wyoming, Idaho, Oregon, and Washington within the United States. These provinces and states occupy the area called the northern Plains and Plateau. To give a rigid geographical definition of the Plains is difficult. The area loosely includes the land between the Mississippi River and the Rocky Mountains. The boreal forest of north-central Alberta, Saskatchewan, and Manitoba forms a northern boundary, and the southern boundary extends down into central Texas. Places such as the Sand Hills of southwestern Saskatchewan, the Cypress Hills in southern Saskatchewan and Alberta, the Badlands of Alberta and South Dakota, the Black Hills of South Dakota, and the Bighorn Mountains of Wyoming contradict the common belief that the Plains are completely flat. Although massive tracts of land are indeed flat, they are pleasantly interrupted by rolling hills, high river banks, wide river valleys, and other formations.

For the most part there are few, if any, trees on the flat prairies but in river valleys, along streams, and in coolies grow poplar or cottonwood trees, willows, sage brush, chokecherry trees and saskatoon or service berry trees,

Beaded bag, c 1900, 34.0 x 30.0 cm, canvas, cotton, velvet, skin, and beads. This Okanagan bag has a plain cloth back, but such bags are often beaded on both sides with different but thematically related designs.

high and low bush cranberries, buffalo berries, blueberries, strawberries, and raspberries. The prairies also provide a home to wild turnips, wild rose bushes, cactus, creeping juniper, sage plants, and various grasses and flowers, all of which provide food and medicine through their fruit, roots, bark, leaves, and stems. Drought and flood can alternate in the same region, and temperature and snowfall vary dramatically from north to south and east to west within the area. Chinook winds coming in from the west over the Rocky Mountains can raise temperatures by as much as forty degrees Celsius in a matter of hours. The prairies are also known for their violent thunderstorms, flash floods, hailstorms, and tornadoes, elements that play an important role in the mythology, stories, and religious beliefs and practices of most Plains cultures.

On the Plateau, Native people tell of Coyote, Old Man, and other trans-formers who moved through their land creating, in the course of their adventures, the mountains, rivers, and unusual landmarks. Whether from geological change or supernatural activity, the resulting landscape is a magnificent set of mountains, rolling hills, and winding rivers. The Plateau encompasses the area of high elevation between the Rocky Mountains to the east and the Cascade mountains to the west. The northern boundary is the great bend of the Fraser River in British Columbia, and to the south the region merges with the Colorado Plateau (Ray 1978, 1). The area is mostly dry and hot in the summer, and the winter months can be very cold with heavy snowfalls. In the valleys and mountain meadows the soil is covered in a variety of shrubs, grasses, and flowering plants. Especially important was the highly nutritious bunch grass. Available early in the spring and late in the fall, even after autumn frosts have killed other grasses, it became the staple food for the first herds of cattle.

The two cultural groups represented in this volume share many ele-ments of traditional culture and beliefs and are linked by common threads of history. Nevertheless, they are unique, with different languages and, depending on the local resources, different tools and technologies. The Plains people used hides to cover their tipis, for example, while some Plateau groups used woven mat coverings. Their social and political organi-zation and religious beliefs could also be quite different.

The cultural distribution of Native people inhabiting the northern Plains and Plateau has changed quite dramatically over the past 200 years. Some cultures no longer exist; others have had their numbers so drastically reduced that their language and traditions are in grave danger of extinction. Several cultures with small populations merged with and adapted some of the traditions of their neighbours. Intermarriage over the past hundred years has also contributed to a sharing of culture and tradition.

Native cultural groups that consider themselves to be members of the northern Plains today are Algonkian, Athabaskan, Siouan, Caddoan, Uto-Aztecan, and Iroquoian speakers. Among Algonkian speakers are the

Nehiyaw (Plains Cree), Anishnaabe (Plains Ojibwa, Saulteaux, and Chippewa), Tse-tsėhésė-stȧhase (Northern Cheyenne), Hinono'eino' (Arapaho), Ah-ah-nee-nin (Gros Ventre), and the Siksika (Northern Blackfoot), Kainai (Blood, or Blackfoot), Apatohsi Piikunii (North Peigan, or Blackfoot), and Amoskapi Piikunii (South Peigan, or Blackfeet). Some of these groups once lived in the Great Lakes region, where they were semi-agrarian hunters and gatherers. Their gradual movement onto the Plains seems to have taken place at various times during the seventeenth and eighteenth centuries. Other groups, such as the Niisitapiikwan (Blackfoot), who were indigenous to the Plains, were territorial hunters and gatherers. Among the Athabaskan speakers are the Tsuu T'ina (Sarcee, or Beaver). Their traditional stories once placed them in a colder, more northern part of Alberta. Once on the Plains they incorporated elements of Plains culture and traditions while maintaining their language. Among the Siouan family are the Nuptadi/Nueta (Mandan), Hidatsa, Absalooka (Crow), Lakota (Sioux), Dakota (Sioux), and Nakota and Nakoda (Sioux Assiniboine and Stoney). The Nuptadi/Nueta and Hidatsa have a very long agricultural tradition, as once did the Absalooka. Other members of the Siouan family come from a background of some agriculture and hunting and gathering. Among the Caddoan are the Sahnish (Arikara). Among the Uto-Aztecan are the So-sonreh (Shoshone). The So-sonreh have always occupied the central portion of the Plains and Plateau. Their southern boundary extended into Mexico and their northern boundary reached into Canada, where they were referred to as the Snake People. Finally, among the Iroquoian are the Kanien' Kehaka/Nehiyaw (Mohawk/ Cree). Several hundred Kanien' Kehaka traders moved west with the North West Trading Company between the late 1700s and early 1800s and inter-married with the Nehiyaw in central and west-central Alberta.

The Métis, halfbreed, or mixed-blood community was created as a result of the intermarriage of English, Scottish, Irish, Welsh, and French fur traders and Native women. Quite often when a fur trader retired from the company he would return to Europe, leaving his wife and children to return to the woman's home community. Of the traders who remained, many followed their wives to their communities, or the two turned to farming. Several started their own businesses as freighters, free traders, and stock producers.

Groups considered to be members of the Plateau culture are the Salish and Sahaptin language speakers, who include the Stl'átl'imx (Lillooet), Nlha7kápmx (Thompson), Secwepemc (Shuswap), Okanagan, Coeur d'Alêne, Salish (Flathead), and Nez Percé, among others. The Kutenai (Kootenay) have their own language and the Carrier and Chilcotin are Athabaskan speakers. At one time, the eastern Plateau communities – the Salish, the Kutenai, the Nez Percé, and the Coeur d'Alêne – were considered part of the Plains cultural groups that hunted buffalo and practised the Sun Dance. The groups living near the west coast were thought to be part of the northwest

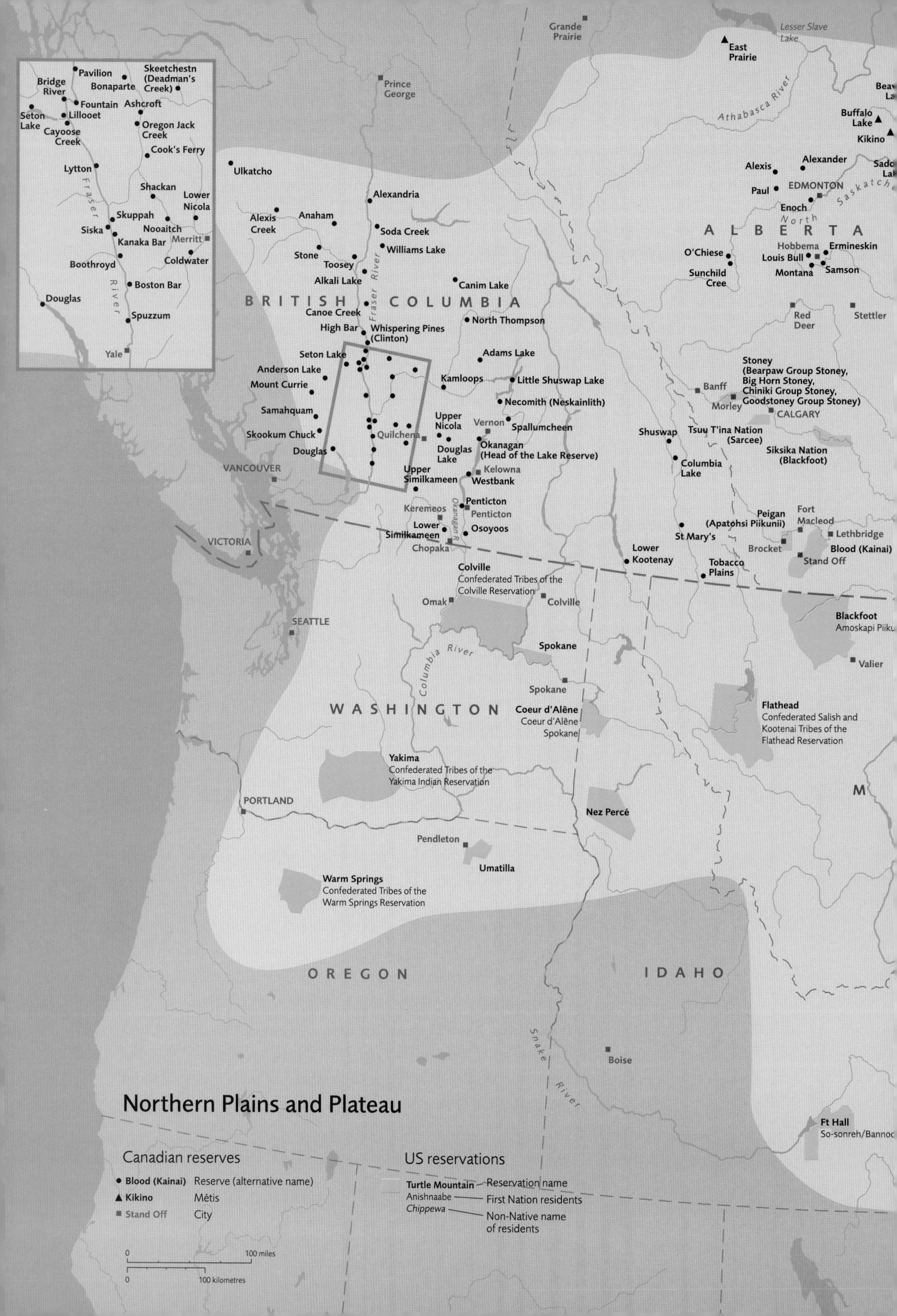

Northern Plains and Plateau
Canadian reserves
Blood (Kainai) Reserve (alternative name)
Kikino Métis
Stand Off City
US reservations
Turtle Mountain — Reservation name
Anishnaabe — First Nation residents
Chippewa — Non-Native name of residents
0 100 miles
0 100 kilometres
BRITISH COLUMBIA
ALBERTA
WASHINGTON
OREGON
IDAHO
M
Pavilion
Skeetchestn (Deadman's Creek)
Bridge River
Bonaparte
Fountain
Ashcroft
Seton Lake
Lillooet
Oregon Jack Creek
Cayoose Creek
Cook's Ferry
Lytton
Fraser River
Shackan
Lower Nicola
Skuppah
Nooaitch
Siska
Merritt
Kanaka Bar
Coldwater
Boothroyd
Boston Bar
Douglas
Spuzzum
Yale
Grande Prairie
Lesser Slave Lake
East Prairie
Prince George
Athabasca River
Beav La
Buffalo Lake
Kikino
Sado La
Ulkatcho
Alexis
Alexander
Paul
EDMONTON
Saskatche
Enoch
North
Alexandria
Anaham
Alexis Creek
Soda Creek
Williams Lake
Stone
Toosey
Alkali Lake
Canim Lake
O'Chiese
Hobbema
Ermineskin
Louis Bull
Sunchild Cree
Montana
Samson
Canoe Creek
High Bar
Whispering Pines (Clinton)
North Thompson
Red Deer
Stettler
Seton Lake
Adams Lake
Anderson Lake
Mount Currie
Kamloops
Little Shuswap Lake
Stoney (Bearpaw Group Stoney, Big Horn Stoney, Chiniki Group Stoney, Goodstoney Group Stoney)
Banff
Morley
CALGARY
Samahquam
Necomith (Neskainlith)
Upper Nicola
Vernon
Spallumcheen
Skookum Chuck
Quilchena
Shuswap
Tsuu T'ina Nation (Sarcee)
Douglas
Douglas Lake
Okanagan (Head of the Lake Reserve)
Siksika Nation (Blackfoot)
VANCOUVER
Upper Similkameen
Kelowna
Westbank
Columbia Lake
Keremeos
Penticton
Penticton
Okanagan R.
Lower Similkameen
Osoyoos
Peigan (Apatohsi Piikunii)
Fort Macleod
Lethbridge
VICTORIA
Chopaka
St Mary's
Brocket
Blood (Kainai)
Lower Kootenay
Tobacco Plains
Stand Off
Colville
Confederated Tribes of the Colville Reservation
Omak
Colville
Blackfoot
Amoskapi Piiku
SEATTLE
Spokane
Columbia River
Valier
Spokane
Flathead
Confederated Salish and Kootenai Tribes of the Flathead Reservation
Coeur d'Alêne
Coeur d'Alêne
Spokane
Yakima
Confederated Tribes of the Yakima Indian Reservation
PORTLAND
Nez Percé
Pendleton
Umatilla
Warm Springs
Confederated Tribes of the Warm Springs Reservation
Snake River
Boise
Ft Hall
So-sonreh/Bannoc

ld Lake
rst Nations
Joseph
Bighead
▲
abeth
Waterhen
Lake
Island
Lake
Flying Dust
win
▲
Fishing Lake
Makwa Sahgaiehcan
(Loon Lake)
Onion
Lake
Pelican
Lake
Big River
Attahkakoop
(Sandy Lake)
Thunderchild
Witchekan
Lake
Shell
Lake
Wahpeton
Moosomin
Saulteaux
Mistawasis
Sturgeon Lake
James Smith
Prince
Albert
John Smith
Little Pine
Poundmaker
Sweet Grass
Muskeg
Lake
Beardy's and Okemasis
Red
Pheasant
One Arrow
Yellowquill
(Nut Lake)
Mosquito-Grizzly
Bear's Head
S A S K A T C H E W A N
Kinistin
(Kinistino)
SASKATOON
Moose
Woods
Fishing
Lake
Keeseekoose
Crane
River
Peguis
Little Black
River
Kawacatoose
(Poorman)
Day Star
Muskowekwan
Key
Cote
Valley
River
Dauphin
Ebb and
Flow
Lake
Manitoba
Sagkeeng
Gordon
Little Black
Bear
Sakimay
Star
Blanket
Standing Buffalo
Okanese
Peepeekisis
Waywayseecappo
Keeseekoowenin
Brokenhead
Ojibway Nation
Muscowpetung
Piapot
Pasqua
Kahkewistahaw
Sandy Bay
First Nation
Moose
Jaw
Fort
Qu'Appelle
REGINA
Cowessess
Ochapowace
Gamblers
Rolling
River
Dakota Tipi
Portage la
Prairie
WINNIPEG
Carry the
Kettle
Birdtail Sioux
First Nation
Sioux Valley
First Nation
Long Plain First Nation
Dakota Plains First Nation
Buffalo Point
First Nation
Brandon
White Bear
Oak Lake
First Nation
Swan Lake
First Nation
Roseau River
Tribal Council
Lake of
the Woods
Nikaneet
Wood
Mountain
CANADA
U.S.A.
Turtle Mountain
Anishnaabe
Chippewa
Red Lake
Anishnaabe
Chippewa
Ft Belknap
Nakota Assiniboine
Ah-ah-nee-nin Gros Ventre
Ft Peck
Nakota/Dakota
Sioux
Devils Lake
Dakota
Sioux
Rocky Boys
Nehiyaw Cree
Anishnaabe Chippewa
Lake
Sakakawea
N O R T H   D A K O T A
White Earth
Anishnaabe
Chippewa
Missouri
River
Fort Peck
Reservoir
Ft Berthold
Nuptadi/Nueta Mandan
Sahnish Arikara
Hidatsa
T A N A
Yellowstone River
Rosebud Cr
Sisseton
Sisseton Dakota
Sioux
MINNESOTA
Billings
Little Bighorn River
Standing Rock
Dakota/Lakota
Sioux
Oahe
Reservoir
Crow
Absalooka
Northern Cheyenne
Tse-tsêhésê-stâhase
Cheyenne River
Lakota
Sioux
Crow Creek
Dakota
Sioux
Bighorn River
S O U T H   D A K O T A
Rapid
City
Lower Brule
Brulé Lakota
Sioux
Missouri
Yankton
Yankton Dakota
Sioux
Pine Ridge
Oglala Lakota
Sioux
Rosebud
Sicangu Lakota
Sioux
Santee
Santee Dakota
Sioux
Wind River
So-sonreh Shoshone
Hinono'eino' Arapaho
W Y O M I N G
N E B R A S K A

Lake
Winnipeg

M A N I T O B A

O N T A R I O

Saskatchewan
River

Assiniboine

River

Red
River

coast cultures, with an economy based on fishing. Now, however, these people are seen as a single cultural group. They occupy the high plateaux and traditionally survived by fishing, gathering roots and fruits, hunting deer and elk, and making forays into buffalo country. They shared a set of beliefs that included vision quests and a role for guardians who appeared in dreams (Ray 1978).

The Plains and Plateau people have been brought together here because of their shared history of ranching and rodeo. They competed for the buffalo, traded horses, and fought battles or formed alliances with each other. Over time, members from each of these communities took their knowledge of horses and herding and found employment as cowboys and ranchers. Using the same skills many found work in Wild West shows, and in the early 1920s people began finding employment in the movie industry. For each community the time, the resources, and the circumstances of change were different. This history of Native ranching and the development of 'Indian cowboys' has recently been explored in several important studies. Sarah Carter, for example, has documented the early history of Native agriculture on the Plains in her book, *Lost Harvest: Prairie Indian Reserve Farmers and Government Policy*. Peter Iverson has written a history of American Native cowboys in his study, *When Indians Became Cowboys: Native People and Cattle Ranching in the American West*.

Legends of Our Times is a different sort of book, presenting the words and works of Plains, Plateau, and Métis ranchers and cowboys themselves. The expression of these voices takes several forms: narratives and legends, research studies, and artistic statements such as poetry, works of art, and objects of everyday use. The book is divided into three sections, and a full range of narrative, poetic, and visual expression is included in each. 'Sacred Beings' explores the roles of the horse, buffalo, deer, coyote, dog, and wolf in Plains and Plateau culture. Accounts of these roles are passed from generation to generation through stories, songs, dances, and ceremonies. These are the 'legends of our times'; they are real in the ways that they link the people to their past and provide meaning for the present. From this background have come the history and contemporary activities of ranching and rodeo. These themes are somewhat arbitrarily divided into two sections, 'Ranching Life' and 'Rodeo and Other Entertainment.' The same skills of riding, roping, and herding, and the same knowledge of horses and cattle, are required for each. For many Native rodeo and ranching families, ranching is done for business and rodeo is done for pleasure; for others the activities and their significance may be reversed. Rodeo is a full-time occupation for some and the main source of income for the men and women who follow the rodeo circuit throughout the year. *Legends of Our Times* is also the story of human survival during difficult periods of change, and of individuals, both historical and contemporary, who have contributed to the sport, art, and industry of ranching, rodeo, and cowboy life.

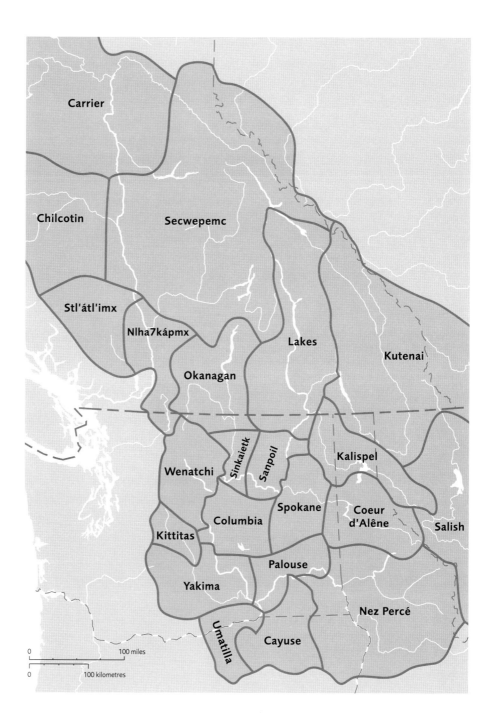

Historical Territories on the Plateau

After Ray (1978)

The following territory labels appear on the map: Carrier, Chilcotin, Secwepemc, Stl'átl'imx, Nlha7kápmx, Lakes, Kutenai, Okanagan, Sinkaietk, Sanpoil, Kalispel, Wenatchi, Spokane, Coeur d'Alêne, Salish, Columbia, Kittitas, Palouse, Yakima, Nez Percé, Umatilla, Cayuse

0   100 miles

0   100 kilometres

Tribal Naming

The use of various terms for Native people has changed considerably over the past few years in both Canada and the United States. Native American or North American Indian appears more frequently in the United States; Canada uses the terms Native, Aboriginal, and Indigenous. Other terms such as First Nations, Inuit, Status, Non-Status, and Métis generally refer to specific, smaller groups within the Aboriginal population. Métis, for example, denotes the descendants of marriages between Native and non-Native people.

In general, this work uses the terms Native and Aboriginal and, whenever appropriate, the Native name for the community. The English equivalents for Native terms are given below.

Aboriginal name	English term
Ah-ah-nee-nin	Gros Ventre
Amoskapi Piikunii	South Peigan (Blackfeet, Montana)
Anishnaabe	Plains Ojibwa and Saulteaux and Chippewa
Apatohsi Piikunii	North Peigan (Blackfoot, Alberta)
Absalooka	Crow
Carrier	Carrier
Cayuse	Cayuse
Chilcotin	Chilcotin
Coeur d'Alêne	Coeur d'Alêne
Dakota	Sioux
Hidatsa	Hidatsa
Hinono'eino'	Arapaho
Kainai	Blood (Blackfoot, Alberta)
Kaiugui	Kiowa
Kanien' Kehaka	Mohawk
Kutenai	Kootenay
Lakota	Sioux
Nakoda	Sioux Assiniboine/Stoney (Morley, Eden Valley, and Big Horn, Alberta)
Nakota	Sioux Assiniboine/Stoney (Saskatchewan and Montana)
Nehiyaw	Plains Cree
Nez Percé	Nez Percé
Niisitapiikwan	Blackfoot people, the First People
Nlha7kápmx	Thompson
Nuptadi/Nueta	Mandan
Okanagan	Okanagan
Pawnee	Pawnee
Sahnish	Arikara
Salish	Flathead
Secwepemc	Shuswap
Siksika	Blackfoot (Alberta)
Sinkaietk	Okanagon
So-sonreh	Shoshone
Stl'átl'imx	Lillooet
Tse-tsêhésê-stàhase	Northern Cheyenne
Tsuu T'ina	Sarcee

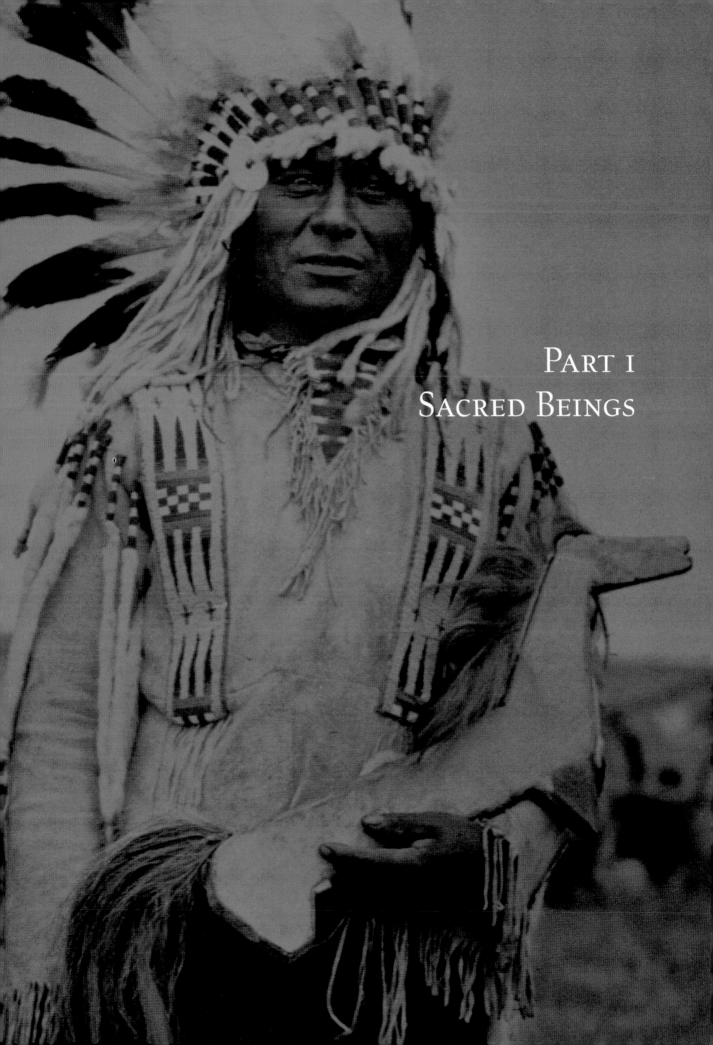

PART I
SACRED BEINGS

Sacred Beings

Cowboys are mainly concerned with the habits and well-being of two types of animal: cattle, the source of their income; and horses, their working partners. For many Native cowboys their relationship with these two animals is based on an alliance established from the earliest days. For many Plains and some Plateau peoples an association with cattle goes back to the time of the buffalo. Indeed in some communities cattle were substituted for some ceremonial purposes when buffalo were no longer available. The dog, coyote, and wolf are still part of the rancher's life, the first as companion and helper, the last two as raiders of sheep and calves. The world view of and historical changes in Plains and Plateau cowboy cultures is told through animal stories and imagery.

These stories tell about the creation of the universe, where animals come from, and why they act the way that they do. They give moral lessons about how people should behave toward the animals that give their lives to sustain human life. Thus both the appearance and the disappearance of the buffalo, for example, are explained through traditional stories. Lessons of proper behaviour and history are taught through stories about animal interactions, especially those between the greedy trickster and transformer, Coyote, and the animals he encounters. Finally, many of the stories are humorous and entertaining; they are remembered and told again and again to each new generation.

Images of the buffalo, dog, and deer date back thousands of years. Images of horses and mounted warriors started to appear as horses spread across the northern Plains and Plateau through the eighteenth century. Sometimes animal images were simply outlined in stones; at other times they were painted with ochres or carved into rock as pictographs and petroglyphs. They are found on cave walls, on the sides of sandstone cliffs, on vertical rock faces, on prairie boulders, on hilltops, or simply laid out on the flat prairie landscape itself. Their purpose is not absolutely certain, although they often appear in areas known to have been sacred, where people came to pray and to seek visions. Some areas are also known to have been camping stops for many different cultures. Images in these places may have served as messages left by one party for another or simply as recordings of recent events. Their true meaning died with the makers and those to whom they passed the information.

It was common practice on the Plains and Plateau to incorporate the image of horses, dogs, buffalo, and deer into the design and construction of items used as personal adornment, dwellings, and sacred and secular objects. On objects used for ceremonial purposes such imagery can convey religious meanings. Some Native people contend that any object used to evoke the aid of sacred and powerful beings is in itself sacred. Others argue that the ritual songs and prayers that accompany the symbol and the healing they bring about are sacred but that the symbols themselves merely act as a reminder of the events, songs, ceremonies, experiences, or visions. Animal imagery also appears on everyday objects such as moccasins and clothing, often simply because people enjoy the memories the images evoke. Today people often want a favourite dog or horse or even a prize bull beaded onto their gloves, jackets, or skirts. A third category of animal imagery is found on objects created for sale to tourists. Such items were particularly popular in the 1860s and 1870s, when beadworkers produced massive numbers of items for soldiers, government agents, and tourists. The images depicted old war accounts, hunting scenes, horse stealing raids, and even cowboys on bucking broncs.

The Spiritual Bond

The Creator placed first minerals, then plants, animals, and human beings, on the earth, giving everything a spirit. Native people generally accept that among humans some are more gifted than others and some have special powers. The same can be said of the animal world. A horse that managed to survive battle wounds and make its way home would be considered powerful and gifted. Gifted animals are generally acknowledged as sacred.

Another kind of spiritual being, or helper, occupies the universe. These beings sometimes choose to reveal themselves to humans in the form of dreams or waking visions. They may appear in human or animal shapes such as horse, dog, coyote, wolf, deer, and buffalo, though sometimes they take the form of an object, such as an arrow, a gun, or a bullet, or even as an unidentifiable shape. These spiritual beings may be benevolent or malicious, but if treated with respect they can act as teachers, healers, and protectors. They can also provide humans with physical and spiritual protection and gifts of power, usually in the form of a song. The power can heal people, help them to be successful in the hunt, or protect them in warfare or on horse raids.

Above: THE HITCHHIKER,
1972, 29.0 x 55.0 x 12.4 cm,
bronze, by Gerald Tailfeathers.
Tailfeathers, a Kainai from
Stand Off, Alberta, may have
based this bronze on his 1958
pen and ink drawing, STORMY
RESCUE. *Spring snow storms*
are a common occurrence on the
northern Plains, often coming at
calving time. We can only assume
that the calf lying across the rider's
lap did not belong to the cow that
walks ahead, or she would proba-
bly be following the horse.

Opposite: Jacket, 1997, 76.0 x
71.0 cm, silk and embroidery
thread, by Shannon Kilroy,
Lower Nicola, British Columbia.
The designs and motifs of
Kilroy's contemporary clothing
are drawn from the traditional
images of the Nlha7kápmx
Nation, of which she is a member.
The colours of the silks and
linens used in her suits and jack-
ets reflect the soft, muted colours
of the Plateau landscape. The
buffalo and coyote embroidered
on this jacket reflect her new
fashion line, which draws from
the legends of her people.

Among Plains and Plateau cultures it is believed that animals could once talk and communicate quite freely with humans. Some specially gifted animals were capable of shifting or transforming themselves into human or other animal forms. The horse, dog, coyote, wolf, deer, and buffalo were among these transformers and gift givers, who stood in a special relationship with the people of the region. They not only helped humans to acquire sustenance but also, in some cases, gave their bodies as food when required. In thanks, humans were expected to respect and honour them. As the traditional way of life changed on the Plains and Plateau, maintaining a relationship with these animals became increasingly difficult. Religious ceremonies, dances, and horse stealing raids were made illegal by governments and church officials in Canada and the United States. For many families and communities, the human-animal relationship took on new forms, partly through daily contact with the horse, dog, and those buffalo-like beings, cattle, as 'Indians' became cowboys.

The Horse

Horses were reintroduced to the Americas in 1493 by the Spanish and spread through Central America and Mexico. They were also brought to the east coast of North America by the Dutch, French, and English in the early 1600s. Their arrival on the Plateau and northern Plains, between the late 1600s and 1770, is attributed to their migration from South America and Mexico into Texas and California, where they were traded for or captured by southern Plains Aboriginal cultures. It is also accepted that many horses escaped their Spanish ranches and found their way onto the Plateau and northern Plains without human aid. As well several accounts document how northern cultures obtained horses from southern Aboriginal communities through either trade or raid.

Mike Bruised Head (Niinaa Piik-sii, Chief Bird), a Kainai from Stand Off, Alberta, comes from a family with a very long and successful tradition of rodeo and ranching. He is an active Native rodeo supporter and organizer, he raises horses, and he is very interested in Niisitapiikwan history.

In the old days you respected your horses – you relied on them with your life. They took you to war, on the hunt, on horse raids, on scouting expeditions and you expected your horse to bring you home. You knew the songs and medicines for your horse to take you into battle and the medicines and songs to cure your horse when it was ill or injured. We were equal with our horses before the residential school. The residential school experience taught us that horses were simply beasts of burden whose purpose was to help us break the land and pull heavy equipment. Our horses were being crossbred with foreign breeds. They were no longer our pets and our friends. They were no longer sacred.

The horse completely changed the lives of Plains and Plateau people. Before its arrival, a community's wealth was limited to the loads that could be pulled or carried by dogs and people. Because of its size and strength, the horse had the capacity to carry 100 to 200 kilograms of equipment, meat,

Right: Native people had many different styles of horse travois, each culture fashioning them according to its needs. This turn-of-the-century photograph depicts a Niisitapiikwan travois style.

Below: Stl'átl'imx people on horseback, 1865. The community has gathered to welcome a delegation of government officials. The fact that almost everyone is on horseback indicates the large number of horses available to this small community.

Horse saddled in traditional Nlha7kápmx style. This rare photograph shows a style of horse gear on the BC Plateau from the mid-nineteenth century, recreated for the ethnographic work of James Teit.

hides, and personal belongings. People thus became more mobile, lived in larger dwellings, carried more belongings, and acquired more possessions. The presence of the horse also brought about new forms of trade, hunting methods, and tribal warfare and expanded territorial occupancy. It magnified the class system among these cultures, and wealth came to be measured by the number of horses one possessed. Aboriginal people became superb equestrians. A warhorse came to be seen as an extension of the warrior and was painted and adorned with war medicine such as paint and feathers, like its rider. Horses were decorated with beaded or quilled equipment and paraded at public gatherings as an expression of a family's wealth and artistic talent.

Horses also became the centre of some ceremonies, and favoured horses were honoured in songs and dances. Powerful equine spirits appeared in people's dreams and visions, bestowing on them secrets for gaining protection in war and on horse raids, for capturing, breaking, and training horses, and for performing curative ceremonies for horses and people. Some ceremonial occasions took the form of horse dances and ritual sweat baths, in which the horse spirit was asked for its healing powers, blessings, and assistance.

Some Aboriginal stories speak of encounters with miniature horses, which roamed the continent during the Pleistocene age. From that time to the present horses and humans have been able to communicate with one another, though now only gifted people have this skill, and the horse has taught Aboriginal people its medicines, songs, dances, and ceremonies. Native people have many stories of the Creator's gift of horses to human beings. Some describe the animal descending from the sky world, from the West, or from the underworld, also referred to as the water world. Horses frequently assisted individuals, particularly someone who faced a difficult challenge. Traditional stories explain the nature of the horse, the gifts it brings, its relationship with people and with other animal beings, and its link to lightning, thunder, and other elements of nature.

Respect, admiration, and pride in the bond between horse and owner were, and still are, expressed through horse imagery and symbols on equipment, clothing, pipes, dance sticks, war clubs, and medicine objects and on warriors' lodges. The imagery is sometimes as complex as a recording of actual events in the person's life. Warriors who had captured horses from their enemies, for example, often recorded their acts of courage and strength on their war shirts, their tipis, or their buffalo robes. In some instances their deeds were painted directly onto their horses' bodies. Occasionally women depicted their husbands', fathers', or brothers' bravery and deeds on their dresses. Alternatively, the imagery can be as simple as a single horse figure represented on an everyday object. Basket makers, for example, wove horse figures and horse brand designs. Some imagery represents these animals as spiritual beings who visited men and women during their vision quests. Their days of solitude, fasting, and prayer were sometimes recorded on objects and frequently included the image of the horses that had appeared to them.

Black Elk (1863-1950), Lakota elder, 1931. Black Elk was a warrior and medicine man of the Oglala. He witnessed the Battle of the Little Bighorn and the massacre of the Lakota/Dakota at Wounded Knee.

The lightning has wings and rides on a horse ... The stallion is said to have power to herd the mares, lead them about, and subject them to his will. His power is supposed to have been given by the Thunder-horse, or the Thunder.

Lone Man, Oglala Lakota elder, 1931.

The swallow's flying precedes a thunderstorm. This bird is closely related to the thunderbird. The action of a swallow is very agile. The greatest aid to a warrior is a good horse, and what a warrior desires most for his horse is that it may be as swift as the swallow in dodging the enemy or in direct flight.

People took pride and pleasure in adorning their horses with paint and horse equipment with paint, beadwork, and quillwork. Several groups in the Plains and Plateau shared similar design styles and equipment. The Absalooka and the Plateau communities of Cayuse, Salish, and especially the Nez Percé traded and travelled together. A similar style of geometric designs in brightly coloured beads that appeared between 1850 and the early 1900s suggests that the two cultures willingly shared ideas and identified

*Above: Basket, c 1900, 11.0 x
23.5 cm, cedar root, bark, and
grass. Horse figures were sometimes woven on cedar bark baskets and corn husk bags. Other,
more geometric designs are said
to be horse brands.*

*Opposite: Horse robe, 1842,
230.0 cm length, horse skin and
paint. Warriors generally painted
images of their war exploits,
horse raids, and various encounters on hides, using buffalo, elk,
horse, and sometimes deer. This
Dakota/Lakota horse robe was
collected on the upper Missouri
River. Its design includes painted
calumets, concentric sunburst or
feather motifs, buffalo hunting
scenes, a camp scene with tipis,
war scenes, buffalo being
butchered, mounted riders, a
mule, and horses. On the fur side
of the hide, at the head, is
inscribed 'Gabriel Amire/1842,'
most probably the owner.*

with each other visually (Loeb 1991, 197). This transmontane style of beadwork appeared on gun cases, bandoleer bags that were hung around the
neck of horses for parades, baby boards that were attached to women's saddles, and saddle blankets.

The horse was also often depicted in a stylized effigy. A memorial horse
effigy – or horse stick – was sometimes made if a warrior lost a horse in battle, and would incorporate the mane and tail of the favoured animal.
Mountain Chief, an Amoskapi Piikunii veteran of the intertribal wars, for
example, was photographed by Joseph K. Dixon in 1913 holding an effigy
horse and rider. Apparently he had been in a battle in which his horse had
been shot several times. Mountain Chief escaped, leaving his horse for dead.
Several days later the horse, to his amazement, arrived at the camp. Out of
respect, he made an effigy in recognition of this courageous horse, which
obviously possessed secret powers.

Long-handled horse effigy sticks were carried in horse dances on the
Standing Rock Reservation in South Dakota until almost the beginning of
the First World War. Men used sticks with carved horse heads and horsehair to beat time to the music while the horses danced (Ewers 1986, 140).
The details of this healing ceremony are generally revealed to someone in a
dream and as a rule are kept secret, though Lakota holy man Black Elk
shared particulars of his vision and of the dance ceremony in *Black Elk Speaks*
(Neihardt 1972). Carved horse effigies were also used in victory dances, in
which warriors carried wooden effigies to remind people of their bravery
and skill in raiding enemy horses (Ewers 1986, 139). Although many war

clubs and coup sticks, which were used to strike or touch an enemy in battle, were carved with human heads or human figures, others had animal figures, including horse heads, possibly because the animal in each case was the warrior's 'medicine' or protector. So-sonreh warriors left behind stakes, carved at one end with horse heads, following a horse raid. H.A. Morrow explained that when a war party wished to mislead its pursuers, a stake would be placed on the trail 'usually at a point where two or more trails intersect, and this is thought to have a charm by which its pursuers were induced to follow the wrong trail' (quoted in Ewers 1986, 146). Horse effigies also appear as stops on both Great Lakes and Plains love flutes, which were used for courting. A common form among the Lakota and Dakota was of a stallion with an arched neck. One explanation is that the suitor would ask the stallion spirit to help him win the attention of the woman he loved.

Small beaded horse figures were employed either as horse medicine to give power over horses when catching them, training them, or capturing them in raids, or as personal amulets for protection. These horse effigies were sometimes made with a large thong, to be worn around the neck, while other pieces had small ties to attach the effigy to the hair, weapons, or piece of clothing. Rawhide or parfleche containers that held horse medicine were sometimes decorated with imagery of horses or horse tracks.

Brian Pratt was a Dakota cowboy from the Sioux Valley Reserve who donated a great deal of his time to promoting rodeo among Native youth in Manitoba.

There is a strong relationship between our people and the horse. We call the horse 'sunka wakan,' which means holy animal. I can't just go put down a horse if a horse is hurt. In the old days we had special people who could do that. That animal is holy to us because it carries us on its back. In the old days they used to make our horses dance in a ceremony. They would dance to the beat of the drum. It is in the Sun Dance that they [people] use them. So they [people and horses] are really close together. Even today that relationship is still there. Our people don't go around beating horses – whipping them or something. You just don't do that sort of thing. This is a holy animal.

A number of painted drums and shields show images of horned horses, or of horses wearing horned war bonnets. Only those who made these objects knew the true significance of the symbols they contained, but horned animals and horned spiritual beings were generally revered for their strength and power. A painted robe collected in 1833 from Mato Tope, a Nueta warrior, shows warriors and horses wearing feathered bonnets (Walton, Ewers, and Hassrick 1985, 103). This rare and early imagery of the horse with a feathered bonnet is important because it indicates that at this date Aboriginal people were providing the same spiritual and physical protection for their horses as they gave themselves.

Throughout the nineteenth century, horses were a popular theme in decoration of clothing and other items, particularly of objects for sale.

Many Plains warriors made memorial effigy dance sticks to honour horses killed in battle, often employing the tails and manes. Sometimes a person would give a horse away when he carried a memorial stick into a dance. This 1905 photograph shows a Nakota man from the Fort Belknap Reservation, Montana, carrying a horse effigy.

Man's shirt, c 1900, 59.5 x 77.5 cm, twill, cotton, ribbon, beads, and glass bugles. Man's beaded vest, c 1900, 53.0 x 33.5 cm, leather, beads, cotton. These Kutenai examples of clothing show the two styles of beadwork commonly found on the Plateau. Both geometric and floral patterns were popular late in the nineteenth century.

During the second half of the nineteenth century, known as the Reservation Period on the prairies, pipes with riders or mounted warriors or soldiers were common subject matter. These later forms of effigy pipes were often sold as tourist items, as they are today, but some may have been made for ceremonial and personal use.

From 1850 to 1900 a completely new style of art developed, depicting animals in beadwork. The beadworkers who made the most representational designs were Lakota, Dakota, Nakota, and Absalooka people. On the Plateau, women began to produce flat beaded bags and cradle boards, whose large surfaces permitted the execution of complex designs. Elaborately beaded horses and mounted warriors were used to decorate personal items such as holsters, vests, jackets, and dresses as well as tourist pieces such as trunks, suitcases, umbrellas, shoes, and clothing. Many of these scenes are similar to those in ledger art, the drawings produced in military and government ledger books, which became popular at the same time. Both Plains and Plateau objects depict war scenes, military encounters, friendly encounters, horse stealing raids, cowboys, and rodeo scenes. Other popular designs on the Plateau showed a horse and sometimes a deer or other animal surrounded by trees and floral patterns. Entire regalia for both horse and rider were crafted out of beads (Duncan 1991, 192). Although this style of beadwork was particularly popular until about 1930, its subjects have again come into fashion and are now appearing on contemporary pow-wow dresses, western style dresses, vests, and jackets.

Today the horse is still used by many people: the working cowboy, the pleasure rider, rodeo cowboys, and horse breeders. Although it is rarely used as a means of transportation, in some remote communities a horse-drawn wagon is still the only means of transporting children to school. The horse also continues to be called on for spiritual guidance and for its powers of healing through various ceremonies. As well it remains an inspiration to many artists.

One such artist, George Littlechild, a Nehiyaw painter from the Ermineskin Reserve in Hobbema, Alberta, provides a particularly good example of the contemporary artist drawing on traditional motifs. The image he uses most prominently is the horse, which he perceives as highly spiritual. Although he neither owns a horse nor rides one, he believes that when he is near horses he can feel their power and metaphorically draw from it. Littlechild had already spent several years incorporating horse imagery into his work before discovering that in Nehiyaw culture the horse is the carrier of visions and messages from the spirit world to this world. On many occasions Littlechild has felt horse images carried to him so strongly that he can visualize them as clearly as if they had been drawn for him. He believes that the horse is the mystical link to the spirit world, a spirit helper who protects people from circumstances and is the channel for ancient memories. In some instances Littlechild depicts the horse as a messenger who imparts

Two Spokane women pose with their beaded bags in this photograph taken early in this century. The horse figures beaded on one of the bags are a fairly simple example of a popular motif. Some skilled beadworkers depicted the breed of horse, such as the Appaloosa, or showed the horse with a decorated saddle, bridle, and other equipment. The horses are often shown bucking, running, or proudly walking with cowboys or warriors on their backs.

Above: THE LAND CALLED MORNING, *1986, 53.3 x 66.0 cm, acrylic on paper, by George Littlechild, Nehiyaw. The horses carry their riders above the earth, flying over the earthly dwellings. Riders are wearing bonnets, which not only offer spiritual and physical protection but also signify the riders' stately position. The riders' arms are extended in a posture of freedom, as they are carried from their earthly dwellings into the sky world.*

Opposite, above: Pipe bowl, late 1800s or early 1900s, 7.5 x 13.5 cm, engraved red pipestone. The double-headed horse is of Dakota/Lakota design.

Opposite, below: Parfleche containers, mid-1800s to mid-1900s, buffalo rawhide, paint, and glass beads. Clockwise from top: northern Plains, Anishinaabe, Absalooka, Siksika, Anishinaabe, Absalooka, Tsuu T'ina, Okanagan. Parfleche containers are made of untanned hide, usually of buffalo but occasionally of deer, moose, elk, or cow. They were used for storing everything from clothes to dried meat and berries and also served as suitcases.*

knowledge or reveals secrets to humans. Probably the most distinctive horse image in his work is the figure of Horsechild, the transformer, who is meant to represent both Native people and, as often as not, the artist himself. Horsechild has the ability to change from human form to horse and back to human again. Littlechild sees this transformation as a change in persona: from an ordinary person into a warrior.

Two horse stories and a poem have been selected for this volume. 'The First Horses' is a Nehiyaw story that explains the origin of the horse in that culture. The second story is a contemporary account of the origin of the name Painted Pony. This name has been passed from generation to generation in an Okanagan/Secwepemc family. The story also speaks of the gift of transformation, the ability of humans to change into animals and back, and of the gift of speech between animals and humans. The poem 'Âyahkwêw's Lodge' tells of the same tradition.

The Buffalo and the Deer

Buffalo and deer have been on the North American continent for many thousands of years. They have helped sustain Plains and Plateau communities by supplying meat, hides for shelter and clothing, and bones for tools. At least 300 different types of items for daily and ceremonial use were traditionally made from buffalo hide, horn, bone, hooves, organs, hair, and other parts of the body. For many Plateau communities deer were available in greater supply than buffalo and supplied the same range of materials for sustenance, shelter, clothing, and tools.

People of the northern Plains and Plateau were skilled hunters who knew the migration patterns and behaviour of deer and buffalo. Hunting methods changed according to the season, landscape, and available tools. People also adapted new technology and techniques over time. Prior to the use of horses, buffalo and deer were hunted on foot. Hunters may have covered themselves with coyote or wolf hides in order to approach the buffalo without alarming the herd. Buffalo were familiar with these animals and not disturbed by their presence. The hunter knew the behaviour of the coyote and wolf and could mimic their movements to get close enough to the herd either to charge the buffalo over a cliff or to use a spear or other weapon to kill the prey. In winter hunters with dogs could chase buffalo or deer into deep snow, where the animals would stumble and be slowed down. By using snowshoes hunters had an advantage over their prey. In other seasons buffalo pounds and deer fences were built. Once inside a pound the animals could be trapped and killed. This method was used particularly on the prairie, where there were no steep cliffs – or jumps – over which to drive the herd. On the Plateau hunters frequently drove deer by burning the grasses behind the herd. Once horses became available hunters could travel more quickly to the buffalo and deer herds and hunt them from horseback.

From the mid-eighteenth to the mid-nineteenth century, the Métis community competed with Aboriginal and non-Native people to harvest and sell buffalo products. The Métis had a rich and complex culture centred on the buffalo hunt. Twice a year, in the spring and again in the fall, a chief of the hunt was selected and rules concerning the organization and start of the hunt had to be followed. Harsh penalties were imposed on those who disobeyed. For the Métis the hunt was an important economic activity as they were one of the main suppliers of pemmican, the newly popular buffalo robes, and dried buffalo tongue to competing fur trade companies. Some Métis also found employment as freighters, and shipped hides and supplies between the various trading posts and recently established towns. As the vast herds began to disappear, competition for buffalo took its toll on both Native and Métis communities.

Several factors led to the decimation of buffalo herds. Mass slaughter was prompted by growing markets for buffalo products and by sport hunting by hobbyists and tourists. The railroad companies also found buffalo herds to be a nuisance. Occasionally trains would stop to allow tourists, passengers, and soldiers to shoot as many buffalo as they could. Buffalo Bill Cody and others like him took tourists and European nobility out on 'hunts' and killed buffalo by the thousands. Both the Canadian and the American federal government also encouraged the slaughter of buffalo herds in order to destroy the traditional life of Plains and Plateau people. The practice created widespread starvation and made the transfer of communities to reserves and reservations easier. Concentrated hunting led not only to waste and overkilling but also to disease, brought on the animals by the stress of constant pursuit. By the late 1800s the buffalo herds on the northern Plains had almost vanished. Some people believed that the buffalo spirit had become displeased with its mistreatment by humans and that the buffalo therefore decided to return to the underworld or sky world from which they originally came. The Creator had given these gifts to human beings for their use, and as long as they respected them the buffalo and horse would be plentiful. If humans showed disrespect toward these beings, they would depart this world. Small herds of buffalo were saved during this period of overhunting, however, and for the past thirty years Native bands and tribes have owned buffalo herds produced from ones preserved by Canadian and US Park Services.

The loss of the buffalo caused Native people a great deal of distress and suffering. During this period a Paiute prophet from Nevada by the name of Wovoka, or Jack Wilson, began to speak of a dance that promised a return of the old ways, of peace and unity, of the disappearance of whites, and of the return of the great buffalo herds. Everyone was encouraged to take part so that all Native people, both alive and dead, would be united and live together in peace. The Ghost Dance movement spread rapidly, and Native followers from communities in Canada and the United States came in great

Left: Coat, mid-1800s, 90.0 x 75.0 cm; trousers, mid-1800s, 100.0 x 48.0 cm; moccasins, mid- to late 1800s, 25.0 x 11.5 x 16.0 cm; fire bag, mid- to late 1800s, 37.0 x 23.0 cm; sash, 1600s, 300.4 x 21.5 cm. Tanned smoked hide, beadwork, cotton mattress ticking, unbleached cotton, metal buttons, stroud, glass beads, silk embroidery thread, broadcloth, sinew, wool, fur, and silk cord. The coat and pants are a Métis Dakota/Lakota design. The style of the fire, or 'octopus,' bag was used by many cultures throughout the Northwest. The 'Assumption sash,' or ceinture flèche, popular during the fur trade, is made using a technique of weaving with the fingers rather than on a loom. It was worn as a belt but had many other uses, including as a tump line to assist in carrying heavy loads of goods. Over the years it has become one of the symbols of Métis identity. This outfit is representative of what a Métis Dakota/Lakota buffalo hunter may have worn in the mid-1800s.

Right: The Head Smashed In buffalo jump in southern Alberta was used for thousands of years. It is located just north of the Apatohsi Piikunii Reserve in Brocket, northwest of Fort Macleod.

numbers to learn the dance and the prophet's teachings. Although the dance caused great joy and ecstasy for many participants, in 1890 it brought tragedy to the Lakota men, women, and children at Wounded Knee. There about 150 people were massacred by the US army for failing to put an end to their involvement in the dance. Word of the massacre spread across the West. The Lakota, Dakota, and their allies – who had already been scattered as a nation and had their sacred circle of unity broken in 1876 at the battle of the Little Bighorn in Montana – were forced to disperse again. The Ghost Dance seemed to have failed. Individuals and communities across the Plains and Plateau were affected, and many who continued to believe in the teachings went into hiding and performed the dance in secret. Others completely abandoned it, believing that the prophecies had been false. Wovoka continued to believe in the dance and his visions and carried on the teachings until his death in the early 1930s. Today some still practise the sacred dance, believing that unity, peace, and a new order will come to North American Aboriginal people. They listen and watch closely for new prophecies and signs.

The deer population also suffered major reduction in areas of the Plateau. Increased demand from fur traders and the introduction of the gun led to overhunting. While less dramatic than the disappearance of the buffalo, the scarcity of deer, elk, and other large animals led to widespread starvation.

Plains and Plateau peoples have songs, dances, and ceremonies to honour and pay respect to the buffalo and deer for their many gifts. Many ritual societies asked the spirit of the buffalo for healing and for guidance in the hunt and everyday life. The deer was often a hunter's guardian spirit, appearing in a dream or vision after a period of fasting and ritual observance. Among the communities that practised the Sun Dance, the buffalo was central for both its spiritual significance and its meat, dried tongue, and other products.

The relationship between buffalo and human is a complex one. Among some cultures it is believed that buffalo originally hunted human beings and ate them. Suddenly the situation was reversed and the buffalo gave itself to humans for their sustenance. One Nlha7kápmx story says the change came because Coyote ran a race with Buffalo and won. If Buffalo won, he could continue to kill and eat humans, but if Coyote won, then people would eat buffalo. Buffalo was very swift and could easily outrun Coyote, but Coyote got the better of him by running *through* the hill, thus always keeping ahead. Coyote transformed Buffalo, saying 'Henceforth you will be a common buffalo, and men will hunt you and eat your flesh' (Teit 1912, 304).

There are many other stories about buffalo and deer. Five representative accounts have been chosen here: three about the buffalo and two about deer. A Pawnee story entitled 'Buffalo Woman Leads the Buffalo out of the Earth' relates how Buffalo Woman led first the buffalo, then all other animals, and finally humans out of their underground dwelling to a warm and grassy place on earth where the Platte River flowed. 'Coyote and Buffalo' is an Okanagan story that describes how Coyote brought Buffalo back to life from a pile of bones. As a reward, Buffalo gave Coyote one of his wives, who could constantly renew herself as a source of food. Through his greed and that of his friends, however, Coyote lost his buffalo wife, which is why there are no buffalo on the northern Plateau. The final buffalo story, 'The End of the World: The Buffalo Go,' is a Kaiugui explanation of the disappearance of the buffalo. 'The Deer,' the story of a hunter who married into a deer family, shows the proper behaviour between humans and animals, while 'Coyote and Wood Tick' shows what happens when someone is greedy.

Every community had individuals with a special connection to the buffalo and deer. Such people had the power to communicate with the deer or buffalo spirit and 'see,' through dreams and visions, the location of the migrating herds. Others were given the gift of 'calling' the buffalo to pounds and jumps through songs and prayers. Some Plains cultures used fossils that resembled the shape of sleeping buffalo to assist them in calling the buffalo spirit in times of hunger. Carved stone buffalo effigies are rare and tend to be found most frequently on the northern Plains. Their function is uncertain but they too may have been used for hunting or to call buffalo during periods of hunger or starvation. Among the Niisitapiikwan an *aniskim*, or small section of a baculite or ammonite fossil resembling a sleeping buffalo, was used in ceremonies by gifted spiritual people to call buffalo to particular pounds and jump sites. In the Hidatsa culture chosen young men would use a wooden stick carved with a buffalo to help them seek a vision of power when the people of the village were hungry. (Ewers 1986, 149).

The image of the buffalo – and sometimes just a symbolic representation in the form of the head, hooves, tracks, or a buffalo pound – was often painted, carved, or embossed on everyday and sacred objects. The buffalo pound image, though commonly referred to as the keyhole design, more accurately resembles the shape of a round corral with a fence fanning out from one portion of the circle. This particular design also closely resembles the shape of earth and medicine lodges. The buffalo track is probably the most frequently used buffalo image in beadwork. On moccasins it generally appears as a full hoof print on each moccasin but occasionally one half of the print is executed on the right moccasin and the other half on the left. According to David Pratt, a Dakota Sun Dance chief, the design may signify that the wearer has taken part in a Sun Dance and thus has walked the 'buffalo trail,' the path inside the Sun Dance lodge. A buffalo spine design also appears on footwear, in the form of two rows of diminishing or equal triangles running down the centre of the buffalo track design.

Like the horse effigies mentioned earlier, beaded buffalo effigies, still in use today, were often found attached to ties that could be worn in the hair or on a piece of clothing. Effigy pipes also carried the symbols and

Below: Moccasins, 1921, 25.5 x 7.6 x 21.0 cm, tanned smoked hide and glass beads. The buffalo pound design on these Tsuu T'ina moccasins was commonly used on the Plains even before European contact. The pounds were built as a means of entrapping buffalo. Once inside, the lead bull or cow would run around a pole positioned in the centre of the pound. The red centre on these moccasins may represent the pole or the sun.

Right: Headdress, late 1800s or early 1900s, 36.0 x 110.0 x 22.0 cm, felt, split buffalo horn, feathers, ermine skin, silk ribbon, stroud, cotton, and glass beads. This Niisitapiikwan bonnet has pencil drawings of horned headdresses and of horse tracks, probably representing scouting exploits, on the inside of the cotton trailer.

Yellow Horse, shown here in 1907-8, was a minor chief from the Siksika community in Alberta. Later photographs of him in the early 1920s show him still wearing his beaded buffalo effigy.

forms of the buffalo and were in frequent use on the Plains as full and partially figured animals or as symbolic representation such as the buffalo leg and hoof design.

Bonnets with buffalo horns attached were common to most Plains cultures. As we have seen, horned beings were generally considered sacred and powerful. A man wearing a horned bonnet might have belonged to a particular society or been a war leader. Both eagle feather bonnets and horned bonnets were believed to offer special protection from arrows and bullets. Some war bonnets were made of split buffalo horn or of material representing split horn. Most also had strips of ermine skin attached to the cap. On the inside cotton trailer of one Niisitapiikwan split-horned bonnet are pencilled pictographs of horned bonnets and horse tracks, probably representing scouting expeditions. The meaning of these pictographs is not fully clear but we may assume that they relate to war deeds and scouting or horse raiding exploits performed by the wearer.

Deer imagery is not as widespread as that of the buffalo, though it does appear on woven and beaded bags, baskets, and clothing. The images are often realistic figures of deer heads or the body in profile. Triangular figures of deer are often found on Wasco root-digging bags made during the last century (Schlick 1994, 167). Among the Nlha7kápmx deer are frequently drawn on items of clothing. They are associated with stories of hunting or show mythical meetings between hunter and deer. One shirt tells the story of two deer that were killed and a third that escaped and was chased by the hunter's dogs. A woman's winter dress of deer skin has a painting of two figures meeting, interpreted as a hunter and a deer standing on its hind legs. A vest has a hunter or possibly a warrior in full regalia with a buck, doe, and fawn drawn below. A rare Nlha7kápmx poncho uses a design of a deer fence, drawn as lattice work. Two deer, represented as dots, have been caught in the mesh while other dots show deer travelling along trails into the corral. The same lattice-work design is said to represent the net used by shamans to capture the soul as it leaves the body.

The White Buffalo

The birth of a white buffalo was an important symbolic event in buffalo-hunting cultures. Its flesh possessed healing powers and its hide offered great spiritual protection. The hide is the highest offering that can be given to the Great Spirit. 'It was a gift to the people but it was returned to the Great Spirit as an offering. The birth of a white buffalo usually means a turn for the good for our people,' explains Rick Two Dog in *Indian Country Today*, 28 September 1994. Because of the animal's sacredness its hide was specially prepared, in some cases with nose, hooves, horns, and tail intact. Some communities evolved great ritual and ceremony for tanning and handling the hide. Sometimes special skinning knives were saved and used only on white buffalo. Other communities were so fearful of the powers of a white buffalo spirit that prisoners were given the task of tanning the hide; if the spirit of the white buffalo became angry, its anger would be directed at the tanner. In other tribes only the hunter who killed the white buffalo could handle the hide and the meat (Pickering 1997, 20-3). White buffalo hides were also traded, sometimes costing as many as ten to fifteen horses.

Some communities hung the hide on poles facing the sun; others hung it near the tipi of the one who killed the buffalo; still others cut the hide and either made garments or sold the pieces at great cost. Among the Nuptadi/Nueta, a women's society called the White Buffalo Society wore white buffalo hide robes and hats while performing a calling ceremony to entice the buffalo close to their village. When not in use the hats were hung on the western or southern side of the tipi – the direction from which the buffalo came (Pickering 1997, 23).

The birth of a white buffalo calf in 1994 on a Wisconsin farm was seen by many Native people as the fulfilment of a Lakota prophecy based on the legend of White Buffalo Calf Woman. Nineteen generations ago she brought

Man's shirt, 66.0 x 45.0 cm, skin, paint, and cotton. The design on the front of this Nlha7kápmx shirt tells of a hunter's experience. The image of the dog chasing the running deer shows that the animal escaped. The two deer the hunter killed are drawn just above. The animals that the hunter encountered near his tipi are shown along the shirt's lower edge.

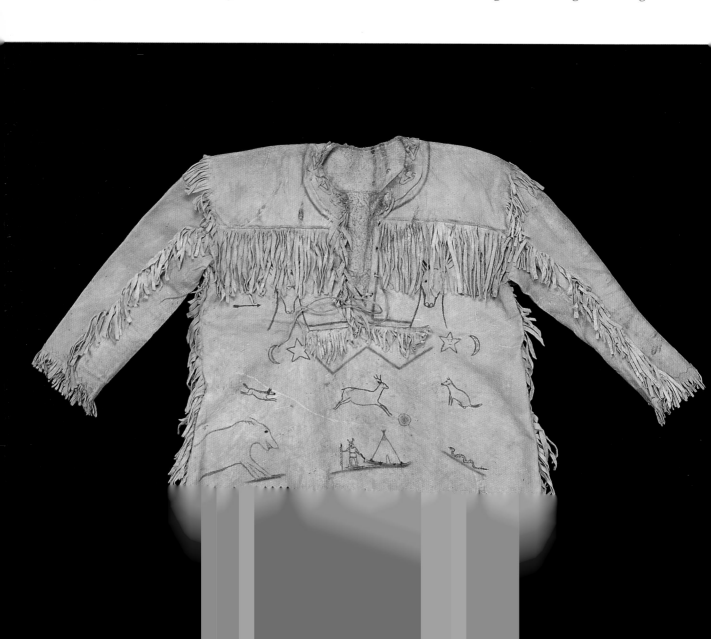

Métis Constable Dennis Fraser, RCMP, and Lakota spiritual leader Arvol Looking Horse with a group of Nehiyaw riders in 1997. The riders came from across western Canada to participate in the Cree Unity Ride for World Peace, which began in The Pas, Manitoba, and concluded at the Sunchild Reserve, Alberta. Here we see the group leaving Rocky Mountain House, Alberta, just sixteen kilometres from their destination.

the sacred pipe, with its moral code and ceremonial teachings, to the Lakota, Dakota, and Nakota nations. White Buffalo Calf Woman promised that she would return again during a time of great need. As she left the village she stopped and rolled over four times. The first time she became a black buffalo, the second time a brown buffalo, the third time a red buffalo, and the fourth time a white female buffalo calf. A white buffalo calf, said to be born only every fourth generation, comes during times of famine, turmoil, and sickness. Miracle, the Wisconsin calf, has also changed colours four times.

Okanagan Nation Unity Riders, 1996. The Okanagan community participates every year in the Unity Ride begun by Arvol Looking Horse. They raise funds to support riders from the community.

The birth of the White Buffalo Calf lets us know that we are at a crossroads – either return to balance or face global disaster. It is our duty to return back to the sacred places and pray for world peace.

Though white buffalo are very rare, an unusual number have been born since 1994. In 1995 Miracle's half-sister was born with white legs. In 1996 two albino calves were born near Michigan, North Dakota, and a white calf was born on the Pine Ridge Reservation in South Dakota. In 1997 another white buffalo was born in Michigan. In response to these events, Arvol Looking Horse, a Lakota and the nineteenth-generation keeper of the sacred White Buffalo Calf Pipe, has called for Native and non-Native people alike to begin mending the sacred circle of life and promoting global healing. Each spring since 1993 people from many different First Nations communities and non-Native people from around the world have joined him in a spiritual ride to pray for unity and world peace.

Coyote, Dog, and Wolf

For many Plateau communities and for some on the Plains, Coyote is an important figure in the stories about creation and the ordering of the everyday world. Sent by the Old One, Coyote was to finish the task begun by the Creator. He changed and distributed people among the various regions of the country and transformed beings who once fed on humans into animals that are now harmless or can be killed for food. In this way, the hummingbird was transformed from a warrior into a swift and agile bird; a woman who killed people by pushing them off high cliffs with a forked white stick was turned into a mountain sheep. Coyote created the mighty Columbia River when wishing simply to cool his feet, and brought salmon for the first time to people along the rivers in return for a wife from their village. These stories often have a moral message about how to treat others, about greed, or about lust. Other tales explain why an animal looks or acts the way it does. Some stories are simply fun to tell and hear. As Roberta Haines notes, 'throughout these legends, Coyote shows us our humanly arrogant attitude towards spiritual guidance and the inevitable price of this foolishness. Coyote provides us a humorous glimpse of the limitations of our own humanity' (Haines 1991, 156).

At one time, the dog was kept at the side of humans as a pack animal, hunter, and guardian. During times of starvation it was an important source of food and at times of illness was used for very special healing ceremonies, such as the dog feast, where dog meat was served to heal the sick. For thousands of years it has been companion, protector, and special messenger. A Nlha7kápmx story tells of a dog who cares for some children stolen from their parents. The dog travels to the sun for medicine to help the children and on the way carries messages from dying trees and a dried-up lake and creek. He returns bringing healing knowledge not only for the children but for the trees, lake, and creek as well (Joe 1996, 89-93).

Today this animal is usually just a pet and watchdog. Among ranching families the dog assists in rounding up cattle and in protecting the property from stray dogs and unfriendly human beings. For many people the dog continues to be a loyal companion. Some families own them to protect their homes from spiritual as well as human intruders. Dogs are said to be gifted with an ability to detect the presence of spirits and they also bark to chase them away. Families who keep ceremonial material may not allow dogs into their homes – they would chase benevolent spirits away during ceremonies – but keep them outside to prevent unwanted spirits from entering. In some communities the dog is still used in healing ceremonies.

Although rare, dog imagery can be found in Plains and Plateau art as well as in petroglyphs and pictographs. It is seen on effigy pipes, although sometimes it is difficult to distinguish whether the image is that of a dog, a coyote, or a wolf. The dog image has also been found on the tips of walking canes, though it is not known what purpose the carved effigy served. Various societies use dog, coyote, and wolf imagery on the religious bundles that hold their sacred medicines, objects, and society material, and on sacred objects themselves. There are far fewer examples of dog imagery than of the horse and buffalo, though coyote and wolf skins were often used for clothing, especially for hats, warm robes, and as status symbols for warriors.

These beings have been an important part of Plains and Plateau cultures for a long time and many stories tell of the relationship between the dog, coyote, and wolf and human beings. David Pratt's poem 'Man's Best Friend,' presented here, is a traditional story put into verse about how the human and the wolf, ancestor of the dog, came to respect each other. In payment for a human saving its life the wolf offered itself as protector, helper, friend, and healer, a role mirrored by the other animals discussed here as sacred beings. The story that follows the poem, 'The Dog Chief,' presents the dog as transformer from beast of burden to human form. It also tells of the gifts received by the children of the Dog Chief and his human wife: they became very fast runners, chiefs, and leaders of their community. This story is found in slightly different versions among Plains and Plateau communities, as are many of the legends that follow here.

THE FIRST HORSES

Collected by Eleanor Brass

This Nehiyaw story explains the origin of the horse in that culture. In the story the young man who eventually brings horses to his culture is on a vision quest, guided by spirit helpers in the form of grandmothers. In fulfilment of his quest the Creator gives the young man the gift of horses, which come from the water world.

There once was an Indian chief who had six sons. Five of them were fine robust men who were noted for their skill in hunting and scouting. However, the youngest son was quite the opposite. He was small and puny and didn't seem to have any desire to leave the camp. He sat around day after day, just dreaming, so he was called 'Day Dreamer.' He was ridiculed by the family and when they couldn't tolerate him any longer, they sent him to live with his grandmother.

'*Nokoom*,' he said to his grandmother when he arrived in her camp, 'my father and brothers have sent me to live with you, to take care of you. They're always teasing me and saying that I'm not any good because I don't want to go out hunting or scouting with them.'

'*Nosesim*, my grandchild, I'm overjoyed to have you live with me and I know it's not true the things your father and brothers have been saying about you. I know that you're going to do something wonderful for your people soon.'

The youth sat down in deep thought and said, 'You know, *Nokoom*, I feel that it's for a reason that I was born not to be robust like my brothers. Perhaps I'm meant to sit at home and think, until I find a way for my people to make a living in some easier way. The thought that always comes to me is that there are large animals somewhere for us to use for travelling and hunting. They are much larger than the dogs we now use.'

'Yes, *nosesim*, I have the greatest faith in you and I'll be glad to help you all I can. I'll make a new pair of moccasins for you, then I'll prepare some food for you to carry along on a trip that you'll be taking. You'll have to do a lot of travelling in search of those large animals but I'm certain that you're going to find them. Now you must rest for you'll start early in the morning.'

When the dreamer went to bed, the old woman chanted to the Great Spirit:
'Great Spirit, great father,
'Guide his moccasined feet
'As he travels further and further
'In search of something more fleet,

Horse dance stick, 1996, 65.0 x 68.0 x 16.0 cm, wood, feathers, horsehair, beads, leather, brass wire, angora, and felt marker, by Nueta/Hidatsa/Lakota artist Dennis R. Fox Jr, from New Town, North Dakota.

'With which to hunt the buffalo and deer.

'A dreamer, they call him,

'In ridicule, for he is small,

'But I know my *nosesim*

'Will find something for them all

'And he will be the greatest ever.'

The next morning, *Nokoom* gave the youth his new moccasins and some food. 'Now *nosesim*, go and search for these large animals; follow the sun and by nightfall you will come to a tepee where another grandmother lives. You will rest there and she will make you another pair of moccasins and give you more food.'

So after bidding *Nokoom* farewell, the dreamer departed, and travelled all day stopping only to eat his midday meal. At night he could see a tepee in the distance and was very weary when he arrived at its door.

'*Astom, nosesim,*' said the old grandmother who lived at the lodge, 'Come, grandchild, and sit down; you must be very weary. I have food and drink ready for you.'

The young man gladly ate for he was hungry. He went to bed early and as he slept this grandmother also sang him a song and chanted to the Great Spirit.

At the first gleam of dawn the grandmother gave the dreamer food and drink, then handed him a new pair of moccasins and food to carry. She also told him to follow the sun.

The youth kept going for several days and each night there was a grandmother waiting to give him food and a new pair of moccasins. Finally, the last grandmother told him that he was nearly at his destination; he had only one more day of travelling. '*Nosesim,*' she said, 'you'll arrive at the place of the large animals tonight. There you'll be met by a great chief who has snowy white hair. He is a magnificent looking man but he's stern and abrupt. You must approach him with the greatest respect, for he's the one who can give large animals to the Indians, if he believes they are worthy of them.'

The young man set out in high anticipation of at last realizing his dreams. His only worry was what opinion the great chief would form of him, as he was so small in stature. By evening he saw a tepee in the distance; it was large with beautiful paintings of animals on it, the kind he had always dreamed about. As he cautiously approached the lodge, he noticed the richly decorated bridles and saddles hanging all around it on racks.

The great chief came out but the dreamer was so fascinated by the magnificence of this stately chief with gleaming white hair that he just stood and stared.

'Well! what do you want?' the chief said in a stern gruff voice.

The dreamer answered falteringly: 'I came to see you about the large animals which my people might use for hunting and travelling.'

'Who told you that I had large animals? Do you think your people are worthy of getting them?'

'My grandmothers told me that you had them. I've travelled for many days; I've worn out many pairs of moccasins; and I've heard my grandmothers sing many songs and chants.'

The chief led the dreamer past the tepee to a big lake and pointing, he said, 'Look at the water.' The young man saw ripples become small waves until they gradually took the shape of horses' heads. Soon he could also see their bodies as they came swimming toward the shore. At last they came out of the water, first the white ones, then blacks, bays, pintos, palominos, sorrels, greys, roans, and buckskins, all magnificent animals.

The dreamer was excited by the sight and exclaimed, 'This is wonderful! Now my people will be able to travel and hunt more easily. I'm grateful to you, my chief.'

'Remember now, grandson, these animals are gifts from the Great Spirit, and must be treated kindly. Never hit them on their heads, for they don't like that. Now take them home to your people and tell them what I've told you.'

The youth picked up a decorated saddle that the chief had given to him and placed it on the horse that he had chosen for himself. Then he gathered up the herd and started for home. He took his time, as he wanted to admire and become familiar with the animals, but even so it did not take him long to get back to his camp.

When he arrived at his father's lodge, the Indians all came out to stare. They were greatly surprised to see the dreamer with all those magnificent strange animals. Then there was a great celebration and the youth was recognized as a great leader for finding horses for his people.

'*Nosesim* is indeed a great dreamer and his dreams have not been in vain,' said his grandmother proudly.

Winston Wuttunee, a Nehiyaw, grew up in Native ranching country. He was always around horses as a child and has tried to remain connected with them.

I was born on the Red Pheasant Reserve in the Eagle Hills of Saskatchewan. I grew up listening to the sounds of drums and men singing old, powerful Indian Sun Dance songs, Horse Dance songs, Round Dance songs, and Pow-wow songs. There were horses all through my life wherever I was, and when they weren't there in the flesh they came to me in my dreams, as powerful medicine. Later on in life I bought a ranch seven miles west of Turner Valley, Alberta, at the entrance to the Kananaskis Mountains, and there I fulfilled my dream of looking out my windows and seeing my horses grazing on our own land. From this ranch I made many excursions into the nearby mountains with many different peoples, sometimes guiding and sometimes just riding along as a friend.

Painted Pony

Garry Gottfriedson

Garry Gottfriedson is of Okanagan/Secwepemc descent. He was born into a ranching and rodeo family on the Kamloops Indian Reserve, British Columbia. For several generations his family has had large herds of horses. Some were sold to the army during the First World War, others were used for horse logging, and some have been sold to racing stables or as bucking stock. Gottfriedson has published widely, and his work focuses on the lived experience of First Nations people in Canada.

Let me tell you of a time long ago when Turtle Island was inhabited only by Native people. Everything on Turtle Island was alive and had its own language. The Mineral People, who were the oldest, had their own language. The Plant People, whom the Creator made next, also had their own language. Then the Creator made the Birds and Animal People, and they, too, were given a language of their own. The last ones the Creator made were the Humans, but their language was a little bit different from the others.

The Creator told the youngest ones, the Humans, that they must show respect for Him and for Older Ones as well, the Mineral People, the Plant People, and the Birds and Animal People. The Creator told the Humans that they could call on the Older Ones if the People needed help. Then He told the Humans that they were free to travel all over Turtle Island because everything on it was made for their use.

This is how this story was told to me when I was a small child. Now, let me tell you of a special story that I remember as it was told to me. It is an old story about where my name came from. It is an old name that was passed down to me.

My story goes back to when only the Natives lived in North America. Our People were happy people then. They roamed all over the land gathering food in the summer and getting ready for Old Man Winter, so they could settle in warm lodges and tell stories about how they were to live a good life. My people loved to tell stories of old times, and they retold stories mostly in the winter when food gathering and hunting slowed down.

They told stories for many hours during the long cold winter days and wished for summer to come so they could travel again all over the land. In the winter many small bands joined together and camped for the winter, but in the summer they broke into smaller groups and travelled to their favourite places in the mountains. One of those small bands was where my family came from. They broke away from one of the main bands and travelled

Bag, 52.0 x 16.5 cm, fringe 32.0 cm, skin, brass, glass beads, wool, sinew, and linen. This Kutenai style of horse design is reminiscent of early pictographs.

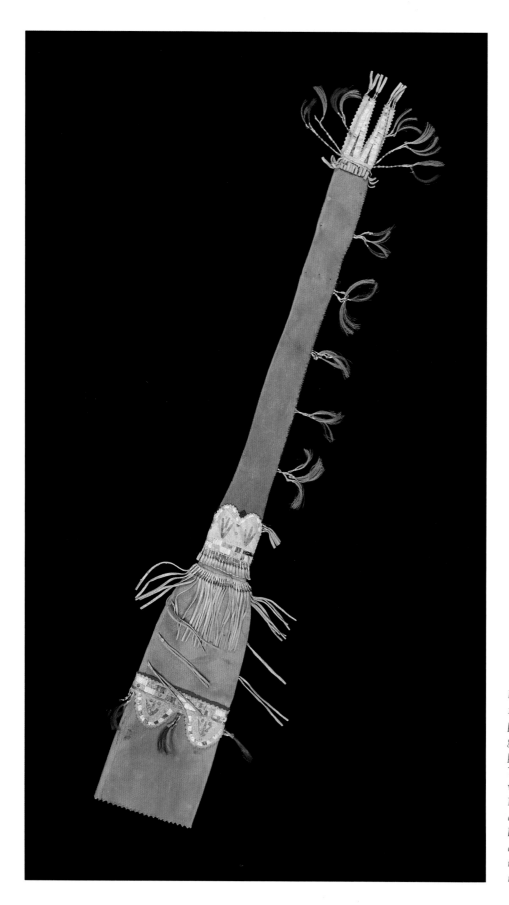

Rifle case, 1875-90, 145.0 x
19.5 cm, tanned smoked skin,
porcupine quill embroidery,
glass beads, dyed horsehair,
paint, felt, stroud, and sinew.
This Dakota/Lakota type case
was collected in the Lake
Manitoba region. Such beautiful
quillwork is difficult to come
by today. The quilled designs
and circular symbols may be
meant to offer the hunter protection and bring luck in the hunt.

to the mountains. The place they went to was deep within the Rocky Mountains. The mountains were beautiful with white snowcaps on them. They were filled with green valleys full of tall grass and colourful flowers. The mountainsides and valley had many spruce trees, pine trees, and poplar trees on them. The Birds sang everywhere. Hawks and eagles soared in the blue skies. Animals roamed freely in the forests. Trout and salmon jumped and played in the clear streams, lakes, and rivers. The water was crystal clear and tasted very sweet. The land was so peaceful that our people even heard the Animal People talking. The band loved this place very much, and each time they arrived there, they became very happy. Besides, they knew there would be a lot of food to gather for winter.

In the summer camps, the men went out hunting and fishing every day. Each day, they brought back plenty of meat and fish for the women to dry for winter. While the men were out, the women went along the hillsides to pick berries and to dig roots. The children helped with chores, and when they were finished, they played. But this was not a happy time for one particular little boy. Often he played alone, sadly, for he had no brothers and sisters and all the other boys and girls teased him. You see, unlike the other children, he did not have a name yet. So, many times he wandered away and played all by himself.

On one of those days, he strolled away through some very tall poplar trees that led to a meadow far from camp. He heard voices in the meadow, so he went to investigate. As he sat at the edge of the meadow in tall bunch grass, he saw many horses eating: brown ones, white ones, red ones, roan ones, and painted horses, too. He saw colts loping and playing with each other and he wished he could play. Naturally, he became very curious and sneaked closer and closer so he could see them better.

The horses looked so happy and fun to be with that he began to wish he could be one of them – a Horse Person. Soon, a painted colt noticed him and came galloping over. The painted colt talked to him, and to his surprise, the boy understood the colt's language. After they talked for a while, the colt asked the boy if he wanted to join his family and be with the Horse People. The boy agreed. Then the colt kicked up his hooves and splattered many colours of earth on the boy. He told the boy to sing these words:

> My name is Painted Pony.
> I am from the Horse People.
> When you are sad or lonely
> You can sing my song
> And I will comfort you.
> My name is Painted Pony.

As he sang this song, he knew that he now had a name. While the boy was singing, the painted colt asked the little boy to imitate him and pretend he was a pony. So the little boy did. He galloped off kicking up his heels and singing the Painted Pony Song. Then something magical happened. The little boy transformed into a beautiful white and brown painted pony. And that night when his mother fell asleep, he sneaked into her dreams and told her what had happened to him. He told her, too, not to be lonely for him, because the Creator would give her a new son who would be named Painted Pony. From that time on, the name Painted Pony was passed on from one generation to the next. And this is how I got my name – Painted Pony.

Kim Colliflower is an Ah-ah-nee-nin/Hinono'eino' from the Fort Belknap Reservation in northern Montana. After a professional career as a bronc rider, he is now often asked to be a rodeo judge. Colliflower is also recognized as a skilled leather worker, whose colourful rodeo chaps are in great demand.

When I was growing up on the Fort Belknap Reservation in the '50s, if you had to go somewhere you went by horseback. There was no other way to get around.
The horse was there for a reason. They were there not for enjoyment but for us to use. They were animals, so you respected them. You took care of them and they relied on us to take care of them. We were always taught to keep them clean and well fed and watered. Before we saddled them up we brushed them and had to make them look good. If that horse looks good – maybe he'll feel good too.

ÂYAHKWÊW'S LODGE

Gregory Scofield
for Garry G.

Gregory Scofield is a Métis/Nehiyaw activist living in Vancouver, where he divides his time between writing and working with street youth. He has three books of poetry. 'Âyahkwêw's Lodge' refers to the practice of holding naming ceremonies, common to all Aboriginal communities on the Plains and Plateau. It is not unusual among Plains cultures for a person to receive from two to four names during a lifetime. An elder or holy person is often approached to name a child, though not always at birth, and children are frequently named after sacred beings such as the horse, thunder, buffalo, or dog, which then act as guardian spirits. *Âyahkwêw* is loosely translated as a person who has both male and female spirits, or is two-spirited.

êkwa êkosi, nikîwêhtatânân ôhi mistatimwak
(And so, we brought these horses home)
and gave them to our women
who in turn
gave them to our men.
That night a baby was born in camp,
eyes clenched shut,
fist in his mouth.

In the lodge
there was an old woman
who had woken in the night
to a lightless presence.
She was instructed
to make offerings,
bring water and blood
from the sacred woman's belly.

These she took to *Âyahkwêw*.

In the blood
a twinning spirit was seen.
The water
was marked by thunder.
Âyahkwêw prepared the rattle,
placing inside
the child's umbilical cord.

At dawn, the time of prayer
they brought the child
to our lodge to be named –
and so we named him twice,
Mistatim-awâsis /
(Horse-child)
He Who Calls *Piyesîwak-iskwêw.*
(Thunder-woman)

THERE'S MORE TO A HORSE
THAN MEETS THE EYE, *1995,
74.5 x 106.0 cm, mixed media,
by George Littlechild. The painting pays homage to the horse for
all its gifts and healing powers.*

*Littlechild also intended to honour
his greatgrandfather, from the
Louis Bull Reserve, Alberta, pictured to the right, who kept a very
large herd of horses and worked
with them in healing ceremonies.*

Buffalo Woman Leads the Buffalo out of the Earth

Collected by Mari Sandoz

This Pawnee story tells of when Buffalo Woman led buffalo and humans out of the underworld and onto the earth, to an area around the Platte River, which has its main tributary in Nebraska. In the 1870s the Pawnee were given land in Oklahoma. In 1980 fewer than 400 Pawnee people resided in the state but today about 2,000 people live on lands originally assigned to them as reservation land. The Pawnee were originally made up of four tribes, the Chaui, Pitahawirata, Kitkahahki, and Skidi. It is not certain from which this story originated.

Once, long ago, all things were waiting in a deep place far underground. There were the great herds of buffaloes and all the people, and the antelope too, and wolves, deer, and rabbits – everything, even the little bird that sings the *tear-tear* song. Everything waited as in sleep.

Then the one called Buffalo Woman awoke, stretched her arms, rose, and began to walk. She walked among all the creatures, past the little *tear-tear* bird, the rabbits, and all the rest and through the people, too, and the buffaloes. Everywhere as she passed there was an awakening, and a slow moving, as when the eyes were making ready for some fine new thing to be seen.

Buffalo Woman walked on in the good way, past even the farthest buffaloes, the young cows with their sleeping yellow calves. She went on to a dark round place that seemed like a hole, and she stood there a while, looking. Then she bowed her head a little as one does to pass under the lodge flap, and stepped out. Suddenly the people could see there was a great shining light all about her, a shining and brightness that seemed blinding as she was gone.

And now a young cow arose and followed the woman, and then another buffalo and another, until a great string of them was following, each one for a moment in the shining light of the hole before he was gone, and the light fell upon the one behind.

When the last of the buffaloes was up and moving, the people began to rise, one after another, and fell into a row too, each one close upon the heels of the moccasins ahead. All the people, young and old and weak and strong went so, out through the hole that was on Pahuk, out upon the shining, warm and grassy place that was the earth, with a wide river, the Platte, flowing below, and over everything a blueness, with the *tear-tear* bird flying toward the sun, the warming sun.

The buffaloes were already scattering over the prairie, feeding, spreading in every direction toward the circle that is the horizon. The people looked all around and knew this was their place, the place upon which they would live forever, they and the buffalo together.

Black Elk (1863-1950), Lakota elder, 1931

The bison is the chief of all animals, and represents the earth, the totality of all that is.
It is the feminine, creating earth principle which gives rise to all living forms.
The animal hunted is sacred-power. To follow his tracks one is on the path of power.
To kill the animal is to obtain power.

COYOTE AND BUFFALO

Herb Manuel

Herb Manuel is an Okanagan storyteller and teacher. He has worked as a ranch hand and band manager and has served as chief and band councillor. This lively story of Coyote and Buffalo is one of the most popular Coyote tales. Slightly different versions are found among other Plateau communities.

Coyote was travelling by one day, just bored. There was nobody around – absolutely nothing around there, and he was hungry. He's always hungry. Seen these pile of bones – buffalo bones – one pile, just the way he died. No scavenger took anything – it was all there, just the way he died. He died fighting for his wives years ago.

So Coyote, he went by there and he sucked on all the bones. He sat down. He got the two ribs and he started beating on them. He started singing, just making no sense. They say that's why you still hear Coyote, still singing around now and then. He does that all the time. He finds a pile of bones or something, or a smell of something dead, and he'll start singing like that again. And he rattled those bones.

And Buffalo told him, 'Oh, leave me alone! I've been dead here since a long time ago. Why don't you just go on your way? Can't you see I'm poor, all faded? Leave me alone.'

Coyote got singing louder. He got through singing and he looked at Buffalo – he laughed at old Buffalo laying there. So Coyote rested his foot on the pile of bones.

And that was all Buffalo needed. He put himself back together – he was just bones. He told Coyote, 'I'm going to kill you, Coyote.'

'What are you talking about, you're going to kill me? You're just a rack of bones there.' So Coyote jogs on quite fast. He hears old Buffalo coming. 'Just, just, just, just, just, just!' Coyote was having a nap, and he looked there. Buffalo's right around over the next hill. He got away from the wind. This went on day and night – Buffalo chased Coyote. He had no peace. He went on and on and on. Pretty soon he was run out of strength. He had no water. He had nothing to eat for days on end because Buffalo bones was chasing him. And he was running with all his might. And he had to climb and he got towards the top, and he couldn't go no further. He stopped and Buffalo was about to gore him, but he had no horns – he was just bony. He was going to bump him. Coyote said, 'Peace! Peace!' He said, 'Let's talk! I'll make you a deal. I'll fix you up, if you quit chasing me. I'll put you back

together and you can go after your enemy. I'll fix you up the way you were – you'll be a young man again.'

Buffalo said, 'But if you lie, Coyote, I'm still going to kill you.'

So Coyote went to work and put him back together – built him stronger than ever. Coyote put thick fur, thick hair, thick skin all over Buffalo – built him just the way he is. But boy, he was just a little leaner!

And he said to him, 'Well, you have to have horns.' So they looked about at all the sticks. 'These pine branches here look about as strong as can be.' He gathered these pine branches, stuck them on Buffalo's head, and told him, 'We'll use that big pine tree there to practise on. You take a run at it. See if it sticks, so it won't break.'

He ran, he hit that thing, and Whamo! – the branches were broken.

'No, we have to find a stick here. Something has got to work.' And he tried the fir tree. That didn't work. Then he thought for a while. He said, 'Well, maybe something a little harder.'

He tried a birch. Birch is hard wood, but it didn't work. He tried that. No. They were trying out horns, the Buffalo and Coyote, and they tried out all the sticks they could find. They were getting disgusted, and Coyote's life was at stake.

So they tried ts'itl' [pitch] from a dead fir tree – an old dead fir tree, pretty well petrified. The pitch would be just black – really solid and hard; but it burns easy. You could make a spear out of it, it's so hard. It's really good wood, and it won't break so easy. So they tried this ts'itl' – pitch for

Left: Drum, late 1800s or early 1900s, 45.5 cm diameter, rawhide, wood, nails, and paint. Buffalo imagery was often incorporated into personal and sacred items to show respect for the animal and to call on its spirit for assistance. This drum is thought to be Niisitapiikwan.

Below: Buffalo carvings, 1996, 14.5 x 26.0 x 15.2 cm and 7.5 x 14.2 x 8.5 cm, Brazilian soapstone, by Charles Brown, Lytton, British Columbia. Charles Brown is one of a number of Nlha7kápmx carvers who are recreating a tradition of stone sculpture in their community. Made of local stone from sites quarried thousands of years ago as well as from imported soapstone, their sculptures draw on archaeological carvings and traditional and contemporary themes.

his horns. Took a run at that pine tree and it stuck. He backed up and hit it again – it stuck. And Coyote said, 'That's the one we're looking for! Yes!'

They were quite happy and Coyote told Kwesp – that's Buffalo in the Okanagan language, 'Let's go down to the lake. Have a look at yourself. See your image in the water – it's a looking-glass.' So he walked down and looked at himself. Ah, he was happy at how he looked! He was satisfied!

'Okay Coyote,' he said, 'now that you fixed me up, I'm going to fix you up.'

They say Coyote at that time had big ugly feet – very big feet, ugly and clumsy – and he had a smashed-in face from fighting so much. He had a little short nose, like a bulldog, and floppy ears and a little short tail – he had a long back and he had short legs, like a baloney dog.

Buffalo told him, 'I'll pretty you up too, partner.' Grabbed him by the ears – like that. Got his nose and stretched it a couple of times. Held it for a while – let him go. He had a nice, long nose. Stretched his eyes back a little, pulled his tail out and fluffed it up a little bit. Pulled his legs out – made nice, cute, small feet on him so he could run faster. Shortened his body up, give him better fur. 'Okay Coyote, go and have a look.' He had a look and he couldn't quit looking at himself. He would run back down there and turn around and pose for himself.

Anyways, 'I'm not quite through with you, Buffalo. I want to see you use them horns. I know where your enemy is. You still got your wives just over the mountain there,' he said. 'We'll go over there and you'll fight and get your wives back. You got all the equipment you need now,' he said. 'I sit up the hill and cheer for you. I ain't going to be part of the fight,' he said. 'Ah,' he said, 'if you get killed, I'll jump over you and bring you back to life – that way I'll owe you nothing.'

'Okay,' said Buffalo.

So they travelled over the hills and through the mountains and out to the Prairies. They came over this big hill, and there was a big herd of buffalo down there. There was a great big bull down there.

Coyote said, 'There's your enemy – kill him.'

Buffalo said to Coyote, 'Yes I'll go fight now – kill him. But I'm going to wait until sunrise – make an event of it.'

So they sat on the hill and waited. Slept over night and waited for the sun to rise. When the sun rose they walked down, Buffalo let out a bellow of challenge, and the big bull, his enemy, came trolling out of the herd.

Buffalo hit him and they had a fight. They fought and fought. They went down – Coyote's friend went down a few times. Buffalo, when he would be right down, Coyote would give him a bracer with his power again and again, and he'd get back up – he'd get at it again. He finally got the best of that big bull, and he killed him and he took over the herd.

So Coyote travelled with his partner. They went around – they were friends for a few years.

And Buffalo told him, 'It's not right that you live with me and my kind. It's unfair for you to live with me.' He said, 'We will part. You go this way, I go that way; but before we part I'll give you one of my wives – not to be your wife, but to be your food.' He said, 'You can cut a chunk. You push her over anytime. Touch her – push her over like that. She'll fall over and she'll fall asleep.' He said, 'Take three or four slices out of the upper rear. When you have enough, slowly rub it over and it will heal and she'll get up and you guys can travel again. Every time you're hungry, you do it.' He said, 'Do it no more than two times a day, sunrise and sunset.'

Coyote was just over the hill, 'Gee, I got to try this out!' Gives her a push – down she went. Hacked a chunk out of her – three or four steaks out of the hind leg there. He cooked it up and ate. Then away he went. He was just barely over the hill there – and he pushed her down again, 'I'm hungry – I'm packing my lunch along. I'm far enough away from my partner – he don't know what date it is.' Down she went again.

It was getting shorter between times – it was getting tiresome.

So the next time he dropped a chunk, he had his friends around. The type of friends that he carried were low-grade. Always Raven and Crow and Magpie and those type of scavengers – those were his people. He invited them over, 'Come on down here,' he said. 'I got the real McCoy! Feast here! Get over here!' So they ate and got past the upper rear and, of course, old Raven, he wouldn't quit eating, and Magpie – they were fighting for it.

Crow said, 'I'm going to eat!'

Magpie would say, 'No, I'm going to eat!'

And they were fighting. Finally, they finished – ate the whole thing up. Coyote was trying to pull them off, and they were biting at him. They ate his wife all to nothing, so he couldn't put the skin back on and it was all dragged away – it was eaten. Just the bones were laying there. He was given trust that he broke. So that was the end of his glory.

THE BUFFALO DANCE OF
THE SIOUX AT FORT
QU'APPELLE, *1881, 22.3 x 33.7*
cm, pencil heightened with grey
and opaque white on laid paper,
by Sydney Prior Hall. The
buffalo dance was performed by
many Plains communities as a
form of supplication to the spirit
of the buffalo to bring the buffalo
herds to the people.

The End of the World: The Buffalo Go

Old Lady Horse (Spear Woman)

Kaiugui, or Kiowa, mythology locates their place of origin on the Yellowstone River. Mount Scott, which is mentioned in the following story, is in Fort Sill, in southwestern Oklahoma. In 1892 the Kaiugui were moved to Indian Territory, reservation land in Oklahoma, where most of them now live. Told by Old Lady Horse (Spear Woman) to Alice Marriott, 'The End of the World' explains the disappearance of the buffalo and the implications for the Kaiugui people. The American government in the 1860s and 1870s realized that the easiest way to get Native Americans to move onto reservations was to remove their food supply. Soldiers were therefore ordered to slaughter the buffalo herds. The story refers to these African American military men as buffalo soldiers, so called by the Kaiugui because their hair seemed to resemble that of buffalo. Spear Woman explains that the buffalo did not give up their lives without a fight. On one occasion at Fort Sill the buffalo herd was so large that soldiers could not shoot fast enough to kill the whole herd.

Everything the Kiowas had came from the buffalo. Their tipis were made of buffalo hides; so were their clothes and moccasins. They ate buffalo meat. Their containers were made of hide, or of bladders or stomachs. The buffalo were the life of the Kiowas.

Most of all, the buffalo was part of the Kiowa religion. A white buffalo calf must be sacrificed in the Sun Dance. The priests used parts of the buffalo to make their prayers when they healed people or when they sang to the powers above.

So, when the white men wanted to build railroads, or when they wanted to farm or raise cattle, the buffalo still protected the Kiowas. They tore up the railroad tracks and the gardens. They chased the cattle off the ranges. The buffalo loved their people as much as the Kiowas loved them.

There was war between the buffalo and the white men. The white men built forts in the Kiowa country, and the woolly-headed buffalo soldiers [the Tenth Cavalry, made up of African American troops] shot the buffalo as fast as they could, but the buffalo kept coming on, coming on, even into the post cemetery at Fort Sill. Soldiers were not enough to hold them back.

Then the white men hired hunters to do nothing but kill the buffalo. Up and down the plains those men ranged, shooting sometimes as many as a hundred buffalo a day. Behind them came the skinners with their wagons. They piled the hides and bones into the wagons until they were full, and then took their loads to the new railroad stations that were being built, to be shipped to the market. Sometimes there would be a pile of bones as high as a man, stretching a mile along the railroad track.

The buffalo saw that their day was over. They could protect their people no longer. Sadly, the last remnant of the great herd gathered in council, and decided what they would do.

The Kiowas were camped on the north side of Mount Scott, those of them who were still free to camp. One young woman got up very early in the morning. The dawn mist was still rising from Medicine Creek, and as she looked across the water, peering through the haze, she saw the last buffalo herd appear like a spirit dream.

Straight to Mount Scott the leader of the herd walked. Behind him came the cows and their calves, and the few young males who had survived. As the woman watched, the face of the mountain opened.

Inside Mount Scott the world was green and fresh, as it had been when she was a small girl. The rivers ran clear, not red. The wild plums were in blossom, chasing the red buds up the inside slopes. Into this world of beauty the buffalo walked, never to be seen again.

THE DEER

Collected by James A. Teit

Stories about the deer do not appear as frequently in collections of legends as do those about the coyote, horse, or buffalo. Deer are more often talked about as sources of food, especially for Coyote, than as the main actors in the story. Humans who marry into deer society find themselves with an ample supply of meat, fat, and bone marrow, along with hides for clothing. This story, collected from the Nlha7kápmx living near Lytton, BC, explains the appropriate actions to ensure that deer remain accessible to the human community.

Nlha7kápmx deer hunters, with horses, Lytton, British Columbia, c 1960. People continue to hunt deer for meat and tan the hides using traditional techniques. Horses still provide transportation through the mountain passes to traditional hunting areas.

There was a man who was a great deer hunter. He was constantly hunting, and was very successful. He thought continually of the deer and dreamed of them. They were as friends to him. Probably they were his manitou [guardian spirit]. He had two wives, one of whom had borne him no children while the other one had borne a male child. One day while hunting, he came on the fresh tracks of a doe and fawn, which he followed. They led to a knoll on which he saw a young woman and child sitting. The tracks led directly to them. He was surprised, and asked the woman if she had seen any deer pass. She answered, 'No.' He walked on, but could not find the tracks. On his return, he said to the woman, 'You must have seen the deer; the tracks seem to disappear where you are, and they are very fresh.' The woman laughed and said, 'You need not trouble yourself about the tracks. For a long time I have loved you and longed for you. Now you shall go with me to my house.' They walked on together; and the hunter could not resist the attraction of the woman, nor help following her. As he went along, he thought, 'It is not well that I am acting thus. My wives and my child are at home awaiting me.' The woman knew his thoughts at once, and said, 'You must not worry or think that you are doing wrong. You shall be my husband, and you will never regret it.' After the two had travelled a long way, they reached a hilly country. Then the man saw an entrance which seemed to lead underground. When they had gone some distance underground, they found themselves in a large house full of people who were just like Indians. They were of both sexes and all ages. They were well dressed in clothes of dressed skin, and wore deer skin robes. They seemed to be very amiable and happy. As the travellers entered, some of the people said, 'Our daughter has brought her husband.' That night the woman said to the hunter, 'You are my husband, and will sleep with me. You may embrace me, but you must not try to have intercourse with me. You must not do so before the rutting season.

Then you may also go with my sisters. Our season comes but once a year, and lasts about a month. During the rest of the year we have no sexual connections.' The hunter slept with his new wife.

On the following day the people said, 'Let our son-in-law hunt. He is a great hunter. Let him get meat for us. We have no more meat.' The hunter took his bow and arrows and went hunting. Two young deer, his brothers-in-law, ran ahead and stood on a knoll. Presently the hunter saw them, and killed both of them. He cut them up and carried them home, leaving nothing but their manure. The chief had told him in the morning to be careful and not to throw away any part of the game. Now the people ate and were glad. They saved all the bones and put them away in one place. They said to the hunter, 'We always save every bone.' When the deer were eaten, the bones were wrapped in bundles, and the chief sent a man to throw them into the water. He carried the bones of the two deer that the hunter had killed, and of another one that the people were eating when the hunter first arrived. The hunter had missed his two brothers-in-law, and thought they were away hunting. When the man who had carried the bones away returned, the two brothers-in-law and another man were with him. They had all come to life when their bones were thrown into the water. Thus these Deer people lived by hunting and killing each other and then reviving. The hunter lived with his wife and her people, and hunted whenever meat was required. He never failed to kill deer, for some of the young deer were always anxious to be killed for the benefit of the people.

IGNACE'S MEDICINE POWER, *c 1842, 10.8 x 17.5 cm, ink on paper, by Nicolas Point, SJ. Point was a Jesuit missionary who spent six years among the Salish, Niisitapiikwan, and Nez Percé. His sketches offer a valuable record of Native life in the 1840s. The deer was often the supernatural helper or guardian spirit of a hunter, and, as in this image, appears in a dream or vision. Also seen in the dream are dogs and a horse, which may have accompanied the man on the hunt.*

Coyote and Wood Tick

Collected by James Teit

James Teit, who recorded this Nlha7kápmx story around 1900, notes that the wood tick is found on deer and horses. It is said to come out of fir or other brush and in the early spring is often found sticking on horses in great numbers and engorged with blood. In this story, Coyote's greed destroys his relationship with the tick and the deer. At the end only Coyote suffers for his actions.

At last he [Coyote] came to a house which was inhabited by Wood Tick (Kîtse'in). He entered and the latter gave him some fat to eat. Coyote said, 'I am hungry and naked, and would like to stay with you as your servant.' Wood Tick agreed to this, and, pointing to a large heap of deer skins, told him to tan them. So Coyote stayed with Wood Tick, and tanned many doe skins for him, and made soft robes and clothes for himself.

After a time Wood Tick trusted him, and sent him to get deer meat. He gave him his staff, and told him to go up to a steep cliff overlooking the house, and to strike the rock once with the staff. He cautioned him particularly never to strike it more than once. Coyote did as directed, and as soon as he struck the rock, a dead deer appeared at his feet. He skinned it, cut it up, and carried it home. When Wood Tick saw that he had done everything right, he made up his mind to send him for meat every day. On the fourth day, when Coyote was up on the rock, he made up his mind to strike it often and see what effect it would have: so he struck the rock with the staff until his arm was tired, and a dead deer fell at his feet each time. Then he said to himself, 'I have now so much meat that I shall never starve'; and returning to Wood Tick's house, he struck him on the head with a stone. After a time Wood Tick revived, and cried out, 'Get up and go!' Then all the deer became alive and ran away. Wood Tick jumped on a buck's ear and made off with the rest. Coyote got excited and ran to save some fat, but it got up and ran away. The robes in his bed, and the buckskin clothes he was wearing, ran away; and every piece of deer's bone, hair, and skin around the place got up and followed the rest: so Coyote was left without food, and with only his robe as before.

James Teit collected this story from the Nlha7kápmx of the Nicola Valley and it was published by Franz Boas in 1917.

Coyote ... said, 'Deer will be game and food for the Indians. There will be deer as long as there are Indians. If the Indians disappear so will the deer.' It was ordained this way. The deer were always animals. They were created as game, and food for people. They were hunted by the ancients, and continue to be hunted by the Indians of the present day.

Coyote

Collected by James A. Teit

There are many, many stories of Coyote on the Plateau and among some Plains cultures. Beliefs about where he came from, what his role was, and if he is still among us in a new form vary from storyteller to storyteller. This brief description from the Okanagan gives one explanation.

Coyote ... travelled on the earth and did many wonderful things. He destroyed the powers of all the monsters and evil beings that preyed on the people. He transformed the good ancients into Indians and divided them into groups or pairs, and settled them in different places; for the Chief [the Creator] desired the earth to be inhabited everywhere, and not only in a few places. He gave each people a different name and a different language. These pairs were the ancestors of all the present Indian tribes; and that is why there are so many Indian tribes and languages now, and why Indians live all over the country. He taught the people how to eat, how to wear clothes, make houses, hunt, fish, etc. Coyote did a great deal of good, but he did not finish everything properly. Sometimes he made mistakes; and although he was wise and powerful, he did many foolish things. He was too fond of playing tricks for his own amusement. He was also often selfish, boastful, and vain. He sometimes overreached himself, and occasionally was duped by persons whom he intended to dupe. He was ugly, and women generally did not like him. He often used cunning to gain his ends. He was immortal, and did not die as we die.

Coyote had done nearly everything he could think of, and was travelling from place to place to learn of other things that remained to be done. Chief looked over the earth, and said, 'Coyote has now done almost everything that he is capable of doing. I will relieve him.' Chief came down, and travelled in the shape of a poor old man. He met Coyote, who said to him, 'I am Coyote. Who are you?' Chief answered, 'I am Chief of the earth. It was I who sent you to set the world right.' Coyote said, 'No, you never sent me. I don't know you. If you are Chief, take that lake and place it yonder.' Chief said, 'No. If you are the wonderful Coyote, let me see you do it!' Coyote did it. Chief said, 'Place it back again.' Coyote tried, but could not do it. He thought this strange. Chief placed it back. Coyote said, 'Now I know you are Chief.' Chief said, 'Your work is finished. You have travelled far and long, and done much good. Now you shall go to where I have prepared a home for you.' Coyote disappeared, and no one knows where he is.

MAN'S BEST FRIEND

David Pratt

David Pratt, Dakota/Nehiyaw, is from Gordon's Reserve in Saskatchewan. He is a working cowboy, rancher, horse trainer, former professional rodeo cowboy, cowboy poet, and entertainer. A featured performer at the Elko Cowboy Poetry Gathering and the Canadian Cowboy Festival, Pratt enacts his unique brand of 'Indian cowboy humour' and brings his audience into the Native cowboy's life.

   'Man's Best Friend' is an old Dakota story put into verse. It relates how people and dogs came to be companions. Several Plains cultures have dog feasts, in which dog meat is served in ceremonies to cure the sick. Because of its healing powers the dog is respected by many as a very sacred being.

There was a time when animals could speak with man,
Back when we were pure enough to understand.
One day my grandfather told me of the change
As we rode together out on the range.

Mother earth shook and opened her mouth
To cleanse herself of the hatred about.
The death of the wolf was certain as he fell into her jaws
But man risked his life and grabbed onto his claws,
'Let go of me brother or you surely will die.'
Man refused, 'If you go brother, so do I.'
Man was laying face down, completely determined.
He used his last strength and pulled wolf up again.

Wolf, grateful to man, said then,
'From now on I will always be your brother and your friend.
I'll protect you with my life and when you're sad I'll sing to you my beautiful song.
I'll walk beside and warn you of danger.
I'll use my keen senses to warn you of strangers.
I will hunt with you, being quiet and sly,
Or if you are hungry, for you I will die.'

Many years have passed but Wolf's promise still stands,
Grandfather's teachings to both wolf and to man.
Today wolf's descendants, the dog, we all know,
Is right by my side, wolf's promise to show.
First thing in the morning and at day's end
My dog is there; he's my best friend.

RETURN OF THE HUNTER, c 1841-7, 10.8 x 17.8 cm, ink on paper, by Nicolas Point, SJ. In his drawings, Point records the different techniques used to hunt animals and birds, usually showing men carrying spears or bows and arrows. This hunter has been successful with his gun and may have taken his dogs along on the hunt as well.

THE DOG CHIEF

Collected by Clark Wissler and D.C. Duvall

Clark Wissler worked for the American Museum of Natural History. David Duvall, Amoskapi Piikunii/French, from Browning, Montana, worked as his interpreter and also collected narratives from older Niisitapiikwan people. This Niisitapiikwan story tells about the marriage of Dog Man and a Niisitapiikwan woman. It speaks of the community's response to the union and of the powerful and gifted children whom the couple raised.

Once there was a very nice girl, the daughter of a head man, and many young men sought her for a wife. One of the men in the camp owned a very large dog. It was a brindle. One time this girl borrowed his dog, hitched him to a travois, and went out for wood. After this she borrowed him many times, and he became used to her. Whenever he came about she always fed him and petted him, and whenever she went for water he went with her. One day as the girl was going along she said aloud, 'I wish you were a young man, then I would marry you.' Now the dog heard and understood. That night he turned himself into a man and went to the lodge where the girl was sleeping. She awoke and found some one kissing her. She put out her hand, felt the man, and noted that his hair was fine and that he had finely shaped limbs. When he went away she wondered who it could be. She never had anything to do with other men. She had two brothers, and for that reason she did not wish to say anything about it. She thought the person might have been one of her suitors. So she thought to herself, 'If he comes, next time I will mark him.' So that evening she took some white earth, mixed it with water in a cup, and stirred it with a stick-weed. That night the strange visitor came again, and, as he caressed the girl, she rubbed some of the white earth on his hair, on his robe, and on his back.

Now the next day there was a dance in the camp, and while it was going on, the girl went out and looked around. Though she could see every man in the camp, none of them wore the marks of her paint. Now she wondered who he could be. As she turned away, she saw a dog in the distance. It was her travois dog, and as he came up she saw stripes of white paint on him, just as she had marked her strange visitor. Now she thought to herself, 'It can't be the dog; but surely that is the paint. Now tonight he will come again, and I will try it once more.' That night the man came again. This time she took his middle finger, and, putting it into her mouth, bit it very hard so as to cut it through with her teeth.

Now she was the daughter of the chief of the tribe. The next day there was to be a dance, and she requested her father to order the young men to dance holding up their hands. Her father did this, and as they danced she looked closely at all their hands but saw no bruises on them. As she looked away, she saw the travois dog again. As he came up, she noticed that he was lame, and when she examined his foot, she found that one of his toes was nearly cut in two. Then she went to the man and asked him for the loan of the dog to go for water. She put him to the travois and went. When out of sight of the camp, she took the dog into the brush, turned to him and said, 'Here, it is you that visits me at night.' The paint was on him yet, and he was very lame.

Then the dog became a man, took off the travois and stood up. He was a fine young man. He said to the girl, 'Well, it was your fault, you wished it.' Then the dog-man took her into the brush. The girl said, 'Let us go far away from the camp. This is a disgrace to me.' 'Well,' said the man, 'I will be a dog again, and you may drive me home with the water; but to-night, when all the people are asleep, we will leave the camp and no one will ever know about this.' So they took the water home, and the girl got all her things together, some food and some moccasins. When it was dark, she told her mother that she was going out for a while. When she was out of sight, the dog-man appeared and they went away together. The next morning the chief called out about the camp, asking if any one had seen the girl. Then the man who owned the dog called out about the camp, saying, 'My large travois dog has gone. Has any one seen him?'

The dog-man and the girl went far off. They were gone four years. They had two children, a boy and a baby girl. The children were real people, for the dog-man was now a person. They all returned to the camp of the girl's people, and the dog-man called at the lodge of his former owner. When he came to the door he said, 'Can I stay here a while?' 'Yes,' said the owner. The dog-man had ten dogs with him. One day the man said to him, 'To what tribe do you belong?' 'Well,' said he, 'I belong to a tribe living far away.' 'Then how is it,' said the man, 'that you speak our language?' The dog-man replied, 'Because our people speak the same language as you.' Now the dog-man always wore his moccasins, and whenever he had occasion to change them he went outside, where no one could see him. About this the people became suspicious. Whenever his wife would cook a meal, he would say that he would eat outside; and some of the people who watched him saw that he ate his meat raw. So one day his former owner said to his wife, 'I believe he is not a person. Suppose we look at him when he has his moccasins off.' So one time, when the dog-man was asleep, they saw his foot sticking out of the bed. He had feet like a dog. During this time the parents of the girl began to see a resemblance in the wife of the dog-man to their lost daughter. They began to have suspicions also. Now the dog-man thought to himself, 'I guess they know all about it.' So one day he said to his former owner, 'Do you know that I am a dog?' 'Yes,' said the man. 'Well,'

Niisitapiikwan travellers with
their dogs. Dogs served many
functions in a Plains camp. As
pack animals, dogs were capable
of carrying from fourteen to
forty-six kilograms, depending
on their size and strength. After
horses became available, dogs
continued to carry lighter loads.
The wagon probably had the
greatest impact on the displace-
ment of the dog as a pack animal.

said the dog-man, 'I am your old brindle.' Now the girl went over to her parents and told them the story. She explained everything as it had happened.

Now, when the news was spread in the camp, all the men stood around and began to make remarks. They said, 'Now, you see all the fine young men refused her, so she married a dog.' The dog-man was very angry because of this abuse, so he requested his wife's people and the people of his former owner to move camp that night. So they moved. When they had camped again, not far away, the dog-man began to call out like a dog, and all the dogs in the camps joined him at once. Now the people were all afoot because they had no travois dogs. So they held a council, and sent four men over to the dog-man's camp to get the dogs back; but when they came there the dog-man barked, and all the dogs jumped upon the four men and killed them. Then the people begged of him to give up the dogs. At last he consented. So they got their dogs back.

Now this dog-man had a dog skin for a medicine, which he gave to his wife's brother. This man called in a number of young men, and organized a society. The society was called 'The Dogs.' After a time the son of the dog-man became a chief, and, like his father's ancestors, he was a great runner. He led the buffalo over the drive, and pursued enemies in battle. His sister became a good woman, a great worker, economical, etc. These children were real persons. There were no traces of dog in them.

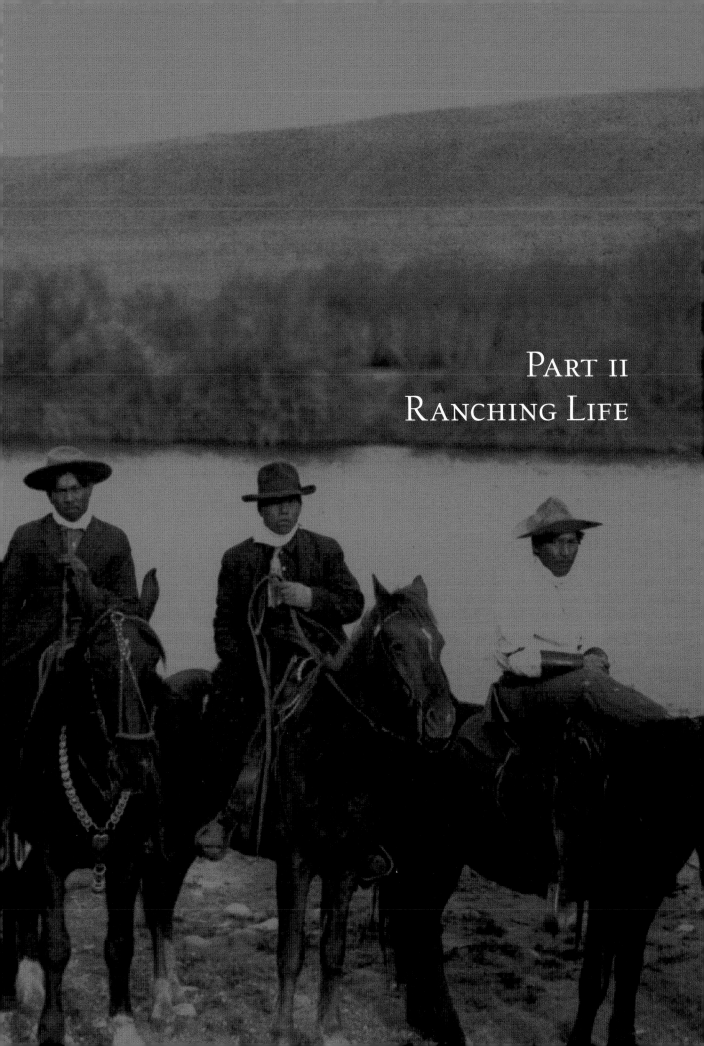

PART II
RANCHING LIFE

Ranching Life

WHEN CHRISTOPHER COLUMBUS made his second voyage to the Americas in 1493, he brought horses and cattle. These animals flourished on the North American continent. Within sixty years there were tens of thousands of cattle and horses in Mexico. Even unsettled regions became populated with wild cattle and horses that had escaped from Spanish ranches and wandered into northern Mexico, Texas, and California (Tylor 1976, 29). The wild herds of cattle became so plentiful that Plains hunters, including Aboriginal people, began hunting them for their hides, meat, and tallow, in the same manner as they did buffalo. By the early 1700s Canadian fur trading posts were keeping livestock. By the early 1800s there were over a million head of cattle in southern California alone, and cattle could be found along the Red River in Manitoba and the Dakotas, and by the 1840s as far north as Fort Edmonton, Alberta. In the 1860s about 22,000 cattle were brought into Canada from the Oregon Territory by way of Osoyoos, British Columbia. During the 1850s and 1860s the cattle population grew, and centres such as Lytton, Lillooet, Caribou, Quesnel, and Williams Lake, British Columbia, became important ranching communities. From 1886 to 1905 the industry of ranching grew in Saskatchewan, though farming displaced it after 1905. In Alberta the cattle industry began to make its appearance between 1874 and 1881 (Slatta 1990, 25-6). Such figures show that the tradition of raising and tending cattle and horses in the Americas is well established.

In 1865, following the American Civil War, Texas was cut off from its eastern markets, and the cost of relocating ranches nearer their markets was too costly. The only alternative was to bring the cattle to the market. Massive cattle drives from Texas to Missouri, California, Kansas, Montana, Illinois, and North Dakota took place between 1867 and the early 1880s, and the best people to do this job were able-bodied horsemen, among them Native cowboys. The drives helped to create the myth of the cowboy. Most of us think of cowboys as ranch workers who ride horses while tending and herding cattle.

Jack Alex and Gabriel Paul were two Okanagan cowboys from the Penticton area in British Columbia. The photograph was taken in the early 1920s and shows them in their working gear: leather cuffs, angora chaps, fancy spurs, boots, hats, and neckerchiefs.

The cattle dip on the Peigan Reserve in Brocket, Alberta, 1940s or '50s. Mange is a very contagious skin disease that affects cattle, horses, coyotes, dogs, and sheep. Infected animals lose their fur or hair, and left untreated the disorder is deadly during winter months. By the mid-twentieth century many families on the Niisitapiikwan reserves had well-established ranches, making the water and kreylon or sulphur and lime dip a necessity.

Horse corrals on the Peigan
Reserve in Brocket, Alberta.
Niisitapiikwan men and women
on the reserve owned thousands
of horses when their reserve was
first established, most of which
roamed freely in the nearby hills.
In 1945 hundreds of horses were
sorted from the herds. Stallions
and brood mares were kept, but
the others were shipped to Europe
for pickled and canned horse
meat to relieve postwar starvation and to work in the fields.

Below: Native cowboys on the banks of the Okanogan River. From left to right are Colville Indians Paul Timentwa, Joe Louie, Joe Thomas, Pierce McCragie, Paul Antoine, and Sam Samuels.

Right: Working cowboys in the Nicola Valley take some time to show off their horsemanship. Note the railroad car behind the fence. Until the arrival of the railroad in the BC Interior late in the nineteenth century, Native cowboys like these drove the cattle over the mountain passes on a long and dangerous journey to the Fraser River. There the animals were loaded onto boats and shipped to the Vancouver market.

We also know them as participants in rodeos and Wild West shows. Popular history and television has almost always chosen to portray these people as Caucasian Americans. When the Spanish began colonizing the Americas, however, they were quick to use the local people as slave labour to tend the growing herds of cattle and horses. Thus the Indigenous peoples of South, Central, and North America were among the first cattle herders, or 'cowboys.'

Native people in western North America had three advantages to help them become successful cowboys and ranchers. First, they already had experience controlling and driving herds of buffalo and deer, and although working with cattle was certainly different the transition was not completely foreign. Second, they were already superb equestrians and had been training and breeding horses in some regions for over 200 years. Third, the land that was now being used for grazing cattle had always been their traditional territory. They knew how to survive its hardships and where to find the best grasslands and sources of water.

Some Native people became cowboys because they recognized and seized new economic opportunities. They established their own ranches by using their knowledge of their traditional hunting and harvesting areas and applying it to the needs of pasturing horses and cattle. Native people were often employed as cowboys by European ranchers because they were knowledgeable and locally available. Other Native people, however, were forced to leave their traditional, territorial, and nomadic way of life and adapt to the new ranching life. The pressure for change arose from depletion of the buffalo herds, restriction to reserve lands, and government policies that tried to 'civilize the Indians' by making them farmers.

The process of adaptation varied from community to community. When it started, how long it took, and how successful it was depended on the resources and the local people involved in implementing the new ranching economy. The amount of government support, the assistance or resistance of the Indian agent, and the availability of land suitable for farming and grazing cattle were all important factors in the success or failure of a community's adaptation to ranching. This brief introduction can provide only a few examples, drawn primarily from western Canada.

Native Ranching on the Canadian Plains
As early as 1811 the Hudson's Bay Company at Red River was raising cattle for milk for the use of the fort's personnel. Oxen and horses were required to haul furs, buffalo hides, and pemmican up and down the Red River trade routes between Manitoba, the Dakotas, Minnesota, and the area that would become Alberta and Saskatchewan. By 1840 a single brigade could have as many as 500 Red River carts. Retired French, Scottish, and Métis fur traders married or kept company with Dakota, Lakota, Nakota, Nehiyaw, and

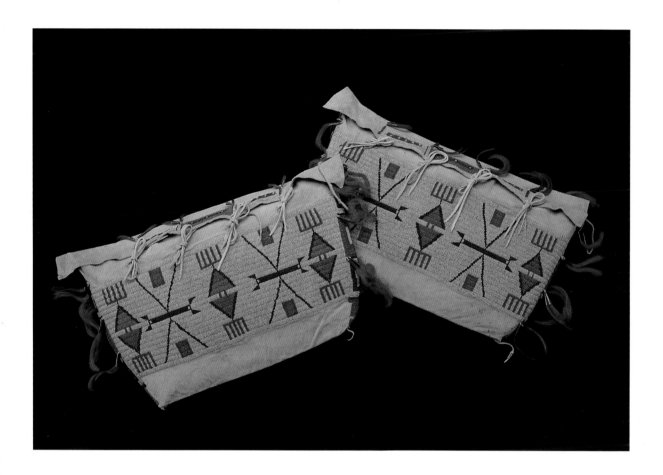

Left: Chaps, c 1930, 105.0 x 83.4 cm, leather and metal; and bridle, c 1930, 270.0 x 22.0 cm, leather and metal, both Nlha7kápmx, Ashcroft, British Columbia. The decorated bridle was sometimes worn for parades, while the chaps were a working pair made from heavy leather that could protect the rider when he or she was moving through thick brush. The long bridle reins could be snapped against the leather chaps to make loud, startling noises that kept the cattle moving on a long drive.

Above: Possible bags, mid-1800s, 35.0 x 57.0 cm, tanned lightly smoked skin, beads, sinew, dyed horsehair, and tin cone, Sioux Falls, South Dakota. During the early Reservation Period, the Dakota, Lakota, and Nakota became renowned for their elaborate beadwork. Some elements of the painted parfleche bags were transferred onto beadwork designs, as can be seen on these Dakota/Lakota style possible bags, so called because they were used to carry anything and everything possible.

Anishnaabe women and settled in the central Plains, where they raised oxen and horses for the Red River traders. Although this may not be viewed as full-scale ranching, the introduction of oxen took place there almost fifty years before white ranchers would bring in large herds of cattle from Texas. Permanent Métis communities were established at Turtle Mountain, Red River, St Boniface, St Paul, Wood Mountain, Milk River, Willow Bunch, Moose Mountain, Fort Qu'Appelle, Cypress Hills, and points farther north and west. When the trade in buffalo hides began to decline, many hunters and traders turned to freighting supplies of dry goods, lumber, and other trade goods.

Some Native communities in western Canada began farming and raising cattle thirty to forty years before treaties were signed. During the 1830s Chief Peguis and his band had already taken up farming at what is now St Peter's, just north of Winnipeg, Manitoba (Buckley 1992, 16). In 1870 the Hudson's Bay Company sold the land within what was then the North-West Territories – now the provinces of Alberta, Saskatchewan, and Manitoba – to the Dominion of Canada. Over the following six years, seven treaties were signed.

In 1873 E.H. Meredith, deputy minister of the new Department of the Interior, was responsible for drafting policy on matters concerning Native affairs in the West. Never having visited the West and having no knowledge of the cultures his policies would affect, he turned to his acquaintances to provide him with advice – counsel that would directly determine the future of Canada's Aboriginal communities. Among his advisers was Alfred Selwyn, director of the Geological Survey of Canada. Although he was a frequent visitor to the West late in his career, at that point Selwyn had only visited the North-West Territories once. He suggested that 'a hardy race of domestic cattle be introduced in areas in which the buffalo were already absent ... Because the Plains people cared well for the horses they raised, there was a good possibility that they could become a content pastoral people, the change being the natural gradation from the hunter to the agriculturist' (Carter 1993, 52).

Aboriginal leaders recognized in signing treaties that the government's intention was to turn nomadic and seminomadic people into farmers and ranchers. To ensure that their communities would be assisted in this objective, several chiefs insisted on having the provisions outlined in their treaties. Treaties 1 and 2, signed in 1871, had made no mention of implements or farm animals, but this was not to be the case for the next five. Nehiyaw chief Sweet Grass addressed Adam Archibald, the lieutenant governor of Manitoba, saying, 'We want cattle, tools, agricultural implements, and assistance in everything when we come to settle – our country is no longer able to support us' (Carter 1993, 55). The Indigenous leaders of Manitoba also demanded farm implements and domestic animals. The Saulteaux of Treaty 3 would twice refuse to sign until their demands for farm implements were met. These prerequisites would set a standard for the treaties to follow, as can be seen in Treaty 7:

> Her Majesty agrees that the said Indians shall be supplied as soon as convenient, after any Band shall make due application therefor, with the following cattle for raising stock, that is to say: for every family of five persons and under, two cows; for every family of more than five persons, and less than ten persons, three cows; for every family of over ten persons, four cows; and every Head and Minor Chief and every Stoney Chief, for the use of their Bands one bull: but if any Band desire to cultivate the soil as well as raise stock, each family of lieu thereof, when settled on their Reserves and prepared to break up the soil, two hoes, one spade, one scythe, two hay forks, and for every three families one plow and one harrow, and for each Band enough potatoes, barley, oats, and wheat (if such seeds are suited for the locality of their Reserves) to plant the land actually broken up. All the aforesaid articles to be given, once for all, for the encouragement of the practice of agriculture among the Indians (Canada 1966, 5).

The motives of the Canadian government can certainly be questioned over the creation of these treaties, as can their intention to honour them. Policy stated that before any farm implements or animals could be issued, reserve land had to be surveyed, bands settled, and land cultivated. The government was not prepared to deal with the number of communities that requested immediate surveys. In fact government officials did not begin to negotiate seriously with community leaders until 1875, at which time only Chief Pasquah's community, in southeastern Saskatchewan, received livestock – two oxen and four cows. In 1876 implements were issued to those who 'would actually require and use the implements: cattle was issued to communities which were felt required them and could care for them' (Carter 1993, 64). Communities that had gone so far as to build log houses and had put up large quantities of hay in the expectation of obtaining implements and stock waited, while ploughs and harrows sat in storage because not all the criteria stipulated in the treaty had been met.

By 1878-9, after two years of starvation, death, or near death for Aboriginal peoples of the Canadian Plains, the government developed a new policy. Native communities were to be furnished with farming or ranching instruction, to be provided by a permanent agricultural instructor serving several communities at once. The presence of an instructor would ensure that nomadic ways would be completely abandoned. Reserves would be divided into lots assigned to each family. Families would in turn build their own houses and barns and become completely self-supporting. Treaties 1, 2, 3, and 5 were excluded from this arrangement, however, because the priority was to assist Plains people formerly dependent on the buffalo, whose means of subsistence had failed (Carter 1993, 82).

This plan, or 'program,' was destined to fail from the beginning. The farm instructors all came from Ontario; none were familiar with farming conditions or ranching in the area or had worked with or even seen Plains Aboriginal people before. None spoke Niisitapiikwan, Nakoda/Nakota, Tsuu T'ina, Nehiyaw, or Anishnaabe. Supposedly the Aboriginal farmer would learn through observation, but the instructors were told by Indian Affairs officials to restrict most of their operations to their own farms, many of which were not on reserve land or anywhere near it. The instructors were to visit community members from time to time to teach animal husbandry, breaking the land, seeding, harvesting, and storage. Some of these communities were as much as eighty kilometres apart. Farm implements often took up to two years to arrive, and when they did were frequently inadequate, of poor quality, or missing parts. Cows were often so wild that they could not be caught, milked, or kept in a barn.

In 1884 the Department of the Interior retired its former policy and increased the number of farm instructors. Their farms were also reduced in size, to allow them time to help Native farmers on the reserves. As well, instructors were now to be chosen from among those familiar with western conditions and experienced in working with Plains people. The concept may have improved but of course it did not guarantee better instructors. Community stories vary about the effectiveness of the new instructors. Some expressed sincere interest in and compassion for the Plains people and the massive transformation they had to undergo. Others used the opportunity to profit their own interests.

The federal government also decided that 'tribes who were not agriculturally inclined would be given cattle' (Kelly 1980, 119). Range cattle were introduced into southern Alberta in the late 1870s but were not immediately turned over to the Kainai and Apatohsi Piikunii people, as Colonel Macleod of the NWMP and other white authorities decided to care for the breeding stock themselves initially. Some, indeed, were never delivered (Hugh Dempsey and Pete Standing Alone, personal communication 1997). By this time, however, the buffalo herds on the northern Plains were long gone and Native people in the area were desperate for meat. In order to survive the winter there was no alternative for the Kainai and Apatohsi Piikunii communities but to eat the cattle held in custody. It seems that the Canadian government was slow to deliver cattle herds because it wanted people to farm instead of ranch. Although small band herds were established in fulfilment of treaty promises during the early 1880s, the larger herds of cattle did not arrive until the early 1890s. Community members had to trade horses for cattle with non-Native ranchers.

Nevertheless, ranching did take hold over the 1880s. The Peigan (Apatohsi Piikunii) and Blood (Kainai) reserves were considered the best ranges in southern Alberta (Yellow Face 1993). Problems continually arose over white ranchers grazing their cattle on reserve land. This sometimes led reserve inhabitants to kill the cattle for food, but in most cases the missing cattle had simply wandered off and the Kainai and Apatohsi Piikunii were blamed for their disappearance (Hugh Dempsey and Pete Standing Alone, personal communication 1997). In 1893 the commissioner of Indian Affairs gave orders that stock belonging to white ranchers would no longer to be allowed to graze on reserve lands.

By the turn of the century ranching was flourishing on the Blood Reserve. As well, several Native cowboys from the Blood, Peigan, Tsuu T'ina, and Stoney reserves came to be good cowhands, working for non-Native ranchers in the area. The years 1910-3 saw no increase in ranch industry in southern Alberta, however, as the era of the cattle barons was over. The Department of Indian Affairs continued to supply communities with farm and ranch managers until the 1960s, at which time many communities began using their own skilled people. Although a band councillor may be given charge of the community farm and ranch operation today, some communities still have not taken over operations and on-site management, hiring non-Native managers instead.

Garry Louis, Nehiyaw, is from the Montana Reserve in Hobbema, Alberta.

It simply is not feasible to be a full-time rancher in central Alberta with a herd smaller than sixty to a hundred head. Given the cost of feed, grain, veterinary bills, pasture, and the time it takes to feed the cattle, it is not possible for someone with ten to fifteen head of cattle to break even. People who keep small herds may kill some of that beef for their own use, but the main reason they keep them is because for us Cree people, it makes us feel good to have them around. It's good for the soul, you know. They're just healthy to have around you.

Despite the federal government's deliberate attempts to ensure that its policies of 'cultivating and civilizing' Aboriginal people did not succeed, farming and ranching became very important industries for most Aboriginal cultures of the Canadian Plains. Today, though there are a few large Native ranches, most ranching operations on reserve are very small, with anywhere from twenty to 200 head of cattle. Unavailability of grazing land, rising costs, and falling cattle prices make ranching a risky and expensive operation. In communities in which the majority of the population have marginal incomes, ranching is a difficult business to move into.

Native Ranching on the Canadian Plateau

By the time early fur traders and explorers made their way to the Canadian Plateau in the early nineteenth century, horses were already present. Native people in the area claimed that they had always had horses, an attitude suggesting that the animal had been used for many generations. Routes from the Plateau into the Plains, used for travel on horseback to buffalo hunting areas, were well established. The riding skills of Native horsemen and women showed long familiarity and experience with the animal. Fur trader

Left: Willard Yellow Face, Apatohsi Piikunii rancher, Brocket, Alberta, 1994. During branding season cattle tags are recorded along with veterinary records.

Right: Some things are still best done by hand. Ross Lethbridge helping his father, Leonard, fence a quarter section of land on the Lakota Reserve in Wood Mountain, Saskatchewan. There are five Lakota families living on this tiny reserve south of Moose Jaw. Ranching and farming are the main occupations.

Alexander Ross noted that 'interruptions which are grievous obstacles to us are nothing in their way; for where a rabbit can pass, and where a horse can pass, the savage, who sticks to his back like a crab, passes over hill and dale, rock and ravine at full speed ... Nor is the fair sex less desterous [*sic*] in managing the horse; a woman with one child on her back and another in her arms still courses the fleetest steed over the most rugged and perilous country' (Ross 1855, 330).

The arrival of the horse had changed Native patterns of hunting and trading. People could travel farther to trade and could more easily hunt buffalo on the prairies. The horse could carry more food and more materials for housing to feed and shelter large numbers of people. Thus people of the Plateau could travel in larger groups for protection from the tribes that

Le Père, la mère et la petite fille appercevant un troupeau de buffles.

Left: *Saddlebags, c 1900, 77.5 x 28.0 cm, skin, cloth, silk, and cotton. Saddlebags of various styles, materials, and shapes replaced the traditional parfleche containers, folded squares of painted hide that held dried meat and berries and household goods. Many of the Nlha7kápmx bags and purses of this period were embroidered with floral motifs using fine silk threads.*

Above: LA PÈRE, LA MÈRE, ET LA PETITE FILLE APPERCEVANT UN TROUPEAU DE BUFFLES, *c 1841, 10.8 x 16.5 cm, ink on paper, by Nicolas Point, SJ. Note the decorated horse gear and quirts as the parents and daughter gallop away to a buffalo hunt.*

claimed the buffalo hunting grounds as their own. Use of the horse also changed the traditional flow and type of trade goods. Larger, heavier items, such as hides and buffalo robes, could be carried for longer distances and trips could be made more quickly and easily, allowing women to travel with their families. New patterns of and ideas for adornment and clothing were exchanged along with trade objects.

The horses on these trading parties required water and range land for grazing, and so new trails had to be found through the mountains surrounding the Plateau. Where once trading partners and meeting places were located along rivers and goods were moved by canoe, new relationships were formed based on accessible horse trails through the mountain meadows. Groups that had been important intermediaries in the trade process now found themselves on the periphery (Teit 1930, 252).

The changes brought by the horse were accelerated with the establishment of fur trading posts in the Plateau. The exchange of furs for trade goods drew some people away from seasonal food gathering to spend more time hunting and trapping. The arrival of cattle and dairy cows and the cultivation of potatoes and other vegetables by the fur traders introduced the idea of ranching and farming to the local Native community.

Fur traders also created a new demand for horses. The fur brigade, which began in 1814, required hundreds of horses to carry supplies. The route in the Plateau ran from the Columbia River through the Okanagan Valley to Kamloops and then north to Fort Alexandria. In the early years the horses wintered over at Fort Okanogan, with pasturage spreading some sixty to seventy-five kilometres along the Okanogan and Columbia rivers. In later years the horses were turned out to pasture at Fort Kamloops, and Native people were often employed to care for these large herds.

The fur traders unfortunately did not record the names of the Native people they employed as stock men, packers, and drovers, but comments about the work of Aboriginal people do appear in their personal reminiscences. In 1860, for example, when Fort Okanogan was being closed, Robert Stevenson recalled, 'At the time of our visit all the Indians in that part of the country were congregated at the fort assisting the factor in packing up the goods preparatory to moving the post to Keremeos in British Columbia' (Brown 1914, 22). Native people were also needed to make parfleches, pack saddles, harnesses, lengths of rope, hobbles, and other horse equipment. Studies of the exchange of goods between the forts and Native people in other Plateau communities list horses and horse equipment as major trade items provided by the Native community.

The discovery of gold in the sandbars of the Fraser River in 1856 began the transformation of British Columbia from the private holding of a trading company to a province in Canada. News of the strike quickly spread to the miners who had come late or unsuccessfully to the California gold rush.

Michel Charlie, a Method Indian from Malott, in his bulky winter coat, and C.B. Suszen Timentwa, who became chief of the Kartar Valley band in Washington state in 1930. Frank Matsura photographed many Okanagon people near his home in northeast Washington in the early twentieth century. Posed in front of Matsura's studio backdrop, these working cowboys show the warm clothing needed to survive the cold Plateau winter.

Within a few years thousands of miners travelled up the Columbia waterways or by boat to Victoria and then to Vancouver and the Fraser River to stake a claim in the BC Interior. The arrival of so many new people began the transformation of the economic base of Native people in the southern Interior from hunting and gathering to ranching, farming, and wage labour. The trading partnership between Native people and Europeans was threatened as miners raided and burned Native winter supplies or killed small groups of Native people. Smallpox and other diseases decimated the Aboriginal population. The demand for horses, food, and transportation of goods, however, offered Native people some new economic opportunities, and they backpacked goods, worked as guides, and marked trails.

The fur brigade was soon replaced by the pack train. The Native people who had worked as packers and looked after the horses were still needed to ferry food, gold mining equipment, and now road building supplies to the rapidly expanding communities in the Interior. An 1860 reminiscence of the arrivals of pack trains in Hope gives a feeling of what the experience must have been like: 'From the doorway of our shack, we could see the Hudson Bay Company Post and watch the pack trains come in from Colville, Keremeos and other places – sometimes there would be a grand stampede and the pack trains would disrupt, horses and men could be seen through a misty cloud of dust, madly dashing all over the Hope flats, lassos flying, dogs barking, hens flying for safety anywhere. Suddenly the tempest would subside as fast as it had arisen. The pack boys would emerge from the clouds of dust leading the ring leaders in the stampede' (Allison n.d.). By 1873 the Indian agent reported that many individuals in the Secwepemc community had 'accumulated considerable wealth by packing and boating for the whites' (Powell 1873).

The greatest transition for Aboriginal people in the area was the establishment of the cattle ranches. Over ten years the number of cattle in just one part of the Interior increased from about 2,500 to 10,000. Though range land was extensive and the grass rich, the area was quickly overgrazed. Unsuccessful miners who were becoming homesteaders and ambitious ranchers who wanted to expand their holdings increasingly demanded more land. The government came under growing pressure to resolve the 'land question.' Settlers could acquire 160 acres at a time, and some entrepreneurs had amassed thousands of acres by purchasing and leasing neighbouring ranches. For legal, economic, and cultural reasons Native access to land was limited. The average land holding among seventy-five Okanagan men in 1877, for example, was nineteen acres (Carstens 1991, 76). Native people were perceived as living on their hunting and fishing activities and not requiring large areas of land for farming or ranching. This view was held despite the census of horses and cattle taken in 1868 by the Indian agent on tour through the Thompson/Nicola area. The smaller communities of fifty to 100 people who lived in mountainous areas with little grazing land still owned

Below: Wilson Pack Train, near Quesnel, British Columbia, c 1890. This pack train was photographed almost a hundred years later than the first fur brigades. Throughout the period Native people continued to play an important role as guides and packers.

Right: Blind Charley Freighting, Nicola Valley, British Columbia, c 1900. As roads were built, people hitched their horses to wagons and offered their services carting goods. The arrival of automobiles and trucks on these same roads put an end to the need for relays of horses and to an entire way of life.

Top: John Chelahitsa, centre, an Okanagan from Douglas Lake, was a chief and a successful rancher. Along with other chiefs from the BC Interior he argued for the Native community's rights for access to land and water.

Above: Native women such as Millie Tonasket, shown here, participated in many aspects of the ranching economy, from looking after the chickens to being camp cook and helping with the round-up and haying. Photos such as this one from the early twentieth century show women engaged in many farm chores, driving the early steam tractors, and getting their horses saddled up for work.

between twenty-five to thirty horses and nine to sixteen head of cattle. In areas with better grasslands the larger communities of 100 to 150 people had twenty to thirty head of cattle and 100 to 200 horses (O'Reilly 1875, 51). Five years later the Kutenai were reported to possess some 300 or 400 head of cattle and 2,500 horses (Powell 1873). A letter to the editor of the *Victoria Standard* estimated 436 head of cattle and 1,300 horses among seven tribes and 'they are only beginning' (Grandidier 1875, 147). Even these figures seem underestimated, for in 1879 a gathering of 1,200 Nlha7kápmx at Lytton had with them 1,500 horses (Harris 1997, 128).

Along with raising cattle and horses many Native communities also farmed, especially where they had access to water for irrigation. The Secwepemc, for example, grew potatoes, as did many other communities, but as well 'without much encouragement produced cereals of all kinds in considerable quantity' (Powell 1873). Rolf Knight, in his study *Indians at Work* (1996, 67), suggests that Native people initiated farming for themselves as an important economic activity after learning the basic skills and receiving the seeds and supplies from the Hudson's Bay Company. Encouraged by missionaries, Native farming spread during the 1830s to 1860s. By the last quarter of the nineteenth century, the Indian agent was calling for the government to supply at cost the best seed grain, agricultural implements, wagons, and harnesses to Native people.

Correspondents to the provincial and federal governments demanded that Native people be restricted to the areas they were already using as homesteads or for farming. The battle over land was especially bitter for the Native community. They had been raising and breeding horses on the bunch grass and open range many years before the arrival of the fur traders and had seen, for at least one generation, the growth of their own cattle and dairy herds. Given an equal opportunity of access to water and the right of land acquisition, some of the great cattle ranches could have been Native owned (Mellows 1990, 110).

As the land question was adjusted and readjusted, with some parcels added and others taken away, Native ranchers and farmers adjusted, petitioned, and adapted as well. Some families counted out their gold and silver coins – earned by packing and working for non-Native employers – and purchased land to start ranches for their children and grandchildren (Brown 1995). Others grazed their herds of cattle over reserve acreage and crown land, mingling personal and band-owned stock with that of non-Native ranchers (N. Louis 1995). Still others made representations to royal commissions, to Indian agents, and to sympathetic missionaries to keep or expand the reserves. While these families continued to breed their own stock and to farm, many took their skills and knowledge of horses and found employment on non-Native-owned ranches. In many cases a ranch was entirely run by Native cowboys, cooks, and maids. (On the bigger ranches, such as

Douglas Lake, near Merritt, BC, about fifty people could be employed year round and 150 to 200 during the haying season, according to the *Family Herald*, 14 August 1931.) On other holdings the employees were a mixture of recent immigrants from Europe and Asia and members of the local Native community. The Native cowboy was welcomed as a ranch hand, one ranch owner stating, 'Years ago the Indians were better cowboys than most whites would ever be' (Guichon 1959, 6).

Joan Perry, Secwepemc, and her family were employed on the Douglas Lake Ranch and also worked their own land, putting up hay. Originally the winter forage for horses and cattle was the local grasses that grew in the Plateau valleys. As the bunch grass disappeared, people on the reserve and on the big ranches planted extensive acreages of hay. The haying season provided employment for many members of the community.

Whoever is working on the ranch stayed working and if they had time off or they asked for time off they came home and helped put the hay up. So a long time ago people worked with each other. There would be a whole bunch of little fields through all the Douglas Lake area and whoever was ready to put up hay, everybody went there. They cut the hay and put the hay up. I drove derrick up there. A derrick is a team of horses and they bring a load of hay in. They hook it up to the slings and you drive two horses. These two horses pull it up onto a cable and onto a stack. I drove that for years up there. I worked for just about everybody up there. I worked for twenty-five cents a day. When I got fifty cents a day I thought I was making a killing. I used to get up in the morning and ride. I would use my own team. Because I used my own horses, I made a little bit more money. I would get up at five and ride up to wherever we had to go. Worked all day and they fed you, go home in the evening.

Left: A view from a nearby hilltop of the O'Keefe Ranch, British Columbia, c 1900, shows the main buildings, the store, and the church that the family built. Surrounding this site are thousands of acres used for grazing cattle and horses and for growing hay and grains. As one of the largest ranches in the area, it employed many Native cowboys from the local reserves.

Right: Chuckwagon and bunkhouse, Douglas Lake Ranch, British Columbia, c 1950. These two photographs show life on the range and back at the ranch. The cowboys spent a lot of time away from the bunkhouse, eating meals prepared from the chuckwagon. In the spring, as the snow melted, the cattle were moved out into the surrounding hills and mountains. In the fall they had to be gathered up again and brought back down the mountain, or if they were going to be sold, herded to the nearest stockyard, railhead, or market.

Work was almost always available for Native people and credit could be had at the ranch stores. The account books kept at the O'Keefe Ranch, near Vernon, BC, show the pattern of ranch employment. In 1924, for example, Pierre Jack was hired to break horses at ten dollars per head with a dollar taken off to pay for his meals and pasturage for his horses. Halter breaking paid three dollars. Joe and Baptiste Nicholas cut wood at two dollars a cord and cleared land at thirty dollars an acre. On the debit side a ten-pound sugar sack was eighty cents, and matches cost thirty cents. Mrs. O'Keefe also extended credit in the winter months to people who would work for her in the summer haying season. A thirty-two-dollar debit incurred between December and June was paid off in nineteen days of 'stooking' hay in July at two dollars a day. More work and more loans in August left the borrower with a debt of three dollars and thirty cents.

The land on reserves was not left idle. Many families who had access to irrigation systems or a source of water put up hay to feed their own stock or to sell to the larger ranches. The government called for more farming on the reserves and more agricultural education in the residential schools. These programs were begun in the 1880s, just as two generations of farming had convinced Native people of its relative unprofitability (Knight 1996, 68).

By the mid-twentieth century many families on the reserves were no longer ranching. The high price of equipment, fencing, feed, and interest payments and unpredictable markets made ranching prohibitively expensive. Some families had a few head of cattle, which were killed as needed for food for their personal use. Many people living on the reserve found work in the lumber industry or as seasonal workers during the haying season. Even so, both the federal government and Native people continued efforts to keep the ranching and farming economy in Plateau communities alive.

A new government program was begun in 1971 to advise Native ranchers. Agronomists focused on the issues of using and improving reserve land, while extension workers offered training and helped to arrange specialized loans. Native people were members of the board of trustees of the program in their communities and served as assistant extension workers. The program stated that 'Indian farmers generally do not have the level of knowledge and experience in the planning and managing of a modern farm business of the farmer at large. There is, therefore, a need for a more intense form of extension service to assist Indian people in planning sound agricultural programs and projects' (Department of Indian and Northern Development 1974, 4). The program met with a mixed response. Some Native people, particularly those wishing to start new enterprises such as rodeo stock contracting, found it useful. Others thought that it did not take into account their own expertise. Nonetheless there was almost universal agreement that its most successful aspect was the establishment of children's 4-H clubs.

Right: Early photographs show stacks of hay so enormous that the people standing on top or the horses pulling sledges at the side are dwarfed by their height and length. These haystacks were usually strategically spaced along the route of a cattle drive, or in a series of pastures so that animals could be moved from area to area throughout the winter months. If there was not too much snow, the animals could graze on the grass, or their food could be supplemented from the haystack.

Below: Horse branding, Nicola Valley, British Columbia, late 1800s. Handling wild horses was and is a dangerous job, and people are often kicked and bitten. The Native families and communities in the Nicola Valley area still come together today to get this job done.

George Saddleman, Okanagan, from Quilchena, British Columbia, is chairman of the Nicola Valley Tribal Association and is working to increase ranching and rodeo opportunities on the reserve.

We learned how to be a board of directors, we learned how to plan, we learned to operate machinery, we learned how to do that all over again. So it was kind of a training package for us and a lot of people that were on the board of directors or worked for the cattle company went home and started working on their own thirty or forty acres and getting that back into production, putting water on it, and bringing the horse herd back up.

A recent survey of people on one of the reserves on the BC Plateau found that ranching was the principal occupation of almost every household head, with logging coming second. Most of the respondents indicated a desire for more employment in ranching and logging, and almost all wanted to continue living on the reserve (Acres Western 1971, 3). Many leaders on different reserves are trying to make those goals possible. For some communities the answer may lie in land claim settlements that will give them access to sufficient land and water to maintain large herds of cattle. Also being considered are new approaches to cooperative ranching and marketing, to the use of horses in lumbering and haying, and to cultivation of cash crops in the hope of establishing a viable ranching and farming economy.

Buffalo Ranching

Over the past twenty years buffalo ranching has become very popular for many Native communities in both Canada and the United States. The first buffalo rancher in Canada may have been Métis buffalo hunter James McKay from Manitoba. In 1873 McKay and his colleague Charles Alloway began gathering orphaned buffalo calves, hoping to raise them in captivity to be used like oxen in farm operations (MacEwan 1995, 84). They managed to acquire a wet cow and to save three buffalo calves. By 1878 the herd had grown to thirteen. McKay died in 1879 and a friend and neighbour, Samuel L. Bedson, bought the small herd for $1,000. One day five of Bedson's buffalo escaped from their enclosure and four were shot and killed, the other wounded. The press and public were outraged that anyone would shoot the last of what was close to becoming an extinct species, prompting a law against destruction of the herd. Nine years later Bedson's herd had grown to 118, and in 1888 he decided to sell it. Parts of the herd were sold around the world, and eventually some became part of the Pablo-Allard herd in Montana, the biggest buffalo herd in the world (MacEwan 1995, 85-9).

In the early 1870s, or so the story is told, Samuel Walking Coyote drove a few buffalo calves on a 241-kilometre trek over the mountains from the Milk River region near the Montana-Canadian border to the Flathead Reservation in Montana (Haines 1995, 220). Two Métis ranchers, Michel Pablo and Charles Allard, then paid Walking Coyote $2,000 in gold coin for thirteen buffalo, and these animals were the beginning of a large herd. In

Top: John Shuter, Nlha7kápmx, Lower Nicola, British Columbia, has brought in his cattle from their summer grazing in the hills and is separating the year-old animals he will be shipping to market.

Above: Lower Nicola Ranch, British Columbia, 1995. The landscape of ranching life on the Plateau shows tall mountains that open out into unexpected valleys or rolling hills with green fields. The ever changing colours and views of the land through the seasons add to the pleasure of the cowboy life.

1896 the herd was divided between Pablo and the Allard family, and over the next ten years the Pablo herd grew to 600 buffalo. Some were sold to zoos, others to Wild West shows, and others to business people starting herds in other areas of the United States.

In 1906 the government declared that the Flathead Reservation would be opened to homesteaders by 1910. Pablo would lose his grazing land. He offered to sell his herd to the US government, but only the Canadian government was interested in purchasing the animals. For more than five years experienced cowboys from the reservation worked to round up the buffalo for shipping by rail to the Wainwright Preserve near Edmonton, Alberta. The round-up included a sixty-five-kilometre fence, log booms in the river, and special corrals built of sixty-centimetre timber (Fugleberg 1991, 9-12). The buffalo were herded into corrals, loaded into custom-built wagons, and hauled to the railhead. Loading the buffalo onto the railcars took days. The cows were fairly easily lured into the boxcars by following their calves, which were loaded first. The bulls were dragged up the ramp, fighting and kicking, by horse-drawn ropes. By 1912 the round-up was complete, though a few buffalo escaped and remained on the Flathead range. Today buffalo can still be seen grazing next to Doug Allard's store and museum near St Ignatius, Montana.

In the early 1970s, almost a hundred years after McKay began building a buffalo herd, a few non-Native, Native, and Métis communities in Saskatchewan began experimenting with raising buffalo. Some intended to crossbreed them with cattle, whereas others wished only to reintroduce buffalo to their communities. The major problem buffalo ranchers face today is the small gene pool. Practically every buffalo in Canada and the United States can trace its genes to the Allard herd, and the effects of inbreeding are beginning to surface. Several bands, Métis communities, and individuals in western Canada have been raising buffalo successfully for many years, among them the Alexander Reserve, Samson Reserve, Enoch Band, Stoney Reserve, Blood Reserve, Peigan Reserve, Kikino Métis Settlement, and Beaver Lake Band. Again, some communities are raising buffalo for resale and meat, while others simply enjoy keeping them even if it is not economically profitable. As Garry Louis from the Montana Reserve in Hobbema, Alberta, pointed out, the animals were so much a part of peoples' lives for thousands of years that it is just good to have them nearby (G. Louis 1997).

Conclusion

Every Plains and Plateau Native ranching community had a different experience as it changed from a traditional hunting and gathering way of life. In some cases Indian agents and agricultural instructors were helpful; in others they impeded or slowed the process of change. Some communities made steady progress, while others were devastated by weather, crop failures, and lack of resources. The Fort Berthold reservation in North Dakota, for example, had a well-established ranching economy until their best pasturage was flooded when the Garrison Dam was built.

A few of these experiences are offered in the following pages through text, images of ranch-related art and crafts, and historical and contemporary photographs. One article presents the work of painter Allen Sapp, which focuses on the daily activities of ranching life on the Red Pheasant and Poundmaker reserves in Saskatchewan. Another describes the ranching and rodeo history of the Lakota people of Wood Mountain. A third colourfully depicts the life of women ranchers. The work of saddle makers, leather workers, bit and spur silversmiths, and fashion designers demonstrates the pride of continuing activities associated with traditional ranching life.

Ranching is still enjoyed by many people in the Native community, although there is a great deal of concern over its future. Despite the support of tribal governments, consultants' reports, and the desire of the communities themselves, it is a struggle to continue ranching. The high costs of

Below: Branding time is still a community event on the Peigan Reserve. This is Henry Potts's annual branding. Henry's brother Ken, left, and well-known rodeo announcer Greg Smith tend the branding irons. Nigel Provost, back centre, has an ear tagger in hand. Apatohsi Piikunii artist William Big Bull, far right, looks on.

Right: Dion Yellowbird, Nehiyaw, on the Diamond 5 Ranch, Montana Reserve, in Hobbema, Alberta. Yellowbird gets a vitamin injection ready for calves missed during the 1994 fall round-up.

ranching and farming equipment, uncertain markets, and the need for large capital investments limit the options of band leadership and individual ranchers. The recent return of many families to the reserve – some wanting to return to their home community, others recently enfranchised – has resulted in the allocation of more land for housing and schools. Pressure on land resources has cut into traditional grazing areas at the same time that environmental concerns are limiting access to federal lands.

Still, Native ranchers and cowboys follow their families' tradition and dedicate their lives to working with horses and cattle. Many have passed on their love of the land and animals to their children and grandchildren. When people talk of losing their traditional way of life, they most often fear the loss of their connection to horses. Dogs will always be companions, even if families move to urban centres, and the bond with the buffalo has to some extent returned with the establishment of buffalo ranches and small herds on various reserves. The horse remains central to the identity of many Plains and Plateau people. They recall the near loss of that relationship as ranches and farms became mechanized and people left the reserves. Now the horse has returned to the communities in greater numbers and one hopes that it will not be lost again.

Left: Saddlebags and thermos holder, c 1995, 54.0 x 24.0 cm, leather, metal buckles, and thread, by Vern Tronson, Vernon, British Columbia. Tronson makes bridles and other horse equipment and tans hides using traditional techniques

Below: Newman Gottfriedson has recently set up a workshop to make and repair saddles on the Okanagan Reserve near Vernon, British Columbia. His customers include both working cowboys and rodeo competitors, particularly saddle bronc riders.

Right: There are cowboy weddings and cowboy funerals — events that recognize a special way of life. For the Shuter family at Lower Nicola, British Columbia, the ranching tradition reaches back several generations. Keith, shown here in 1996 with his new bride, Lorna, has been a cowboy most of his life and started competing in rodeos when he was eleven.

LONELY COWBOY

Tim Ryan Rouillier

Tim Ryan Rouillier, Salish, is from St Ignatius, Montana. He is a singer, songwriter, and recording artist whose music reflects the social and working life of rural and ranching people in western Montana.

They sang and they danced, and shot for a while
And quietly went on their way.
To a passage of time, buried deep in my soul.
Oh, how I long for those days.

Ooh ... lonely cowboy,
The coyotee sings a sad song.
To the trail of life and the tracks left behind.
Now my high ridin' heroes are gone,
I've been roping the wind for too long.

From the big sky of Montana
To the west Texas plains,
The life of the cowboy was born.
Where flowers now blossom,
Their spirit remains
In tin cans and circles of stones.

Ooh ... lonely cowboy
The coyotee sings a sad song.
To the trail of life and the tracks left behind.
Now my high ridin' heroes are gone,
I've been roping the wind for too long.

Sometimes late at night,
I swear I hear the sounds
Of herds off in the distance
And the rumbling of the ground.

Horse and rider, Merritt, British Columbia, early 1900s. Wearing his decorated gauntlet-style gloves and chaps, this Native horseman embodies the romantic image of the cowboy.

Ooh ... lonely cowboy
The coyotee sings a sad song.
To the trail of life and the tracks left behind.
Now my high ridin' heroes are gone,
I've been roping the wind for too long.

Allen Sapp

Bob Boyer

Bob Boyer is a Métis artist from Prince Albert, Saskatchewan, and a descendant of the Red River Métis at Portage La Prairie, Manitoba. For the past eighteen years he has been head of the Indian Fine Arts Department at the Saskatchewan Indian Federated College, Regina. He writes about the art of Allen Sapp, which is internationally known. Curiously, Sapp has never been recognized as a western artist although a great deal of his early art deals with Native rodeo and ranching life. His rodeo and ranching art is neither contrived nor romantic; he paints life as he remembers it.

Allen Sapp is a Plains Nehiyaw painter from the Red Pheasant Reserve in Saskatchewan. His work has been widely collected throughout North America and Europe. In Canada, when the buffalo herds were gone, Indian Affairs replaced them with departmental cattle herds tended by Native wranglers. In due time some of these Indian cattlemen, cowhands, and wranglers developed herds of their own. Allen Sapp's maternal grandfather had a herd of about 175 head during the 1930s – quite good by the standards of the day. Sapp's father came from Poundmaker's Reserve, Saskatchewan, to work as a wrangler for the man who was to become his father-in-law. Early photographs capture him wearing the large brimmed hat, neckerchief, and boots universally recognized as the cowboy's uniform.

Throughout Sapp's career it has been well documented that he grew up with his Indian traditions, but it is not often remembered that he also grew up around horses and cattle. As he has humorously recalled, as a young boy he dreamed of becoming a full-time cowboy, but he fell off the horse too many times. He would play horse by sitting on the pole that connects the horse to the wagon and going for a ride. At other times he would ride a longer stick while using a shorter one as a riding whip. These imaginative scenes later became the inspiration for a series of paintings of children playing horse on wagon poles. Anyone old enough to remember Roy Rogers or Gene Autry can easily relate to these fanciful rides across the lone prairie, on what would be, in one's mind, the best horse in the West, perhaps the world. *Playing Horse*, one of the paintings from the series, shows a young boy astride a pole, holding some traces and wielding a willow whip. Sapp has employed the stop-action that he favours, as if to stop and capture time. Helen Hladin, in the *Albertan*, 17 December 1997, remarked that 'his paintings can relate not only to the Indian People, but also to many prairie people.'

PLAYING HORSE, 1975,
40.6 x 50.8 cm, acrylic on canvas, by Allen Sapp. As a child
Allen Sapp would play horse
by sitting on a wagon pole,
holding the traces and wielding a willow whip.

It is this broad experience and interest that inspires and informs Sapp's work honouring Native cattlemen and rodeo cowboys. *Chuckwagon Race at North Battleford* (1993) commemorates the excitement and pride felt at being on the winning team. Of this painting the artist says, 'Indians have always been very good horsemen, so it only seems natural that they would like rodeos and chuckwagon races. Many of the races are held on the reserves and, of course, the goal is to be in the Calgary Stampede' (Sapp 1994). Sapp sponsored his nephew's chuckwagon team for a number of years and takes great pride in Edgar Baptiste from Red Pheasant, the 1996 Calgary Stampede chuckwagon champion.

Western wear is the clothing of choice for Allen Sapp, who insists that cowboy shirts developed from traditional Native beaded war shirts and chaps evolved from buckskin leggings. Before 1969, he attempted to fit into the urban environment by wearing suits, ties, horn-rimmed glasses, and keeping his hair short. In 1970 he had a change of heart, began to grow his hair long, and went back to the familiar western clothing style of his community. Later his explanation was simple: 'Better to be a good Indian than a poor White man' (Sapp 1989). To him, clothing is a political statement.

This was apparent in June 1986, when at a First Nation Business Summit, Sapp was presented to Princess Anne wearing denim jeans, denim jacket, ten-gallon hat, and cowboy boots. Princess Anne engaged him in a brief conversation, apparently not concerned that he did not remove his Stetson. Later, he and some friends went to a restaurant with a good reputation. Sapp was refused entrance because he was not wearing a suit and tie. Angered, his friends tried to tell the *maître d'* who the artist was, and that he had just been presented to Princess Anne. Sapp managed to calm his friends and persuaded them to leave. On his way out, he turned and said, 'By the way, sir, this is my suit. It is matching denim pants and matching denim jacket. This beaded [western bolo] tie is the tie of my people. I'm so sorry you don't understand this' (Sapp 1986). A year later, in June 1987, he created quite a stir by refusing to wear a suit or tuxedo when receiving the Order of Canada from the governor general, choosing instead to wear his familiar denim 'suit.'

The figures in *Talking about the Round-Up* (1988) are distant enough to be made out as cowboys only by their western wear. They could be from any community, except for their braids. The anatomy of the cowboy's stance is unmistakable. The easiness of the posture could only be depicted by someone very familiar with the lifestyle. *Cowboy and His Horses* (1983) also exhibits Sapp's firsthand knowledge of cowboy life in the relaxed, sitting position of the rider taking a break. One can only marvel at the artist's innate knowledge of the human anatomy. He also knows how to portray animals. Whether it is a chuckwagon race with horses thundering down the track, an old horse drinking from the river, a colt at rest, or a steer about to be

bulldogged, Sapp has an instinctive ability to convey the individual personalities of animals. He has the wonderful gift of observation, combined with a
great skill for illustration.

His work is much more than illustration, however. Sapp breathes life
and spirit into all of his characters and animals, going beyond pure painting
to what the Native world views as a spiritual gift. You cannot learn it or buy
it. It comes only to individuals we call gifted. There really are Indian cowboys, and Allen Sapp knows this.

Western style shirt, 1980s, 80.8 x 57.5 cm, textile, metal, and plastic, by Jackie Colombe. Colombe is a well-known Nueta/Hidatsa clothing designer who now makes her home in Mission, South Dakota. Worn by South Dakota cowboy Phil Baird, Sicangu (Brulé) Lakota, in the 1980s, the shirt is reminiscent of those worn by western actors during the 1940s and '50s.

Western style shirt, c 1994, 71.5
x 68.5 cm, cloth, leather, and
beads, by Ruth Edmonds,
Ashcroft, British Columbia.
Edmonds, Nlha7kápmx, has been
sewing for most of her life and
makes western style shirts for
men and women. These brightly
coloured fabrics are particularly
popular among women barrel
racers. Though she has recently
opened her own craft store,

Feathers of Hope, on the Ashcroft
Reserve, like many other artisans she must sometimes travel
to her buyers, following the
rodeo and pow-wow circuits.

Tried, True, and Tested

Alex Harvey and Tim Ryan Rouillier

Alex Harvey grew up in the American South and has been writing music for over thirty years. His best-known songs are 'Rubin James' and 'Delta Dawn.' He and Tim Ryan Rouillier have a great love of stories written by Louis L'Amour, to whom they pay tribute in this song, which mentions characters in L'Amour's western novels.

When I read from the pages he wrote I get hungry
For the days when a cowboy rode tall
A good horse and saddle was all a man needed
Ol' Louis was the best of them all.

He was rough tough and ready, steel-eyed and steady.
He could weather whatever life has in store
For a man's at his best, when he's tried, true and tested,
Like a page out of Louis L'Amour.

The best of his heroes still ride through my memory
Flint and Chick Bowdrie, the last of a breed
I feel a kin to his straight talkin' men
In the old dog-eared pages I read.

He was rough tough and ready, steel-eyed and steady.
He could weather whatever life has in store
For a man's at his best, when he's tried, true and tested,
Like a page out of Louis L'Amour.

When the lonesome gods call me, to the hill by the river
And I take one last look at my life, I'll be proud
If they say he rode tall, looked you straight in the eye
You knew he was praying if he had his head down.

He was rough tough and ready, steel-eyed and steady.
He could weather whatever life has in store
For a man's at his best, when he's tried, true and tested,
Like a page out of Louis L'Amour.

Stock saddle, 1994, 70.0 x 53.1 cm, leather, wool, and cord, by Duane Lafferty. Lafferty, Minneconjou Lakota, is a custom saddle maker who works out of Hot Springs, South Dakota. Custom saddles are built to fit the horse and rider. This particular saddle can be used for ranch work or for calf and team roping. The leatherwork has been stamped. The alternative method, hand tooling, involves carving into the leather.

Boy's rodeo chaps, 1993, 97.5 ×
72.5 cm, leather and metal, by
George Saddleman. Says
Saddleman, Okanagan, from
Upper Douglas Lake Reserve,
British Columbia, 'Leatherwork and rodeo involvement
makes me second generation,
and with my family competing, a

third generation rodeo family. I
have been ... promoting rodeo in
all circuits within BC and ...
Indian rodeo across North
America. At the same time I
have taken on the wonderful on-
the-scene job of rodeo announcing with several rodeo circuits.
This pair of chaps I designed

and created myself in the summer of 1993. I do some leatherwork. In the last five years I
have designed and created ten
pairs of chaps, mainly for my
sons and nephews.'

At Wood Mountain We Are Still Lakota

Leonard Lethbridge, Harold Thomson, and Thelma Poirier

Leonard Lethbridge is Lakota and a member of the Wood Mountain Band in Saskatchewan. Harold Thomson is also Lakota. He and Betty Thomson, who edited this research, ranch in the Wood Mountain area. Thelma Poirier is a Saskatchewan historian and an active member of the Wood Mountain Historical Society and Museum. All four were active participants on the Lakota Committee of the Wood Mountain Historical Society.

In the early 1800s, the Lakota migrated from the midwestern woodlands of the Upper Mississippi River to the plains beside the Missouri River. They acquired horses, and their remarkable skill with these animals gave them an advantage as buffalo hunters and warriors. Within 100 years, Euro-American settlers began moving onto Lakota hunting grounds. Land that

Wood Mountain

was promised by treaty to be Lakota 'as long as the sun would shine' was preempted. Some bands moved to reservations but many chose the independence and freedom of the traditional ways and ignored requests from the federal government to surrender. Major confrontations between the US militia and the independent Lakota took place in June 1876 on Rosebud Creek and the Little Bighorn River.

At the Battle of the Little Bighorn, the Lakota and their allies annihilated the troops commanded by General George A. Custer and turned back those led by other officers. Lakota leaders such as Sitting Bull realized that the battle was won but that their future as an independent people was lost: the US army would pursue the Lakota until they surrendered, met death, or went into self-imposed exile.

The first Lakota arrived in Canada in the fall of 1876 with Chief Black Moon. Others came the next spring with such chiefs as Four Horns and Sitting Bull. Eventually about 4,000 Lakota sought sanctuary between Wood Mountain and the Cypress Hills. Bands of Nehiyaw and Nakota and several hundred Métis hunted buffalo in the same area. As the buffalo were depleted, most Canadian Natives moved to reserves, while the Métis settled in other communities. The Lakota had no place to go. The Canadian government pressured them into returning to the United States, and by the fall of 1880 most of them had left Canada. Sitting Bull and his band of some 150 men, women, and children were among the last to leave in the summer of 1881.

Just before Sitting Bull's departure two small bands split away from the main one. One of the bands, led by Black Bull, settled near Moose Jaw. The other band of sixteen families, led by Lean Crow and Red Bear, moved to Moose Woods, where the men worked for Métis people. During the Resistance of 1885, led by Louis Riel, some of the men fought for the Métis. Both Lean Crow and Red Bear were captured by Canadian forces and sent to prison at Stony Mountain. The rest of the band joined the main Lakota camp at Moose Jaw.

By 1887 most of the Lakota families in Canada resided on the banks of Moose Jaw Creek. A census taken in 1892 revealed 107 'Alien Sioux Indians' living there: twenty-five families with fifty-five children. The Lakota families experienced great poverty. Their traditional skills – tracking, hunting, tanning, and beading – were not required in an agrarian society. They received no allowance from the government of Canada and were often dependent on the benevolence of the citizens of Moose Jaw.

According to the 1892 census the men sold firewood and worked as harvesters on farms, and the women worked as domestic labourers in the city. A few men became scouts for the North West Mounted Police. Others worked for ranchers. Lakota hunters gradually became Lakota cowboys. The Lakota maintained small bands of horses in the Dirt Hills south of Moose Jaw.

In the early twentieth century many Lakota women married Euro-Canadian ranchers at Wood Mountain. Shown here are, from left to right, Wanbli Sunpagewin (Julia Lethbridge), John Okute Sica, Christina Okute, an unknown child, Auta Naswin (Mrs. Little Eagle), an unknown woman, Tiopa (Mrs. Brown), Ruth Brock, Iha Wastewin (Mrs. Thomson), Tasunke Hin Hotewin (Mrs. Ogle), and, in front of her, Nora Brown. Wood Mountain Historical Society, #1253

THE SIOUX TREK TO
CANADA, 1975, 122.0 x 61.0
cm, oil on wood, by Wasu Mato
(William Lethbridge), Lakota,
from Wood Mountain,
Saskatchewan. Following the
Battle of the Little Bighorn,
several thousand Lakota and
Dakota, including Chief Sitting
Bull, came to Canada, passing
through or settling in Wood
Mountain. This painting depicts
the arrival of Wasu Mato's
father, Matoa Luta (Red Bear),
and his family in Canada.

Each spring they travelled to the Pinto Horse Buttes to visit the sacred sites where some of their people had been buried between 1877 and 1881 and to hunt antelope. From there they went south along the Frenchman River to the Milk River and east to Poplar on the Missouri in time for annual celebrations. By the time of the annual Wood Mountain Races on 1 July the Lakota were back in Canada. Many of them entered the horse races and won small monetary prizes. After the Races they stayed in the area to pick berries and hunt and dry meat. When winter came they were camped at Moose Jaw again.

In some ways the Lakota lived as they had for many years – they kept horses, they moved about following wild game, and they dried meat and berries for winter. In other ways life had changed. Their horse herds dwindled as they traded some animals for food. One by one their warm buffalo-hide tipis wore out and were replaced by thin canvas tents. Leather clothing was replaced by cotton. Sickness, especially diseases such as smallpox, took its toll and many people died. Game was scarce and hunger was prevalent. The Lakota had little or no money in a cash-driven economy. The women sold beadwork and the men sold polished buffalo horns.

For one group of Lakota, life was somewhat easier. In the 1880s and 1890s several young Lakota women married white ranchers and settlers. A warm home, a pantry full of food, and a wardrobe of much-needed clothing may have attracted many of them. The marriages may have been crucial to their survival as well as that of their families. Parents and siblings often went to live with or work near their married daughters and sisters. The marriages were a way of putting down roots in Canada, of avoiding expulsion.

Among the Lakota women who married white men were: Iha Wastewin, who married rancher James Thomson, formerly of the NWMP; Tiopa, who married rancher Fred Brown, another former member of the NWMP; Wanbli Sunpagewin (Julia), who married surveyor Charles Lethbridge; Tasunka Nupawin (Emma), who married Archibald Lecaine, a member of the NWMP; and Tasunke Hin Hotewin (Mary), who married William Hall Ogle, a young rancher from England. The Thomsons, Browns, and Ogles raised large families on horse ranches at Wood Mountain. Many skills of the Lakota buffalo culture were equally useful on a horse ranch: riding, breaking horses, skinning, tanning, and butchering. The women helped with all these tasks although most of their time was spent in domestic work and caring for their children. The children learned to ride at an early age, and by the time they were youths the boys were adept at breaking horses.

It took thirty years for the Lakota band to gain a reserve in Canada. In 1909 homestead rights were granted in the Wood Mountain area. Most Lakota resisted the idea of homesteading. Only one Lakota man, John Okute Sica, actually took out a homestead before the reserve was organized. The

Lakota wanted to live communally, as they always had, and the next year a land reserve was set aside for them. By 1911 more than thirty families were settled there. The lives of those on the reserve and those on nearby ranches were quite similar. Horses played a major role, not just out of necessity but because of the special bond the Lakota had with them.

When the Lakota first came to Canada they brought hundreds of horses with them. Most were runners for hunting, some were war horses, and some were women's horses for pulling travois. The currency of the Lakota was the horse. The more horses a man owned the more he could give to the poor, and the more respect he could gain in return. A Lakota child learned to walk and talk quietly among horses and to become an expert rider, balanced and adept at guiding the horse.

When the Lakota moved to the reserve at Wood Mountain, they brought their horses with them. Bob Lean Crow and Alex Wounded Horse each had over forty head of horses, mostly broncs, though other families had fewer. Young horses were broken in the traditional method of Lakota, a technique of gentling that included stroking their hides and talking to them. Older horses were broken with the aid of ropes and hobbles, throwing a horse to the ground and releasing it until it was pacified.

On the reserve horses were part of daily life. A team hitched to a buckboard or wagon took the family to the post at Wood Mountain to buy groceries or to the Races. A saddlehorse was used to go to the Indian agency, to herd cattle for a rancher, to go for the mail, or to ride to a local dance. The custom of donating horses as a dowry continued in some families. At the Wood Mountain Rodeo, which evolved from the Wood Mountain Races,

Wood Mountain rodeo parade, 1927. The Lakota of Wood Mountain, Saskatchewan, led the Wood Mountain Rodeo parade every year from about 1912 to 1955. In the background among the hills can be seen the Lakota camp. Wood Mountain Historical Society, #249

some horses were decorated for the parade, others were entered in the Indian pony races, and still others were bucking stock.

Off the reserve the Lakota children of ranch families were also brought up with horses. Unlike their counterparts on the reserve, who owned horses for the sake of it, the Browns and Ogles raised horses for sale. The ranchers employed the Lakota method of breaking adult horses; it did not always produce the gentlest horses, but it did train some of the best rodeo cowboys. Horses kept for personal use, however, were gentled. The method was passed down from generation to generation so that even in 1995, a grandson of James Thomson and Iha Wastewin, Harold Thomson, remarked that his horses responded when he called them by name. Another Lakota descendant, Joe Ogle, explained that when he broke his roping horses he never let them buck. By snubbing the bronc to a well-broke horse until it was accustomed to a person on its back, he maintained control of the animal.

The sport of rodeo grew out of the working life of the ranchers. One of the main reasons for the initial success of the Wood Mountain Rodeo was the participation of the Lakota people. Having learned to ride and break horses at an early age, the Browns and Lethbridges excelled at bronc riding. Others, including the Ogles, the Thomsons, the Fergusons, and the Lecaines, were skilled calf ropers, a skill that developed as the Lakota on and off the reserve switched from raising horses to raising cattle. Most of them took part in one type of horse racing or another: Indian pony races or chariot and chuckwagon races. Bucking stock was contracted from Alex Wounded Horse and James Ogle. Other Lakota participated in parades and pow-wows at rodeo time, donning their traditional costumes and dancing the traditional

dances not only for the crowd but with the crowd. And then there were Lakota arena workers, pick-up men, flagmen, repairmen, gatemen, and booth operators. Elizabeth Ogle served roast beef sandwiches and saskatoon pies in her booth for more than thirty years.

The Wood Mountain Rodeo had some of the attributes of earlier Lakota celebrations: the gathering, the sense of being a whole people once all the relatives arrived and the tent village was pitched on the hillside west of the arena, the donning of ceremonial dress, the sharing of a feast. The rodeo committee donated a beef animal, stories were told of success in the various events, and success was shared. There was also a commercial aspect to the Rodeo. Cash prizes were offered in all categories, including special events such as the best dressed man and woman in the parade, and the Indian pony races. For several decades Lakota entrants often won the top money in bronc riding and calf roping.

The Rodeo lasted a only few days, however, and the money earned was not enough. The rest of the year the Lakota had to find other ways to supplement their income. As refugees they received no cash allowance. They were expected to earn their living on the reserve by raising livestock or farming but only a few hundred acres on the reserve were suitable for farming. Many therefore worked as cowboys for other ranchers in the area, helping with round-ups, brandings, and horse breaking. Sometimes they built cattle sheds or corrals or fences. Others went about the community butchering livestock.

Dennis Fraser, a Métis, grew up in Shell Lake, Saskatchewan, where he worked on his grandfather's farm and ranch. It was common practice on reserves and in Métis communities, particularly poor ones, for people to help each other during haying season, round-up, and harvest.

We used to have what you call branding parties. And our different neighbours used to get together, and one weekend we would do one person's farm or ranch, and then the following weekend we would do somebody else's, and we kept on moving like that 'til whoever participated in the surrounding area was all done. You'd brand them, vaccinate, de-horn, all at the same time.

Some of the Lakota applied their natural artistic talents to ranch-related industries. Three brothers, Bill, Pete, and Jim Lethbridge, became saddle makers. Beginning with rawhide saddles they went on to make carefully carved and tooled leather saddles. Others crafted a variety of ranch gear. Willie Thomson braided hackamores; John Okute Sica sewed angora chaps; Elizabeth Ogle and Christina Okute beaded western vests and moccasins.

By 1996, only two of the first generation of Lakota born in Canada were still living, Joe Ogle and Ida Thomson Braaten. Their families have taken over most of the work on their places, although they continue to own them. Other Lakota families have also passed their places on to their children.

On the reserve it has become too costly to grow and put up winter feed for small herds of cattle. The scale of ranching and farming has changed and now most reserve residents rent their farm or pasture lands to others. Technology means fewer people are involved. Only one large ranch exists on the reserve. As fewer Lakota work less and less with livestock, their involvement in ranching and rodeo declines.

Very few of the younger generation understand the Lakota language, yet the feeling both on and off the reserve is very much that they are Lakota. Ties to a common past and to the shared experience of the horse have perpetuated that feeling. The descendants of the small band of Lakota that stayed in Canada after 1881 continue to celebrate their heritage on the reserve, on the ranches, and in the rodeo arena at Wood Mountain.

Victor Runnels, an Oglala Lakota from Pine Ridge, South Dakota, is a rancher and cowboy poet.

Our dad was a foreman for one of the biggest ranches in Nebraska, the McGinnley Ranch. And he put us boys down to work down there when we were, like, twelve, thirteen years old, and we were working with men, you know, did the same jobs they did, got the same wages they did, all the way from breaking horses to working cattle and putting up hay, all of those things that ranch hands do. So we grew up as working cowboys basically. And our dad always had good horses. We were real poor, I mean we, we didn't have any stock or any range or anything, we just, we were working cowboys. But my dad, even though we were real poor, we had real good horses. Some of the best horses in the country, my dad had. And the way he did this without money, you know, he'd trade around, get a real good mare, then those ranches that he worked for, he would take the mare down, get bred by his, his ranch's prize quarter horse, and from that colt then we'd get a real good quarter horse and trade around get another, another mare, just through all this horse trading, he wound up with some of the best horses in the country.

These two cowgirls have been identified as Niisitapiikwan women. It was not uncommon for Native women to assist in working cattle during the early Reservation Period, just as they do today, but at the turn of the century, when this photograph was taken, it was unusual for women to dress in cowboy fashion.

WOMEN AND THE RANCHING LIFE

Clara Spotted Elk

Clara Spotted Elk is a member of the Tsė-tsėhėsė-stáhase community in Lame Deer, Montana. She is a rancher, mother, writer, storyteller, and poet. In January 1995, as part of the Salute to the Indian Cowboy celebration, Clara was a guest at the Cowboy Poetry Gathering in Elko, Nevada. There she performed to an audience of thousands over four days.

My father was Irish and my mother is Northern Cheyenne, but I do live and make my home here on the reservation now, where I'm involved in ranching and various other kinds of menial labour such as timber thinning, fencing – things like that. My background in ranching goes back to when I was kid. I was raised on a ranch in southeastern Montana that was homesteaded by my grandfather, Ramsey McMegan.

I write a lot about ranching or western lifestyle from a woman's point of view. I don't think there are too many women out there that are writing that kind of poetry. There's a lot of women ranchers but most of them are probably too busy to write poems. The second theme I focus on is Indian themes that are unique to our culture. It seems there's a lot of interest in that. The thing I think about a lot, you know – people tell me this and I also observed it when I lived in a big city – I think Americans as a whole are really hungry for something spiritual and something meaningful. And the third thing I like to write about is rodeo 'cause it's my favourite thing to do. So those have been the kind of three areas that I focus on. It's been a lot of fun.

There's a lot of people who write cowboy poetry but not too many that write it to incorporate the Indian part of the West. The other thing I've noticed about this whole area of cowboy poetry is that the emphasis is all on men, famous bronc rides by men, famous bull rides by men. All things that men do. I guess one of the reasons I'm real glad to have an opportunity like this is, I think the role of women in the West has been really neglected. I think the more opportunity we have to remind people, 'Hey, women were at least 50 percent of what went on,' and even though their role historically has not been looked at with the type of glamour that men are looked at, the West wouldn't have been settled if the women hadn't been here.

The other thing that I like to focus on is there are a lot of women who are ranching by themselves. You know, it's tough; there's a lot of physical manual labour. It's not really that romantic when you get right down to it, and it's a real hard way to make a living. Most of us that do it are fortunate

Western style blouse and skirt, 1996, 157.0 x 96.0 cm, textile, metal, and plastic buttons, by Cathy Sparvier, a Nehiyaw western clothing designer from Bragg Creek, Alberta. A blouse and skirt set such as this would be worn to a dance or other special event.

Late 1800s style western wedding dress, 1996, 140.5 x 58.5 cm, rayon gabardine, fusible interfacing, poly and serger thread, shank buttons, and poly lace, by Risa Fritz. Fritz, a Nehiyaw/German western clothing designer, operated a saddle shop, shoe repair, and western clothing store in the mid-1990s with her father, Ross Fritz, in Fort Macleod, Alberta. It has been popular over the past few years for both Native and non-Native couples to have 'old-time' weddings in which the wedding party dresses in period clothes from the late 1800s.

in that we have one or two good hired men that we can rely on. You know, I think people need to recognize women's contribution in all of these areas. Not just in the past but things that are going on now.

There are several Native women who have inspired me in this region. One of them is an older woman named Eva Small. She ranched with her husband for years. He died at an early age and she carried on and runs, like, 600 head of cattle. She must be eighty years old and she's still doing it. She still gets up in the morning and loads up salt and takes it out, and checks her cows. But Eva, it's interesting to me that most of the women who are doing that kind of thing, myself included, are considered to be ... somehow we're not considered to be really feminine. Kind of looked at as being half ornery and that sort of thing, you know. I think we can be real feminine when we want to, but we're in a man's world doing man's work. We still live in a real patriarchal society and there's a ... that's changing you know as time goes by, but there's a real bias that this is man's world and a woman's place is at home, preferably not talking too much. There's still that real strict view on the role of women, and that's why I think some of us who are doing this kind of thing are kind of bucking the odds and breaking new ground, so to speak. You know they look at us as being kind of a little bit beyond the pale I think.

Women worked on the ranch alongside men. For many years, Joan Perry looked after the animals in the family's rodeo stock contracting business. She would secure her baby to her back with a large bedsheet and ride the range tending to the needs of the bucking stock. She would always know when the baby had gone to sleep by the gentle rocking of the baby's head against her back as the horse quietly walked along.

Well, my grandmother was a cook, she cooked all her life. She was up early to cook breakfast and if they took lunch, then the lunches were made, they took them with them. They stayed in camp for so long and then, I guess when they moved the cattle to certain areas and it got farther and farther to ride they had different areas for the camp. There was a camp in one area and then the cattle would get too far, so they would move to the next camp and they all moved by wagon. They hauled all her stuff to wherever the camp was to be set up again. She wrote down what she needed and they would have a boss that came out to the camp. She would send with him what she needed and they would bring it back out again.

My grandma had a flunky, a person who helped her. She did the cooking and the flunky did the dishwashing, set the tables and she had desserts that had to be made. Whoever her helper was helped her do all that stuff. It seemed like long days because it seemed like you just got up because it was daylight and worked until it was dark and you lived in tents. There were no houses because the camp would be set up right where the fields are, close to it. So the men came in at noon and then they came in at supper. They make the bread, I remember they used to make pies and it was nothing to bake twenty-five pies you know. They made all this big bunch of dough for the pies and one woman that's all she did was bake pies.

I myself don't have that many cows. I almost worked up to a hundred but not quite, and that's not enough to make a living. You have to have about 250 cows if you're going to depend on ranching for a full-time income.

So by desperation I got involved in ways to supplement my income, and so I do a lot of contracting, building fences, and what's called timber thinning. I'm going out and thinning the forest reserves of the other trees that are left that'll make better logs.

I think one of the reasons you see so much [Native] involvement in ranching and rodeo is it's very compatible with our culture. You know, you're talking about horses and being outside and all of these things. So it's worked very well here. The mainstay of our economy is ranching but [you have to have] a land base to have grass and hay. We're in a little better situation than most people because the policy of our tribe is they want to see our land and grass used by Indians.

I have a few stories to share with you. This is a true story you know. There's a whole family, and they're all my partners, and the youngest one is Jimmy. They're full-blood Cheyenne Indians; they speak Cheyenne. So, I was driving down to Lame Deer one day and Jimmy's on the side of the road, and he pulls me over. The name of this story is 'Bilingual Blue.'

Jimmy says, 'Clara, I've been looking for you.' I said, 'Well you found me, Jimmy. What's going on?' He said, 'Clara, I've got a dog,' and he said, 'I want to give it to you.' He said, 'It's a Blue dog, it's got blue eyes.' I said, 'Really, that'd be great. I'd like to have a dog like that, you know.' 'Yep,' he said, 'valuable. Valuable cow dog.' 'Well, thank you Jimmy,' I said.

'There's just one problem,' he said. 'What's that?' 'I need five dollars.' 'What do you need five dollars for? Are you going to get a jug or what?' 'Yep,' he said, 'hangover. Bad hangover.'

So I said, 'That's a hell of a deal. I'll give you five dollars for your old Blue dog. Let's go into the store and I'll get some change.' So he follows me and we get two fives for a ten. I said, 'Here you go, Jimmy.'

He says, 'There's just one problem with Joey' – the dog. 'What's that?' I said. 'Joey only understands Indian.' 'Is that right?' I said. 'Well that will be kind of a problem, because you know I don't talk very much Indian.' 'Well,' he said, 'for five more dollars I'll teach him English.'

I said, 'Jimmy, take the five. It's worth it for this story.'

One of the great things about living on an Indian reservation is you don't ever have to make up any stories, you just tell what actually happens, you know. Like there's one other story I'll tell you about this old boy that lives down the road, Jimmy. He's about eighty years old. He's a character, and he's a mule skinner. He still puts up his hay with the wagon and the team. He's a white guy married to a Cheyenne. And Jimmy, he took his calves to town to sell, and got his cheque, and he was up there for a couple of weeks – went on a toot, you know. So he's ready to come home, so he calls his daughter up and he said, 'Thelma, can you come and get me?' he said. 'I'm ready to come home.'

She said, 'Well where are you?' He says, 'I'm in Billings.' 'No, I mean where in Billings are you?' He said, 'Oh I'm on a busy street, lots of cars and

Crupper, c 1860, 65.0 x 22.5 cm, canvas, cloth, beads, buttons, and metal. Cruppers keep the saddle from slipping forward. The back strap passes beneath the horse's tail and the front ties are secured to the saddle. The side pieces are often elaborately decorated. The patterns and designs on Nlha7kápmx articles such as this often have symbolic meaning. On this crupper, according to James Teit, the bands of zigzag designs may represent mountains, sandwiching a wavy line representing a stream. The circular design may be a camp with the dance lodge in the middle and an outside line of hills surrounding the camp. Alternatively, the whole design may represent the sun and stars, or simply flowers. The straight beaded lines could be trails.

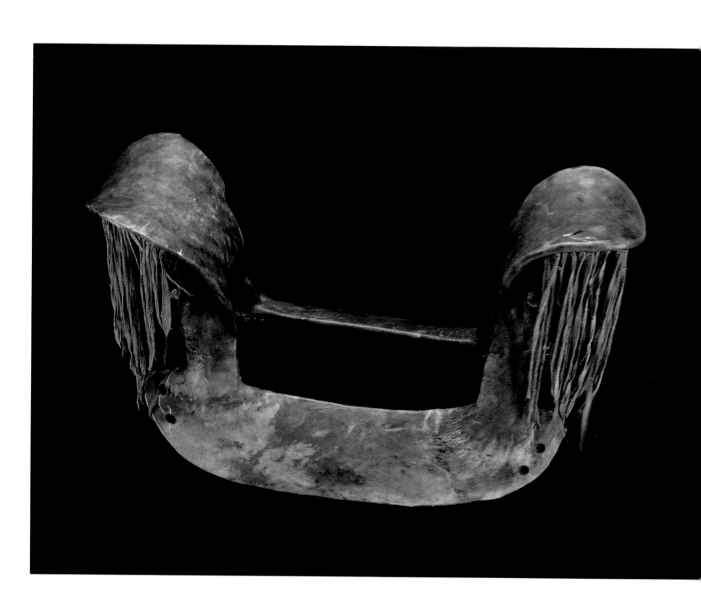

Saddle, c 1900, 62.0 x 35.5 x
29.2 cm, wood, rawhide, sinew,
and skin. This Kutenai style of
wood frame saddle was often
considered a woman's saddle or a
pack saddle because bags,
parfleche containers, and baby
cradles could be easily attached.
A pad saddle, on the other hand,
was a square or oval leather
cushion stuffed with grass or
horsehair and decorated at the
corners with beads or quills.

Opposite: Inlay silver mounted ring bit, c 1990, 14.9 x 19.9 x 16.5 cm, silver and steel, by Thomas Pierre. In exploring the craft of horse gear, Thomas Pierre, Okanagan, from Shingle Creek, British Columbia, experimented with making this early style of ring bit, rarely seen or used today. Once popular among the Spanish, it was used mainly as a decorative bit on older horses that were very well trained and required little or no use of the reins.

Below: Thomas Pierre in his studio, 1995. A desire to have some authentic, top quality, silver decorated tack for his horses, and severe frustration at finding poor quality imitations, prompted Pierre to take matters into his own hands. A working cowboy and ranch hand, at the age of fifty-seven Pierre decided to take a new direction. He had always admired the few pieces of good silverwork he came across over the years and saw no reason that he could not learn to make what he wanted himself. In 1988 he enrolled at the silversmith school of Elmer Miller. His two sons soon followed him into the course and the family established the Snow Mountain Bit and Spur company.

big old tall buildings and pretty big places.' She said, 'What street?' 'I don't rightly know,' he said. 'Well,' she said, 'Dad, put the phone down and go over to the street corner there and look at the signs and come back and tell me what they say. Then I'll know where to pick you up.' 'Okay.'

He comes back. 'Well what did it say, dad?' 'Well I reckon I'm on the corner of Walk and Don't Walk.'

That's a true story! This guy's a classic. Yeah, there are some characters around here. But I think one of the things that's so wonderful about Indian people as a whole, or people who are in ranching and everything, is we've seen so much adversity and hard times and been broke so much and everything that they've developed a wonderful sense of humour. You know, they could find something to laugh about or jokes to make even when everything has gone to hell. And to me that's a wonderful thing about Western people you know and Indian people. It's part of what makes our life so rich, I think, even though materially speaking we don't have that much, you know.

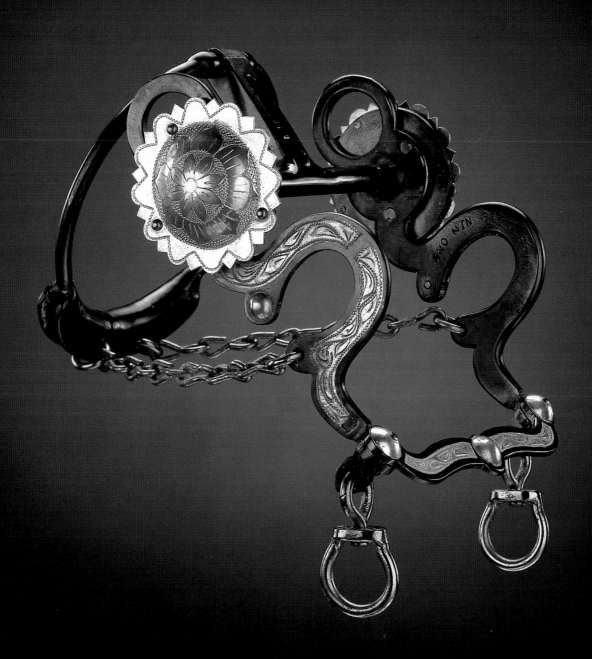

Left: Horse bit and stand, 1997, 22.0 (with base, 30.5) x 14 cm, cold rolled steel, sterling silver, sweet iron, copper, metal, and wood, by Vernon Lynes. The coyote plays an important part in Secwepemc mythology. Lynes, a Secwepemc Métis from Bonnyville, Alberta, has incorporated into this bit the howling coyote, a western icon for nearly a decade, and the Métis Nation of Alberta logo, the Red River cart and map of Alberta.

Right: Vernon Lynes, Métis, manufacturing pieces required in constructing a horse bit.

Coy Fisher is an accomplished Oglala Lakota rodeo cowboy from Scenic, South Dakota. Here he is seen in the saddle repair shop he operated from 1992 to 1994. Today he ranches and operates Badlands Leather, his saddle repair and leatherwork shop out of his home. Fisher is best known for his rodeo chaps and beaded horse tack, which can be seen hanging on the wall over the saddles.

Belt, 1993, 110.8 x 3.3 x 0.6 cm; breast stall, 1993, 52.0 x 150.0 x 5.5 cm; head stall, 1994, 14.5 x 48.5 x 27.0 cm; reins, 1994, 258.0 x 2.5 cm. Leather, glass beads, and chrome, by Coy Fisher. The breast stall is used to keep the saddle from sliding back on the horse, particularly when riding uphill. The head stall accompanies the bit and reins.

Clockwise from top: wooden fork with horn, 1992, 28.2 x 29.0 x 13.3 cm; wooden tree with metal horn, 1992, 20.2 x 56.2 x 34.5 cm; wooden cantle, 1992, 18.3 x 36.5 x 9.3 cm; complete saddle tree covered with rawhide, 1992, 29.1 x 51.6 x 34.2 cm. Wood, cow rawhide, and metal. These saddle tree pieces were made by Nehiyaw saddle maker Wally Soosay from the Samson Reserve in Hobbema, Alberta. The tree is the most important part of saddle construction. Here we see the various stages in tree construction. Both fork and cantle fit into the sidebars, the fork at the front of the saddle and the cantle at the back. Once the tree has been built, assembling the fork, cantle, and body into a single piece, it is covered in wet cow rawhide, as on the finished saddle tree on the right. When applied properly, the rawhide then dries and keeps the wooden tree intact. Fork and cantle design and shape vary a great deal with the style of saddle, which in turn varies according to the intended use. A high cantle was fashionable during the late 1800s and early 1900s, when cowboys spent long hours in the saddle.

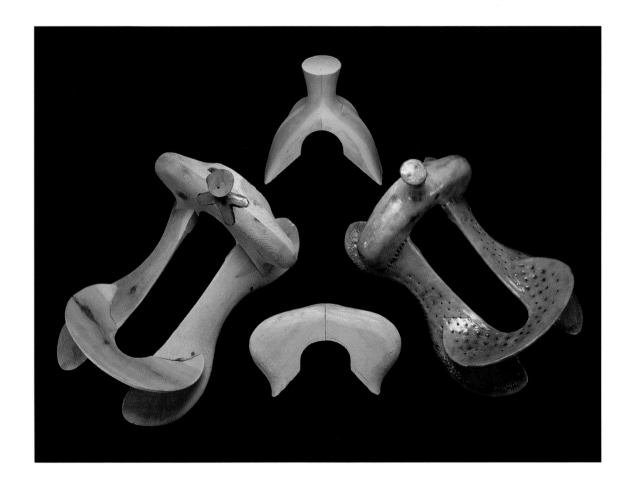

Horse blanket, 1994, 219.0 x 81.5 cm; riding quirt, 1994, 113.5 x 6.5 cm; saddlebag, 1994, 43.5 x 31.9 cm. Textile, beads, leather, wood, tanned deer hide, broadcloth, dyed horsehair, tin cones, hawk bells, and brass buttons, by Harrison Red Crow. Red Crow, Kainai, from Stand Off, Alberta, comes from a family with a long history of ranching life. He began to create traditional style Kainai horse equipment several years ago. Such equipment — handmade saddle blankets, riding quirts, and possible bags — were used with pad or frame saddles. They are sometimes seen today at the Calgary Stampede, Crow Fair, and Cheyenne and Pendleton rodeos.

*Right: Western saddle, 1992,
103.2 x 71.9 x 64.3 cm, leather,
metal, brass, wood, tin, wool,
and foam, by Pete Standing
Alone. Standing Alone, Kainai,
from Stand Off, Alberta, taught
himself how to tool leather from
a Tandy's leather kit, and prefers
to work in tooled floral designs
over hammer and stamp designs.
When Prince Charles was made
an honorary chief of the Kainai,
Standing Alone was asked by
his community to make the
prince a western stock saddle
trimmed in silver.*

*Below: Tooled stirrup covers
under construction, by Pete
Standing Alone, Kainai.*

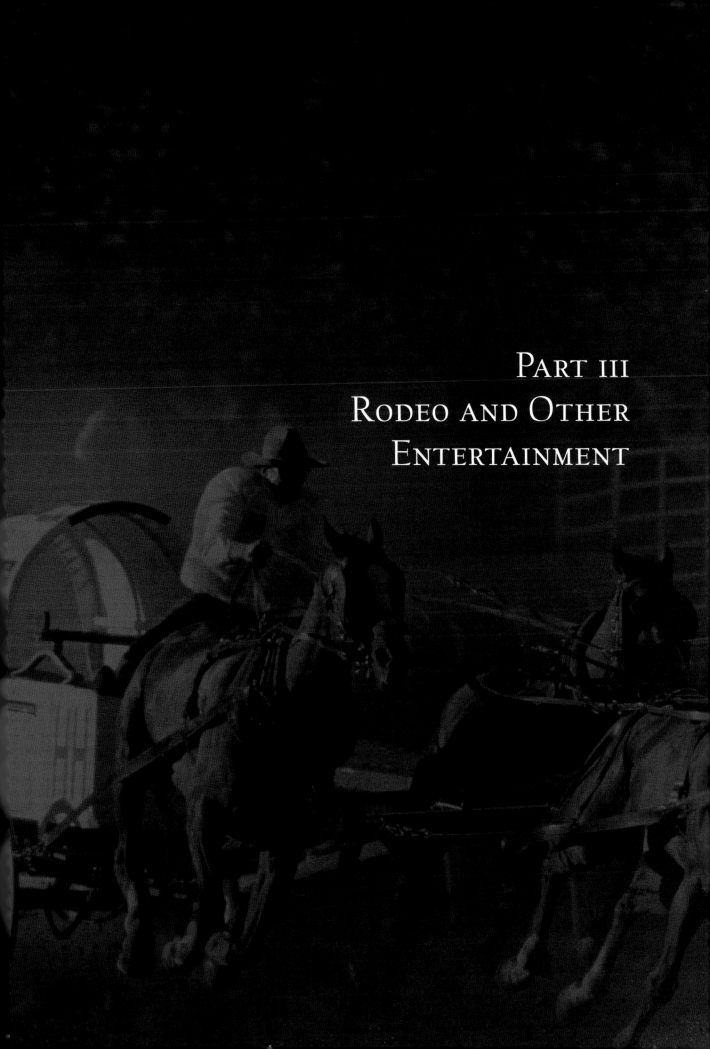

PART III
RODEO AND OTHER
ENTERTAINMENT

Rodeo and Other Entertainment

Late in the nineteenth century the cowboy's skills of horsemanship, roping, and herding stock became popular forms of entertainment and sport. Wild West shows incorporated traditional Native culture and elements of western American history to produce theatrical performances to educate and entertain the public. Rodeos moved away from the ranching environment and developed into organized sport. They were frequently opened by parades of cowboys and Native people in traditional dress. Tipi villages and pow-wows became associated with the larger, internationally known rodeos of the Plains and Plateau.

The idea of using the skills of the cowboy in this manner began in 1883 with William F. Cody. He popularized the Wild West show and it captured the public's imagination. Soon troupes of Native actors were travelling in Europe, the United States, and Australia. Such performances continue today with Disneyland Paris's Wild West Show and with smaller, Native-owned operations such as Apatohsi Piikunii cowboy Pat Provost's Wild Horse Show and Buffalo Chase, and Tse-tsêhésê-stâhase cowboy Philip Whiteman's troupe of Wild West show performers.

At the beginning of the century traditional Native culture and skills were also expressed through parades, pageants, horse races, and 'Indian Villages,' which became part of the fall fairs and larger rodeo performances in western Canada and the United States. People from many different Native cultures came together to share stories and dances, sell their art and craft, and celebrate their heritage. In recent years Aboriginal people have also developed their own opportunities to express their skills, culture, and traditions in conjunction with wider community events. Some people use their horsemanship in other forms of public entertainment, such as the Royal Canadian Mounted Police Musical Ride.

What originally began as friendly competitions at the end of a cattle drive or round-up developed into the sport of rodeo. Thousands of people

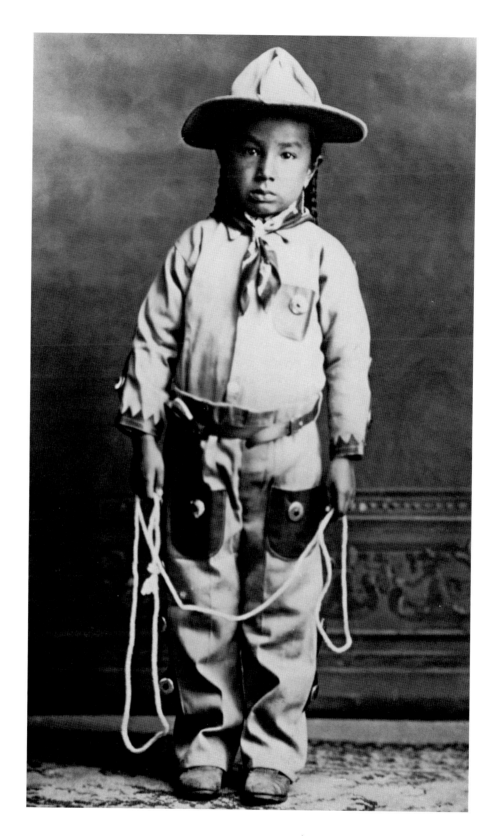

Buffalo Thigh, Tse-tsĕhĕsĕ-stăhase, Clinton, Oklahoma, 1914. By the turn of the century many Native communities were very involved in ranching and rodeo life and the culture of cowboy life was already making an impression on children.

Left: 'Young man in fancy dress,'
Fort Belknap, Montana, 1905.
Following the Reservation
Period many men and boys
were forced to cut their hair.
The photographer, Sumner
Matteson, remarked that 'since
it was a disgrace for any
Indian to appear in fancy dress
or ceremonial attire without
long hair, wigs became the only
remedy. This man is wearing
a braided horse hair wig.'

Above: Wood carving of bronc
rider, 1997, 48.0 x 65.5 cm,
cedar and paint, by Travis Ogle,
Hunkpapa Lakota from Wood
Mountain, Saskatchewan.

are attracted to the Calgary Stampede, the Pendleton Rodeo, the Williams Lake Rodeo, Crow Fair, and the Omak Stampede, and rodeo is regularly broadcast on television sports channels. At first Native cowboys participated in local competitions on reserves and in nearby towns. As the sport grew so did their involvement, including the development of Native rodeo associations. Many of the rodeo legends who serve as role models for young people are Native cowboys from the Plains and Plateau.

Wild West Shows

Aboriginal people in the United States have been closely involved with circuses, staged buffalo hunts, Wild West performances, and other forms of public entertainment for more than 150 years. As early as 1843, P.T. Barnum included Native dancers as part of his 'Grand Buffalo Hunt' in Hoboken, New Jersey (Rosa and May 1989, 66-7). Aboriginal people's greatest involvement in Wild West shows, however, would come about forty years later through the entrepreneurship of Buffalo Bill Cody and others like him.

Having lived in the West, and having 'lived' the West before the onslaught of easterners and European settlers changed his romantic universe, former Indian fighter and scout, Pony Express rider, and buffalo hunter Colonel William F. Cody, better known as Buffalo Bill Cody, became concerned that the experiences and memory of his 'glorious days' would soon be forgotten. He envisioned a theatrical performance that would take place not on stage but in an arena, with live horses, buffalo, Native people, and famous men and women of the West. In the summer of 1882 Cody took part in a July 4th celebration at North Platte, Nebraska, called the 'Old Glory Blow Out,' which had cowboys, Natives, and much spectacle. He was inspired to recreate the West using cowhands, sharpshooters, buffalo hunters, trick riders, trick ropers, mountain men, soldiers, and most important, the first peoples of the Plains. His dream became a reality around 1883 with the creation of Buffalo Bill's Wild West and his Congress of Rough Riders.

Bill Cody was not responsible for inventing rodeos, but he may have been the first to bring what we now call rodeo events into a public arena. He was also among the first to popularize mock battles between North America's Aboriginal people on the one side and the United States Army and 'cowboys' on the other. The tradition of parades associated with rodeos and Wild West shows may be directly related to the period in which Cody joined forces with the Barnum and Bailey circus because of financial difficulty.

Cody had a close relationship with his Aboriginal cast members. They were certainly a very important part of his show and its popularity. Some members remained with him almost throughout the show's career, and the children who were born while the show toured grew up to join the cast.

John Nelson had once served as a scout, interpreter, and guide for the US army. He and his Lakota family joined Buffalo Bill's Wild West and toured with the show for years.

JOHN NELSON, AND FAMILY,
SCOUT, INTERPRETER AND GUIDE.
Buffalo Bill's Wild West.

ELLIOTT & FRY   Copyright.   55, BAKER STR, LONDON. W.

Above: Cornhusk bag, 17.0 x 16.5 cm, fibre, wool, cotton, and skin. Bags such as this Kutenai one, and often much larger and more ornately designed ones, were attached to women's saddles as decoration for parades.

Right: Beaded bag, c 1996, 25.0 x 26.0 cm, deer skin and beads, by Mona Williams, Okanagan. Beaded bags such as this one have been made by generations of beadworkers to carry at pow-wows and in parades for sale and for trade. The patterns are usually of flowers or animals, especially horses or deer, scenes of rodeo events, cowboys, and 'Indian princesses.'

Opposite: Baby board, 100.0 x 37.0 cm, wood, skin, wool, canvas, beads, sinew, and cotton. Baby boards served as cradles and were attached to the side of the saddle when riding. Often the board was hung in a nearby tree while the mother picked berries or dug roots. The wind rocked the baby and kept it out of reach of coyotes and bears. Heavily decorated baby boards such as this Kutenai one were often part of a woman's parade outfit.

Cody liked to recruit traditional Native people who had not adapted to a European way of life. A number of well-known Aboriginal people worked with him: Chief Sitting Bull of the Hunkpapa, Lakota; Brave Chief, Chief of the Witehitos; Gabriel Dumont, the military leader of the 1885 North-West Rebellion; Chief Irontail; Black Elk, Lakota; Lame Deer, Lakota; and Red Shirt, Oglala Lakota. They all joined for their own reasons, of course, but considering their circumstances the most important factor was probably that Cody provided them and their families with a living.

Although the Wild West show representation of Aboriginal people was not a positive one, their decision to become involved with Cody stemmed from several factors. People on the reserve lacked adequate food and housing. Wage labour was often paid in ration tickets or scrip, whereas work off the reserve was paid in cash. Reservation life often meant confinement to land that was inadequate for farming or ranching and had no wild game. Involvement in the show meant an opportunity to travel and maintain one's language, culture, and a traditional form of life, even at the expense of being on public display. Performing in front of an audience did mean popularity and, for some people, a boost to self-esteem.

Life on the road for cast members of Buffalo Bill's Wild West show wasn't all work. A table tennis game draws quite a crowd, c 1900.

From 1883 into the 1930s there were well over 100 Wild West shows touring North America and Europe, many going on at the same time (Farnum 1992, 11). Among others were Major Gordon W. Lillie's Wild West, Pawnee Bill's Wild West, and the Miller Brothers' Ranch 101. Not all of them treated their Aboriginal cast members with dignity and respect. Several shows were owned and operated by con artists, who often left town with cash in hand while creditors, sponsors, subcontractors, and cast members were left behind without compensation.

Numerous Plains and Plateau people also travelled to Australia over the years. A troupe of performers from British Columbia travelled to Sydney in 1911. Alberta sent six Native cowboys to Sydney in 1939 to perform in a Wild West show and compete in a rodeo. Since 1980 several members of the Nehiyaw community at Hobbema, Alberta, have performed in Australia as trick ropers, bronc riders, and traditional dancers.

In recent years Disneyland Paris has revived the Wild West style of performance. With some curatorial advice from the Buffalo Bill Historical Center in Cody, Wyoming, Disney has worked its 'magic' at interpreting American history. Once again Native equestrian experts from Canada and the United

Lakota/Dakota warrior in Buffalo Bill's Wild West show, photographed by Sydney Prior Hall (1842-1922) in Montreal, Quebec, 1887.

Above: Jack Real Bird,
Absalooka, from Garryowen,
Montana, getting ready to
attack the 7th Cavalry in a
Buffalo Bill Wild West reenact-
ment in Cody, Wyoming, 1996.

Right: Native Man from
the Buffalo Bill Wild
West Show, *1887, 35.1 x 25.2*
cm, watercolour on wove paper,
by Sydney Prior Hall (1842-
1922). When Buffalo Bill
brought his Wild West show to
Montreal, Hall photographed
and painted several portraits of
participants.

States have the opportunity to reenact the 'Wild West.' Several times a year, in communities across North America, Disneyland Paris holds auditions for new cast members, and hundreds of Native people have performed in France. Considering the work that so many Aboriginal interest groups have done over the past twenty years to combat stereotypes, it may seem unusual that Native people would want to participate in Disneyland Paris , but the reasons they give are not very different from those offered more than 100 years ago. People

Carter Yellowbird, Nehiyaw, an Indian National finalist from the Samson Reserve in Hobbema, Alberta, has also worked as a cast member for the Disneyland Paris Wild West show.

What a culture shock it was. I went from Hobbema, Alberta, to Rapid City, South Dakota, to New York City and Paris, all in one weekend. It was really frightening going to New York City by myself. In Paris everything is small. Small cars, roads, and such tall buildings. It felt very closed in. Paris is such a fast world. There are so many people.

With the Wild West Show we learned how to do man falls, fall offs, get shot off a horse and take a roll. One day I was taking a man fall after getting shot. My foot got caught on the reins. Man it just whipped me around. Somehow I managed to drag myself out of the arena. They took x-rays of my hip and said that something was broken. At this point I lost my translator. He had to go back to work and I was left alone with this doctor who wanted to cut me open. Boy, the French in me came out then. 'Non! Non! Non!' I spent two days in the hospital. I couldn't move my leg. My back was also sore. I called Willie Littlechild and he and Rick Lightning came to the hospital. They gave me sweetgrass and prayed over me. The next day the doctors took more x-rays and couldn't find anything broken. I discharged myself after two days.

You know in a lot of the scenes they made us wear wigs because we needed long hair. We would do these rescue performances. Timing is crucial. You have to get the momentum right with the horse. Well the first time I did this I didn't get the momentum right. I vaulted over the horse and hit my head full force on a beam. Somehow only half my wig fell off and I was wandering around the arena dazed. People thought I had split my head open because half my hair was hanging. The crowd went crazy. It was really funny when I realized what was happening. You know it was all part of the show.

We also had this act where we chased fifteen head of buffalo on foot. This was not a safe thing to do. They would fill the arena with smoke and music. Out of the canyon prop, a door would open. Then there would be lightning and thunder! The buffalo could come running out. Tonka Yo!! The buffalo would roam around for a minute or two, then two people would come out on foot and chase the buffalo. We would have buffalo robes on our head. We would chase them around the arena and chase them together in a corner then, bang! The music got louder, mounted warriors would come out! Then the buffalo would go out a door. The crowd loved it!

Europeans were really astounded by our culture. We were the only Indians in Europe. It really made you feel very special and proud of your culture. Some people thought we looked Spanish, Moroccan, Italian. We had to tell people what culture we were. Then they wanted to buy all of our stuff. It was surprising that a lot of people knew we didn't live in tipis any more but you got some people who thought we still did. My sister and mother sent some beadwork and it sold very well. The profit margin was incredible.

I really missed Canada when I was there though. I missed the open country and fresh air. It was polluted and very crowded in Europe. Sometimes I would ask myself, 'What am I doing here,' but it was a good experience. If there was a chance to go back I would consider it. Right now, I'd like to get some education. I need to get a degree under my belt – a business or commerce degree.

sign up for the money, for the work, for the travel to Europe, to have fun, and for an opportunity to leave their community and do something different.

A Tradition of Celebration: Treaty Days and Indian Days

Over the centuries Native people have come together for a variety of reasons – to trade, to hold sacred ceremonies, and to participate in Native and non-Native celebrations such as Treaty Days, Canada Day, and Independence Day in the United States. Usually these celebrations took the form of foot races, horse races, family and children's activities, betting games, singing, traditional dancing, fiddle and jigging competitions, and quite often a rodeo. On most reserves in western Canada the anniversary of the day on which the community signed its treaty was marked with celebration and festivities. The event was intended to celebrate not the signing of the treaty but that people from the community who had been working all year in various parts of the countryside had come into town. It was one of those rare times when everyone could count on having money; treaty payments were five dollars per person, which was a lot of money at the turn of the century. Such a large gathering provided a perfect opportunity for people to celebrate. William M. Graham, the Indian agent at Fort Qu'Appelle, Saskatchewan, provided what may be the earliest recording of such a celebration in his 1905 journal:

> Treaty days on an Indian reserve was, until recent years, the most eventful day of the year for the Indians. Three days before the appointed time, usually in June or July, the Indians gathered in one large encampment, bringing with them all their ponies, dogs, etc., and for two days before the annual payment of money began, much time was spent in visiting, renewing friendships and feasting at all hours. There was dancing and horse racing and old men sat in groups of three or four, telling stories. They were waiting for the traders to arrive ... Before [Treaty] payments were completed the horse racing was resumed and Indians gathered at a point selected near the camp for this sport; there they would remain till sundown ... Old people would be cooking food making a feast for friends ... They also had boiled beef as it was the practice of the Department to supply one or two steers to be killed and issued to Indians on Treaty Day (Graham 1991, 116-8).

On the Plateau celebrations were not linked to treaty payments but to times when different communities traditionally came together to trade. The early fur traders wrote about these temporary market villages, where hundreds of people spread their camps over a wide area. Arranged like a large city, certain areas were allocated to particular groups or activities. Horse races, gambling, wrestling, dancing and playing music were all part of the festivities, which went on for weeks (Ross 1855). Autumn was the traditional time for these gatherings, when people would bring dried foods such as salmon or berries to sell or trade. Groups that had access to herds of deer or elk brought hides to exchange with other groups that had access to buffalo skins. Small but rare items such as dentalium shells, found only on

the west coast, or brightly coloured ochres were coveted materials for decoration. By the mid-eighteenth century horses became one of the most important items of exchange, and these markets were an important factor in the spread of the animals across the Plateau.

Such gatherings continued after the fur traders vanished and ranching became the new economy. Though the encampments, now termed 'Indian Villages,' were often centred on a rodeo, they served other purposes as well. In the early twentieth century, for example, a village was set up at the Omak Rodeo and remained as an encampment until the local apple crop was ready for harvest. Many Native people were employed by the local orchards, and while they waited for the harvest to begin they passed the time in the village playing stick games and being with friends.

These gatherings were limited to the few days a year when people had time off from their work on the big ranches. Usually the cowboys and sometimes their wives, if they were employed as cooks, moved from camp to camp over the summer months as they herded the cattle to new grazing lands. The only holidays were Victoria Day, 1 July, and Christmas, when people went into the nearest town or came back to the reserve for the day to join in the celebration. Today people reminisce about gatherings when they were children. Near Lytton, British Columbia, for example, an area of flat land in the mountains, now a landing strip for airplanes, once provided

Opposite: Doll, c 1900, 34.5 × 26 cm, fibre, cotton, skin, glass, metal, tin, quill, porcupine, hair, and paint. This Dakota/Lakota doll is quite representative of the pride and dignity with which women of that culture dressed themselves for celebrations, parades, and Wild West shows.

Below: Julie Hawkins, Tse-tsêhêsê-stâhase, early 1900s, dressed in her dentalium shell dress, concho belt, fully beaded moccasins, and leggings. Boys and girls learned to ride at a very early age, a skill that became most useful when tending herds of horses or cattle during the Reservation Period. The amount of dentalium on this young girl's dress indicates that she must come from a well-to-do family, as the shells were very costly.

sites for camping and a space for horse races. This location had traditionally been a gathering place for trade between Nlha7kápmx, Stl'átl'imx, and Secwepemc people (Spinks 1997). Events often included foot races, horse races, fireworks, and a local rodeo. These gatherings were, and still are, a time to renew old acquaintances, pick up some new jewellery, clothing, and design ideas, play the stick game, dance, and celebrate traditional culture.

Muriel Gottfriedson Saskamoose, Secwepemc, remembers the Indian Days on the Kamloops Reserve in British Columbia. Her family were active supporters of these cultural events, teaching the traditional songs and dances and making traditional clothing to be worn at pow-wows and in parades.

The Indian Days started in the '20s on the Kamloops Indian Reserve. They had all kinds of events and rodeo, horse racing, lacrosse games, baseball games, Indian dancing, lahal games, which was a gambling game that the Indian people used to play. We always had a parade and a lot of authentic Indian foods and stuff, and the Indian school used to participate and they would sell food. Then I think it was in the late '40s, I was very young, it moved into the city of Kamloops at the old exhibition grounds and we had all of the events: the horse events and the tipi villages, and the parades, and the dancing, and the singing, and the entertainment and storytellers. There used to be an old man on the reserve, his name was Johnny Capro and he was our storyteller. He told stories, he predicted weather, and did all kinds of things like that, and it would go on for weeks. My mother always had a float. Dad always had a great big truck and they'd fix it all up and she'd have Indian dancers on there, and there'd be all of the kids from the reserve that she was teaching Indian dancing to. There were a number of people in those days that really kept the culture alive. The amount of things that happened in those days it was just mind boggling.

Then eventually it sort of went to the horse events, and it was about mid '60s, I should say about 1964-5, somewhere in there where other groups of people started to get involved and then it completely died out. Then my mother revived the Kamloops Indian Pow-wow Rodeo. We had the pow-pow and rodeo right down here at the ranch, and that would involve about four days. People from all over – like even California, Oregon, Washington, Montana, Dakotas, Saskatchewan, Alberta, Manitoba, British Columbia – Indians from all over would come and compete for all the games and events and dancing.

Perhaps the most famous example of Indian Days celebrations are the Banff Indian Days. These began in the mid-1880s and are still celebrated today. In 1885 an order in council created Rocky Mountain Park, Canada's first national park: sixteen square kilometres around the sulphur springs at Siding 29, which later came to be known as Banff Hot Springs. In 1889, when heavy rains washed out the Canadian Pacific Railway line at the Banff Springs Hotel, Tom Wilson, a Banff resident, met with Hector Crawler, Chief Buffalo Calf of the Nakoda Reserve at Morley. He asked the chief's permission to allow people from the reserve to entertain the hotel's stranded guests. Chief Buffalo Calf welcomed the project, and within a couple of days 250 Nakoda arrived in Banff on horseback, in wagons, and pulling travois. They entertained guests with songs, dances, races, and traditional games. The event was so well received that the Nakoda were invited to return the following year. Within a few years a popular afternoon rodeo was added to the program (Parker 1990). Banff Indian Days would became an annual event, known world wide.

The Native celebrations in Banff provided a venue for Aboriginal people to hold horse races. While many of the traditional flat races continued to be held, a number of new races emerged from the Banff event and other similar gatherings. The one-mile dash with relay involved riders with two horses each. Each rider ran 91.5 metres, saddled a horse, raced around a track, unsaddled the horse, saddled a second, and finally raced once more around, the race totalling one mile. The democrat, or wagon, pie race involved a wagon driver and an assistant. They had first to eat a pie each, then to harness a team of horses to a wagon, and finally to race around a track to a finish line. Native wrestling on horseback was a favourite sport not only on reserves but also among the North West Mounted Police. Sitting bareback, legs pressed against their horses' bellies, two contestants tried to unseat each other. The horses walked around one another, alternately bumping into and pulling away from each other. The rider to fall off first lost (Parker 1990, 16). The rawhide race had a horse and rider, and dragging behind was a passenger seated on a rawhide tied with a long rope to the horn of the saddle. The passenger had only two small rope handles to hold. The team to come in first with its passenger still sitting on the rawhide won. The rubber band race required

Niisitapiikwan men ready for a rodeo parade early in the century. Horses were greatly respected and honoured for their skills and accomplishments. Note the horse on the far right. Hanging from its chin is what may be a man's hair extension, similar to the type worn by members of the Niisitapiikwan Parted Hair Society. Also evident here is a painted horse with a horse mask, third from right, and two horses with feathers attached to their brow bands, second and fourth from the right. Horse masks and feathers were forms of medicine meant to offer the horse protection in battle and when on raids. Feathers were used by warriors as medicine power as well.

Above: There was plenty of open space for this women's race for May Day celebrations in the Nicola Valley, British Columbia, 1910. Women participated in many of the same racing events as men. Some of the more courageous young women competed in the mountain races.

Right: Woman's saddle, c 1930, 85.0 x 32.0 cm, leather, metal, wood, and cloth. This all-purpose Nlha7kápmx woman's saddle was sometimes used for racing.

a mounted rider to race around a track to a point where a second horse waited. Removing the horse's saddle, which was attached with a large rubber band, the rider put it on the second horse and raced to a third, waiting horse. After saddling the final horse, the rider raced to the finish line. The three-horse relay race involved several horse teams with one rider each and three saddled horses. The rider raced a horse around a track, mounted a second horse, raced around a second time, mounted a third horse, and raced around one last time. Another variation of this race involved riding bareback. The bareback pony race was once a popular children's race and has recently become popular again. The horse and travois race had riders mounted on horses hitched to travois and racing against each other around a track. Flat races and mountain races had men, women, and children racing within their own categories either across a flat field or down a steep hillside. Several of these races were so well received that they were adopted by Native people and taken home to become part of their community rodeos and fairs.

For a thirty-seven-year span between 1915 and 1952, the years in which Norman Luxton was in charge of organizing Banff Indian Days, rodeos were not allowed in Banff. Luxton, a prominent Banff businessman, believed that rodeos and cowboy music were not a part of Indian culture. One year a Nakoda youth from Morley went on stage with a guitar and began singing a western song. Luxton got up, took the microphone away, and asked the drumming group to take over (Parker 1990, 82-3). Banff Indian Days was attempting to present the 'true Indian' in a romantic way, but anyone who lived in the West knew that by 1915 Aboriginal people had already made a name for themselves as working and rodeo cowboys.

During the 1970s a number of disagreements developed between the community at Morley and the Banff Indian Days Committee, and for several years the Nakoda refused to take part in the celebrations. Today few people from the three Nakoda communities take part, but the Indian Days celebrations continue to take place at Banff. Now Native people from across the West camp and take part in the activities.

Other Forms of Entertainment

Native people also used their skill with horses to work as scouts or as police, assisting the United States Army and the North West Mounted Police toward the end of the nineteenth century to maintain order on the newly established reserves and to ensure that European settlement was a peaceful process. Today not many mounted military or police units remain, but among those still in existence some Aboriginal people can be found. The Sacramento Police Mounted Unit in California has several members of Native American ancestry. The Royal Canadian Mounted Police have several hundred Aboriginal members. Two of the force's Aboriginal members, Constables Dennis Fraser from Saskatchewan and Tyrone Potts from Alberta, have

A Western saddle competition during a break in the pow-wow, 1958. Drummers and singers provided the music at this North Peigan Reserve event.

participated in the Musical Ride, a travelling goodwill show demonstrating equestrian and military skills. Their ranching background, knowledge of horses, and riding skills have been a tremendous asset to their work.

Constable Dennis Fraser, Métis, is from Shell Lake, Saskatchewan. He was with the Royal Canadian Mounted Police Musical Ride from 1992 to 1996. The Ride consists of thirty-six mounted police who perform a variety of equestrian and military manoeuvres to both military and popular music, touring North America and occasionally Europe.

One show in particular was very special for me. We went to a reserve to do a show and it was the first time in Western Canada that the Ride had shown on a reserve. It happened to be showing a couple miles from where my grandfather was born ... We stopped a few miles from the show site and the community did a traditional re-enactment of the days when the Mounties used to come, or anytime they had a visitor, into a Native encampment. You would stop a ways out and they would send two riders in to come and meet you to see what you wanted, to see what the business was, and they would tell the Chief who the visitors were and what you wanted. Then the Chief would send a welcome to welcome you in. So, we waited there, the whole Ride, until the two riders, who were all dressed up in feathers, with their ponies all painted up, went back and got permission for us to enter as they did in the olden days. When they got the permission they came back and they told us we were friends, they were friends, and they welcomed us in to do a performance.

Constable Tyrone Potts Jr, Apatohsi Piikunii, from Brocket, Alberta, is a rancher, rodeo cowboy and horse trader. From 1992 to 1994, he toured with the RCMP Musical Ride.

One of the things that the Musical Ride is based on is public relations and police community relations. I did a lot of school talks prior to coming here and I guess I was a real role model to them [the children]. I feel very honoured to be with the Musical Ride, being the first Blackfoot Native to be on the Ride. I know I've talked to a lot of the people back home; they're very proud of me. Coming on the Musical Ride was a goal that I had set years and years ago. I'm glad I've accomplished it ... From here I'd like to go back, work with Native people in a public relations aspect of the job.

Native people also use their skills and knowledge to bring programs of learning and entertainment to the local community. They help to organize children's gymkhanas or horse events and offer riding and horse-care clinics. Many people are involved in children's 4-H clubs and other horse- and ranch-related activities for their communities. In this way they share their enjoyment of working with horses and other animals.

Rodeo

Rodeo has its roots in cowboy culture and grew out of daily ranch life. In time the sport gained popularity, gradually becoming more professional in its judging, prizes, rodeo stock, and level of competition. No one seems to know when the first Native rodeo was held. Native communities had been raising and breaking horses for several generations when rodeo first began. In some communities horses were bred for racing, both on the flat tracks and as mountain racers. Competitions were held on Victoria Day, on 1 July, 4 July, Treaty Days, in the spring and fall after round-up, or in the fall after the

7. NELSON, B.C. HORSE RACE, JULY 1ST, 1898.   HADDE BROS. VANCOUVER AND NELSON B.C.

A horse race through the centre
of Nelson, British Columbia,
was part of the 1 July celebrations in 1898. The same street
was probably also used for
parades, when Native people
would decorate their horses with
traditional regalia.

harvest. People on the Plateau recall that as children they cleared the mountain path of bushes and rocks for the downhill races or competed in the flat races at places that had been traditional intertribal gathering grounds for hundreds of years. Photographs taken around the turn of the century show horse races through the centre of small towns in the BC Interior. One of the first rodeos may have been held in 1896 on the Blood Reserve when the federal government tried to provide an alternative to the Sun Dance ceremonies.

During the first part of the century rodeo grounds were created by people pulling their wagons and later their cars into a circle to form the performance ring. Later, more permanent rodeo grounds with seating, chutes, and announcer's booths were built on many reserves. A few of these remain, but many were torn down or fell into disuse. Fewer people had horses or worked on ranches, so interest in riding and roping declined. Many young people left reserves for work and education in the cities, while others began to play different sports. Softball and slowpitch leagues have been very popular on many reserves for the past twenty years. Today parents often spend their time driving children to hockey tournaments or synchronized swimming competitions. Nevertheless some new rodeo arenas are being built or refurbished as part of new economic enterprises. Among those still in use or being built in British Columbia, for example, are arenas at Quilchena, Head of the Lake Reserve, Whispering Pines, Chopaka, and Deadman's Creek.

The first rodeos were casual affairs. Meeting on a Sunday afternoon or on a holiday, cowboys continued their work activities of roping calves and

Jay Louis, Okanagan, from Head of the Lake, British Columbia, has been participating and winning at rodeos since high school. The Louis family has been involved in rodeo for many years. The action behind a rodeo chute shows the camaraderie and support that riders give to each other. There are always willing hands to saddle the animal or to give encouraging words or a pat on the back. After each ride the contestant is welcomed back to the group with handshakes, friendly joking, or concern for injuries.

I'm on the road probably four to five days of the week, fifteen to eighteen hours a day, and I don't know how many miles I put on this year. I started by going to Denver and I went as far south as Kasumi, Florida, and down to Brownsville, Texas, and then all the way to Tucson, Arizona, then all the way up into Canada, northern Alberta, High Prairie, saw that area of northern Alberta and northern BC too, and across to Brandon, Manitoba. I don't go to many rodeos where you stay in the same town for four days in a row. Travel actually helps me ride better, I feel it helps me think about things. Like when I usually work at home driving a tractor or something, I've got lots of time to think about riding and that helps me a bunch. It's kind of, not relaxation, but time where nobody's there and it's noisy but you still have time to think about what you like to do and how you want to ride and stuff like that.

There are a lot of fine points people really can't see because they don't know too much about rodeo. In the stands here they just come to watch rodeo once a year in the summer. You are trying to better yourself every day, thinking of new ways to improve and either look a little better, have a little better form, or just a little faster speed or ride a little more consistent. I like the challenge, I guess. Everything else I have ever done before this seems to be that I got to a point where I kind of got the handle on it and it lost the excitement. When you are riding broncs, every time you get on it's different.

Lillooet Stampede, 1951.
Throughout the 1950s rodeos
like this one were held through-
out the Plateau area. Note the
wooden corral and bucking
chute, replaced today by steel
fences and gates.

Left: Jay Louis at the Head of the Lake rodeo grounds, Vernon, British Columbia, 1995. The Louis family and their Native and non-Native neighbours have used these rodeo grounds on the Okanagan Reserve for generations to host local rodeos and for weekend practice.

Below: Denny Bish, Tsuu T'ina, 'mutton bustin' at the Tsuu T'ina Nation Rodeo, Alberta, 1990. The purpose of this event is for children to have fun whether they can ride their sheep for more than a few seconds or not. Jim Goodstriker (1937-97), who took the photograph, was a Kainai from Stand Off, Alberta, and western Canada's best known Native rodeo photographer.

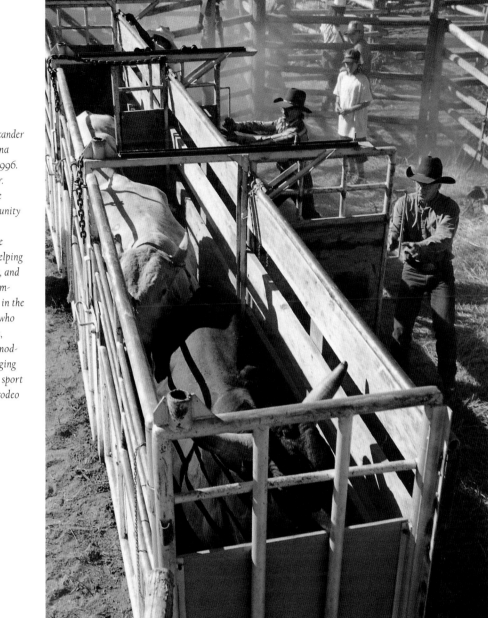

Keith Shuter and Wade Alexander loading the chutes, Quilchena Rodeo, British Columbia, 1996. Photograph by Troy Hunter. Rodeo is a labour-intensive sport. At the smaller community rodeos people often take on numerous tasks, loading the chutes, opening the gates, helping their friends get saddled up, and competing in the events themselves. Note the young boys in the background. The cowboys, who may be their older brothers, uncles, or fathers, are role models and often teachers, bringing the young boys along in the sport through riding clinics and rodeo schools.

Troy Hunter is a young Kutenai photographer who is starting to build a portfolio of images of Native life, including rodeo and ranching scenes.

My first camera was given to me by an elder when I was a child. I can still remember how much fun I had taking pictures with that camera. I was always looking for that something extra-special that I could capture on film. When I'm behind the camera lens and I'm looking through the viewfinder at a great image, I get very excited. Nothing pleases me more than to hear that sound of the lens shutter clicking as it opens and then quickly snapping shut. That sound is the sound of artwork. The feeling, the passion, the joy – they all give to me a natural high.

riding bucking horses. On some afternoons the adults organized races and games on horseback for the children in the community. The younger competitors tried to stay on the backs of sheep or steers; the adults were challenged by riding bulls and wild horses. Announcements were made through handheld megaphones. The pace of the rodeo was leisurely, sometimes taking three or four hours as the animals were herded in and saddled. Sometimes the stock bucked and gave good sport for the competitors and spectators; at other times the animals did not.

Gradually rodeo became more formally structured. The competition broadened as cowboys began to travel to neighbouring towns or nearby ranches where they knew rodeos were being held. A number of Native ranchers saw a new economic opportunity. Instead of simply bringing horses in from the neighbouring field, they would drive their bucking stock into towns or hold their own rodeos. In the 1930s men such as Leo Moomaw from the Colville Reserve worked to convince small towns to hold rodeos to bring in tourist dollars. By the 1950s stock contractors were providing the pick-up men – who help the rider dismount at the end of the ride and herd the animal out of the arena – the portable corrals, and the organizational expertise to develop the sport. One of the best known was David Perry, who, first with Gus Gottfriedson and later with Gary Hook, developed and expanded the professional rodeo circuit. The rodeos organized by Perry and Hook were 'fast, smooth and therefore pleasing to the spectators and contestants alike, which added much to the expansion and improvement of the performances' (*Canadian Rodeo News* 15 March 1970, 3)

Many cities and small towns in the West held an annual rodeo as part of their fall fair or in the spring. Some attracted just a local crowd, who came to cheer on their friends and families. Others drew cowboys from as far away as the neighbouring province or state. Only a few have reached international prominence, among them the Calgary and the Omak Stampede.

Calgary, Alberta, has long been a gathering place for Native people on the Plains. At the turn of the century Native people participated in the Calgary Exhibition, riding in parades, horse races, and rodeo events. When Calgary organized a 'blockbuster' stampede in 1912, it was only logical that Native people would become involved. The first rodeo reported in Calgary was in 1901 as a part of a local fair; the second took place in 1906. In 1912 H.C. McMullen, general livestock agent of the Canadian Pacific Railway, and Guy Weadick, who once rode with the Miller Brothers' Ranch 101, conceived the idea of organizing a celebration for Calgary that would be bigger than any of the round-ups, stampedes, and shows done south of the Canadian border. Later they enlisted the assistance of the most prominent cattle barons in Alberta, A.E. Cross and A.J. MacLean. The first Calgary Stampede was meant to be a spectacular celebration to honour the land barons, cattle barons, cowboys, small ranchers and pioneers, and Aboriginal

Right: Rodeo can be a leisurely afternoon activity, as chutes are loaded with horses or bulls, or barrels are set up for the women's barrel racing. Here, Ken Manuel waits for the next event to start. Behind him is the transport truck that brought in the rodeo stock for this Quilchena Rodeo in 1993.

Below: Women and a young girl ready for the Omak parade of almost a hundred years ago. The horses are not elaborately decorated, lacking the masks, blankets (or draps), and breast plates common today. Still, each rider displays with pride one or two beautifully beaded or woven bags.

people of the Plains. Guy Weadick wanted it to offer a reunion of old-timers, to show how the West evolved, and to bring together the province's Aboriginal people in their original costumes, along with the finest ropers and rough riders of the North American continent in competition (Kelly 1980, 431-3):

> The parade had two thousand of the Province's Indians participating; wearing war paint and feathers, guiding their mounts by leather thongs tied around their jaws, travois, papooses, buxom squaws, hundreds of cowboys, Hudson Bay carts, half-breeds, stage coaches, Mounted Police of 1874, and Mounted Police of 1912. Sacred warriors, painted and half-naked, rode in line with Indian cowboys in spurs, chaps, and western saddles, or beside a wagon that carried some sturdy young Indian farmer who had erected a display of the crops off his little farm. The past and present were plainly shown (*Calgary Herald*, 3 September 1912).

Below: Native people gathering at the Indian Village for the Calgary Stampede, 1912.

Opposite: Two thousand Native people were reported to have taken part in the first Calgary Stampede, in 1912. Here we see part of the parade.

By 1923 the stampede featured a wild cow milking contest, wild horse race, and chuckwagon races (Belanger 1983, 13-6). Native people have competed in all of these events over the years. Hundreds of Native participants have been attracted to the pony chuckwagon and chariot races. The big chuckwagon races seem to carry the most prestige, particularly at the Calgary Stampede and Cheyenne Days. Although they seldom won during the early days at Calgary, some of those early Native chuckwagon racers –

Many women and young girls on the ranch break and train horses, rope and brand calves and colts, and herd, feed, and care for the animals. In rodeo, however, their participation is generally limited to barrel racing and break-away roping. These events demand excellent equestrian skills and good timing. For some women, these two events are not sufficiently challenging and they have created the Professional Women's Rodeo Association (PWRA). The other type of competition offered to young women is for rodeo queen. Rodeo queens are usually drawn from the competitors in the women's events. A contestant is rated on her knowledge and ability to handle horses. Each is interviewed by the judges, answering general questions about horses and then guiding a horse that she has never ridden through a complicated series of commands. The contestant is also judged for her appearance, poise, and knowledge of her Native heritage during a fashion show highlighting the work of Native fashion designers. Sarah Boensch, Oglala Lakota, was Miss Rodeo Colorado 1994.

I have rodeoed since I guess I was seven. Right now I college rodeo and pro-rodeo also. I guess that's pretty much what I do. I was in some high school queen contests. It's been proven that barrel racing is the fan's second favourite event right after bull riding, so it definitely shows that the fans enjoy seeing women at pro-rodeos. I also think that women can add maybe a little bit of class to a definitely very masculine sport. But we also have to keep in mind that there's also women's rodeos. The PWRA is an association where women ride bulls, they do everything that men do. They do tie-down calf roping, they do everything but bulldog, I believe. So if a woman does want to do these things it's not like the doors are closed to them. There's also a lady from Texas, she got her PRCA card this year and she actually entered some bull ridings. I think she got hurt pretty early so I don't know if she kept going. The doors are not closed to women in the PRCA. And I think the PRCA also recognizes that they need women by supporting the queen contests.

Dick White Elk, Slim MacMaster, Tom Jerry, Rufus Goodstriker, and Mindy Shingoose – are remembered for the excitement they brought to the track (Goodstriker 1993). In recent times Ray Mitsuing and Edgar Baptiste, both Nehiyaw from Saskatchewan, Brian Laboucan, a Saskatchewan Métis, and Keith Woods, an Albertan Nehiyaw, have distinguished themselves in chuckwagon racing at the Calgary Stampede and pony chuckwagon racing in Saddle Lake, Alberta.

While Native cowboys from the Plateau frequently competed and sometimes won at the Calgary Stampede, as well as at other well-known rodeos such as those at Pendleton, Yakima, and Ellensburg, they also had a famous stampede in their own area – the Omak Suicide Race and Stampede. Leo Moomaw and his partner Tim Bernard were among its founders. Moomaw started as a rodeo contractor in 1915, when he was just nineteen. Returning from the First World War, he then worked with various partners providing bucking stock and travelling from Louisiana to Texas and throughout the Northwest. In 1932 Moomaw and Bernard decided that their season should include one show in their home town. They drove stock up from their ranch and across the river and stabled them in a nearby barn. The first Omak Stampede was in the high school athletic field. The rodeo began with the first 'mad scramble' in history – riders and broncs came out of all six chutes at once. There was no fence, no gate, and no means to collect admission fees. The first exhibition drew a big crowd but was not profitable. Two years later, however, on 24 August 1934, the *Omak Chronicle* was announcing that thousands of people were expected to attend and that world and state champions would compete. Today the stampede grounds and Indian Village are on the Colville Reserve, and the Native community is closely involved with the city in planning the annual event.

The Omak Suicide Race has received a great deal of publicity. The suicide race, or mountain race, was started in 1935 as a special attraction for the Omak Stampede. Mountain races were common in many communities on the Plateau. At Omak the hill goes sixty-nine metres straight down to end in the river. Riders scramble down the hill, into the water, and then across to the finish line in the centre of the rodeo arena. Most competitors have been Native people, particularly from British Columbia and Washington state. Some racers, such as Alex Dick, Les Moses, Kerry Carden, and Casey Nissen have won many times over the years.

Native rodeo kept developing through the century, hitting a peak in the 1980s. From 1978 to 1990 the sport experienced a boom, as many Aboriginal cowboys from the northern Plains and Plateau began making a name for themselves. In Alberta a number of Native communities became extremely wealthy from oil discoveries on their reserves, and some directed resources toward the development of professional quality rodeo and horse racing. New facilities such as the Panee Memorial Agri-plex and the Diamond 5 Rodeo

Opposite, above: Members of the Aboriginal Elders Advisory Committee for the Calgary Stampede Board, Thelma Chalifoux and Harold Healy, Kainai, sitting in back seat, in the Calgary Stampede parade, 1995. Only vintage cars are allowed in the parade. When treaties were signed on the Plains, chiefs were given a Union Jack, which is why these parade members carry one. Today only 200 to 400 Native people take part in the Stampede parade, compared to 2,000 in 1912.

Opposite, below: Stan Waddell, a Métis chuckwagon racer originally from Saskatchewan, competing at Calgary Stampede, 1997. In the early days of racing there were three wagons to a heat; today there are four. Four outriders are assigned to each wagon. Each team is then lined up beside a barrel. When a horn sounds the outriders throw a 'stove' and two tent poles into the back of the wagon and the teams then race around a five-eighths-mile track.

Pony chuckwagon and chariot
racing is a Canadian sport with
only about 200 participants,
almost half of whom are Native.
Over the past few years the
National Pony and Chuckwagon

Finals have been held on the
Saddle Lake Reserve, Alberta.
Marcel Paul takes the inside rail
in this 1996 race.

Ranch in Hobbema, Alberta, offered Native cowboys big prize money and the opportunity to advance to the National Finals. For the first time some could afford to buy horses worth $10,000 to $20,000. Good year-round facilities meant that Native cowboys could practise regularly and develop their skills, competing with others at their own level. During these years there was a noticeable increase in the number of Native cowboys who rodeoed professionally throughout the year, sometimes moving to the southern United States in the winter and back to Canada in the spring. Although many Native cowboys from Alberta continue to rodeo professionally, however, the boom has passed and some of the big facilities are no longer operating.

Rodeo Heroes

Rodeo has provided many heroes for both the Native and non-Native communities. Skill and physical grace are only a small part of what makes a rodeo hero; for many it is the courage and generosity of spirit shown to others. Many communities on the Plains and Plateau have been lucky enough to have one or more such role models. Two rodeo greats who made their mark early were Tom Three Persons and Jackson Sundown.

Tom Three Persons, a Kainai from Stand Off, Alberta, was the only Canadian to take first place in any of the 1912 Calgary Stampede events. He rode his horse Cyclone to a standstill to win the world saddle-bronc competition, winning $1,000, a saddle, and a championship belt:

> Three Persons' ride was a wonderful performance. 'Cyclone' tried every art known to his craft. He stood and pitched, started to stampede several times, then stopped and tried the trick that has sent 129 men to earth. He reared straight up and feinted as if to throw himself backward, then took prodigious leaps and twisted and corkscrewed his body in a fury of contortions that threatened to tear him in two. The Indian sat in his saddle as if glued to it, with hands up and a challenge to 'Cyclone' to do his worst.
>
> Again and again the horse stopped, but only for a few seconds, when he renewed the struggle. Again he tried to throw his rider backward and then, acknowledging he had met his master in the aborigine, he surrendered (Belanger 1983, 12).

Three Persons had worked for close to ten years as a ranch hand in the Fort Macleod district before the 1912 Stampede. He had always been considered an excellent rider by his peers. His riding skills were developed by working as a rough rider, and people in the community boasted that he could ride any horse (Standing Alone 1993). At the 1912 Stampede Three Persons not only made his mark in a newly developed western North American sport but also cleared the path for upcoming Aboriginal cowboys to enter into serious competition with the European and American cowboys who were quickly planting their roots in western Canada and the United States.

Indian Village, Omak, Washington, 1916 and 1996. These villages and their pow-wows are part of a larger circuit of gatherings. Many people travel every weekend, especially during the summer months, to rodeos or pow-wows at nearby communities. In the early 1900s families travelled by horse and wagon, whereas today they use pick-up trucks and campers, but many of the songs and dances are the same and the enjoyment of the traditional gambling game continues.

Mountain racing is a favourite sport on the Plateau and has been part of local rodeos for many years. The Omak Suicide Race is perhaps the best known of these races, and Native families have been participating for generations. The riders must race down the hill, across the river, and into the middle of the rodeo arena.

The riders, the horses, and the cars are all decorated to participate in the annual Omak Stampede parade, 1996. Note the different styles and types of saddlebags and personal bags used, particularly the one with the fine deer design on the horse. The car also carries a beautifully beaded bag of a warrior on his high-stepping horse.

Tom Three Persons and his wife, Ambush Woman, Kainai, 1912. Three Persons is pictured wearing his gold buckle and silver medal. Tom Three Persons, from Stand Off, Alberta, is one of the most important rodeo cowboys in Canadian history. Aside from being a world rodeo champion, he was also a very successful rancher. Prior to his death in 1949 he was said to have owned about 500 head of Hereford cattle and almost as many horses.

Nez Percé cowboy Jackson Sundown was the first Native American to become world bucking champion and to hold the all-around title at the Pendleton Rodeo, which he did in 1916. Born in the 1860s, Jackson Sundown became a symbol of Native American traditional culture and of Native cowboying. His skill with horses was quickly recognized, and he was given his first pony at the age of five. Caught up in the Nez Percé Wars of 1877 as a young teenager, Sundown survived the massacre at the Battle of Big Hole by hiding under buffalo robes in a tipi until the tipi was set on fire. He escaped from the battlefield at Bear Paw Mountain by clinging to the side of his horse, remaining out of the soldiers' sight. Seeking refuge in Canada at the village of Chief Sitting Bull, Sundown travelled wounded and without food, moccasins, or blankets through the late autumn cold. After a few years he returned to the United States and eventually settled on the Flathead Reservation in Montana.

Virginia Baptiste, a member of the Osoyoos Indian Band, is currently researching its history and compiling a resource of family and community photographs and oral records. Her uncle, the late Francis Baptiste, an Okanagan artist, rancher, and rodeo rider, was born in Omak, Washington, and was raised and lived on the Inkmeep (Osoyoos) Indian Reserve in Oliver, British Columbia. His painting *Indian Boys in Training*, on buckskin, won first class in the Royal Drawing Society's Exhibition in London, England. In 1938 he spent a year in Santa Fe, New Mexico, studying art. His niece talks about his rodeo career.

Francis did not restrict himself to one area in rodeo. He rode saddle bronc, bareback, bulls, as well as being an accomplished calf roper. The excitement of rodeos kept him on the road for twenty years. In his whole rodeo career there was only one broken nose and one broken leg to report. At a rodeo in Omak, Washington, he rode under two names, Jimmy and Francis. He came in first and second in one event. Francis said Jimmy left for home so advised them to mail him his prize money. What people didn't know was that Francis and Jimmy were the same person! When both would win, one would go home early.

When Jackson Sundown was about forty, he began to ride bucking stock at rodeos and to give demonstrations using the name Buffalo Jackson. His reputation grew to the extent that people refused to ride against him, and stock contractors removed their bucking horses from competition. Sundown would stay on the bull or horse until he rode it to a stop; some bulls and horses never bucked again. Wearing shaggy orange angora chaps with black spots, brightly coloured scarves, and his hair in two long braids secured under his chin, he became a favourite with rodeo crowds (Alcorn and Alcorn 1966, 1983). Sundown was in his fifties and at the end of his rodeo career when he rode Angel to win his championship at Pendleton. The ride has often been described:

> The instant the blindfold was pulled from Angel, the outlaw whirled twice and made a bone-jarring, jackknife leap. 'Sundown held fast as the huge bay thundered to the ground from leap after leap,' witnesses to the event described it. 'As the superb riding exhibition continued, the capacity crowd rose to its feet yelling

Above: Jackson Sundown.
Right: Sundown's bridle, 304.0 x
25.0 cm, horsehair, metal, and
hide. Sundown won many sad-
dles, trophies, and prizes in his
successful career. It is still possi-
ble to find his championship sad-
dles and other memorabilia in

the proud possession of people
who admire his skill and
courage. This bridle is an excel-
lent example of the skill of horse-
hair hitching.

*Barney Old Coyote Sr,
Absalooka. All dressed up and
ready to rodeo, c 1920.*

'Sundown! Sundown! Ride 'em Sundown!' Then the shot rang out signaling the end of the ride and the crowning of the fifty-year-old (sic) Indian as the Champion of the World' (*Idaho Country Free Press*, 16 June 1966).

Toward the end of his life Sundown posed for paintings and sculptures embodying the romantic image of the Native American. Today the figure and legend of Jackson Sundown continue to intrigue. Novelist Ken Kesey, for example, has recently published his version of the Pendleton competition in *Last Go Round* (1994).

Native Stock Contractors

In the world of rodeo acknowledging the ability of the animal is as important as acknowledging the skill of the cowboys. Horses and bulls that are difficult to ride become as famous as the cowboys who ride them. The animals are honoured with trophies and ribbons, and their owners receive cash prizes. Rodeo committees work with stock contractors in choosing the best stock for their shows as well as the best people to coordinate and run the event.

Todd Buffalo, Nehiyaw, comes from a family of working and rodeo cowboys from the Samson Reserve in Hobbema, Alberta. His whole family has rodeoed professionally and belonged to several Native and non-Native rodeo associations. For many years he was a rodeo stock contractor and hosted an annual rodeo at his ranch.

Part of our heritage, and part of our ability, too, as athletes, is to be able to compete one on one with the animal, the animal that was set on earth here by the Creator. We are probably closer to the animal – bucking horse and bulls, roping cattle, and everything involved in the rodeo – than any of the other cowboys are. We have a bond, a closeness with the livestock, because of the Indian way of life. Horses have been part of our way of life right from day one. Same with cattle. It all ties in together. We have a respect for the animal, which makes me feel mighty good. Once they are cowboys, first of all they have to be proud that they are cowboys, but most of all they must be proud that they are Indian cowboys.

You realize that Hobbema is noted as the rodeo capital of Canada, 'cause at one time we used to average thirty-five rodeos a year, ranging anywhere from youth rodeos, high school rodeos, low-budget rodeos, to professional and Indian rodeos. Any kind of rodeo that you could think of, girls' rodeos, we produced them in Hobbema. But it took a lot of commitment – that made all that possible. Rodeo is a tough sport, and as Indian cowboys we have to strive a little harder. We have never really had anything easy. Now it is starting to fall into place, 'cause we have starting going ahead with our own Indian stock contractors, our Indian announcers, and everything else in rodeo. Now we have the ability to do it ourselves. Our stock is just as good as anybody's that's producing rodeos. Our cowboys are just as good as anybody going down the road. The one thing about Indian cowboys, as I mentioned before, is that they are mighty proud to be cowboys, but most of all they are proud to be Indian cowboys.

Native stock contractors are among those who provide the finest animals for both Native and non-Native rodeos. They are often in charge of the entire event and provide an exciting, well-run sport. The Medicine Shield family from Siksika, for example, supplied stock to the Calgary Stampede for over thirty-five years (Medicine Shield 1992). Long Time Squirrel, or Mesamikayisi, from the Blood Reserve, also provided the Stampede with outstanding bucking animals. Cowboys came to know that a horse bearing Mesamikayisi's B161 brand would offer them a challenging ride. Dave Perry is another example of a successful stock contractor. In the 1960s his horses were in demand by rodeo organizers throughout British Columbia, at Omak, and as far away as Oklahoma. The stock contracting industry on the Plateau continues today with ranching families such as the Lindleys, the Draneys, and the Labordaises, among others. In recent years, Pat Provost and Butch Little Mustache, co-owners of Sundance Ranch in Brocket, Alberta, have supplied stock for the Calgary Stampede (Provost 1992; Little Mustache 1992). The Bobtail Ranch on Montana Reserve, Alberta, supplied stock for steer wrestling events at both Calgary and the Canadian National Finals Rodeo in Edmonton, Alberta for almost twenty years (G. Louis 1995; Potts 1995).

In team roping, one person tries to rope the horns of the calf and the second tries to rope its back feet. For calves that do not offer horns for roping, an artificial set are provided.

'There is only one real cowboy left in this community — Butch Little Mustache,' say many people on the Peigan Reserve, west of Fort Macleod. Little Mustache is a rancher, working cowboy, rodeo stock contractor, and often a pick-up man for southern Alberta rodeos. He spends a great deal of his time in the saddle. You can usually count on seeing his dog Blue not far from his side. An experienced cattle dog is as good a ranch hand as any.

Standing with his clipboard in
hand, Ken Manuel acts as a
judge for the 1993 Quilchena
Rodeo. A former bull rider, now
retired, he is asked to judge
many Native rodeos. Sitting on
the fence directly behind him is

Gus Gottfriedson Jr, another
experienced rodeo cowboy, who
qualified several times for the
Indian National Rodeo Finals.

Native Rodeo Associations

Native cowboys have always rodeoed alongside their non-Native counterparts, from early ranch competitions to the days of amateur and professional rodeo. For the most part rodeo is rodeo, and it does not matter who the participants are. As in most sports, however, events that use handheld stopwatches and human judgment to determine a winner are open to problems, especially when prize money or trophies are involved. Three events, in particular, fall into this category: bareback, saddle bronc, and bull riding. All other events also use stopwatches, but these three require a high level of personal judgment to determine a winner. All cowboys or cowgirls who have ridden in a town other than their own would probably say that at one time or another they were judged unfairly, but large numbers of Aboriginal people began to perceive judging bias regularly. Bad feelings developed, not with other cowboys but with the rodeo committees and rodeo judges. Native cowboys therefore began to organize their own rodeo clubs, with their own rodeo committees and judges.

Though few people raise heavy horses today, some Native people still take part in the horse pull event at rodeos and fairs. Albert Primeau, Métis, is the government ranch manager at Mayfair, Saskatchewan. He still enjoys raising heavy horses and likes taking part in the heavy horse pulls throughout the province. One of his teams is shown here competing in a pull at the Saskatoon Fair in 1996.

Kim Colliflower, Ah-ah-nee-nin/Hinono'eino' is from the Belknap Reservation in northern Montana. He lived and worked on the Samson Reserve in Hobbema for almost twenty years before moving to Phoenix in 1997.

I started judging rodeos in 1976 or '77. I worked rodeos in the four western Canadian provinces. In previous years I worked Pro-Rodeo in the United States. Lately I've been doing Indian rodeos. Indian rodeo is harder to judge. There are more contestants in Indian rodeos. The other problem is I know a lot of people. Some people think I should bend the rules and I don't believe in bending the rules. There are already enough variables in there anyway, that you don't need any unfair advantages over anyone else. So, I like to keep thing honest, just stay above board and strict.

I was fortunate enough in 1996 to be invited to judge the Indian National Finals Rodeo. I felt really honoured to do this because they haven't used too many Native judges for this rodeo. Bob Gottfriedson from British Columbia once judged it and I always had great respect for Bob. He knew what he was doing. That's the key thing to judging. You have to know all the rules and know how to interpret them and how they apply to different situations that arise. It's hard but if you do your job correctly it's really rewarding. I think the best praise comes from the people who hired you. When the committee comes up to you, shakes your hand, and says thank you, you've done a good job – that's real praise.

In 1945 a substantial number of Native cowboys joined the Cowboy's Protective Association, which later became the Canadian Professional Rodeo Association. In its early incarnation the organization was primarily interested in the betterment of rodeo and was not yet a professional rodeo club, though it would become one. When Native cowboys later formed their own associations, they used the same rules and many kept their membership in the non-Native professional association.

In the late 1950s seven cowboys from the Blood Reserve in Stand Off, Alberta – Rufus Goodstriker, Floyd and Frank Many Fingers, Ken and Tuffy Tailfeathers, and Fred and Horace Gladstone – formed the Lazy-B 70 Rodeo Club. They had a deep interest in rodeo and wanted to attract younger Native cowboys to the sport. As dissatisfaction grew among Native people over unfair judges and timekeepers, Patty Rattlesnake, from Ermineskin Reserve in Hobbema, wrote to Rufus Goodstriker with a proposal for an all-Native rodeo association, and in 1962 the All-Indian Rodeo Cowboys Association (AIRCA) was formed. The two organizations eventually amalgamated in 1974.

At first the AIRCA only allowed Treaty Indians as members, but within a few years it was being asked to give membership to Métis, non-Treaty Indians from British Columbia, and Montana Native cowboys. In an attempt to foster the growth of Aboriginal involvement in rodeo and to expand its membership, the association changed its name in 1967 to the Indian Rodeo Cowboys Association (IRCA) and formed a new executive with board members from different regions in the province, enlarging its membership to include non-Treaty Indians and Métis cowboys (Goodstriker 1993). Since its inception the association has used the rule book and followed the guidelines of the Canadian Professional Rodeo Association, receiving tremendous support from that group in the process. The IRCA hosted its first International Rodeo Finals in Lethbridge, Alberta, in 1969 and in the same year registered under the Societies Act of Alberta.

The first people to splinter from the IRCA were the BC cowboys, mainly because of the distance they had to travel to get to the rodeos. The British Columbia Indian Rodeo Association (BCIRA) was then established as a 'loosely knit' organization to help co-ordinate Native rodeos in the province (WIREA n.d.). As the membership grew people gradually perceived the need for a more formal organization that would be accountable to its members, and in 1981 the Western Indian Rodeo and Exhibition Association (WIREA) was incorporated through the efforts of the BCIRA board of directors. Its objectives were and are to promote the sport of rodeo among the Native population by providing training and advice and upholding the rules and standards of the association. It also encourages greater participation by Native stock contractors, concessionaires, and craftspeople.

Today there are five Native rodeo associations in Canada: the IRCA; the WIREA; the Prairie Indian Rodeo Association, which covers Saskatchewan; the Northern Alberta Native Cowboy Association, which takes in northern Alberta; and the Indian Pro Rodeo Association, covering Saskatchewan (Yellowbird 1997). In 1974 members of Native rodeo associations in both Canada and the United States began to discuss forming an association of all the Native rodeo associations and holding international Indian rodeo finals. A committee was established with Pete and John Fredericks, Jay Harwood, Mel Samson, and Fred Gladstone and in 1975 the first world Indian rodeo finals were held in Salt Lake City, Utah. The organization came to be known as the Indian National Finals Rodeo (INFR) Commission. Thirteen Native rodeo associations in Canada and the United States are now recognized by the Commission.

Women judges are usually limited to rodeo queen competitions, but a few women have judged the rodeo events. The number of women who move from behind the scenes as organizers, managers, and fundraisers into the rodeo arena as participants, announcers, and judges may slowly increase as women search for a more prominent role in the sport. Pamela Word, Oglala Lakota from Kyle, South Dakota, is a rodeo queen judge.

What I look for in these girls is how they prepared for the competition. I look at their personalities and how much they know about their cultures because being Miss Rodeo Indian America, that's very important. Of course they have to know some things about their horses and that's also very important. It's like second nature to be with horses, so I expect them to handle their horses very well. I think if they know things about their culture, it makes them realize who they are and where they come from. In today's society the younger Indian generation doesn't really have a grasp on where they come from.

I grew up on a ranch and I had to do my horse training and breaking my own horses and things like that all by myself. I think women should be able to judge the bareback riding and such things. Men judge the queen contests, and so women should be able to do the same with the men. There are women that ride bulls and ride barebacks and things like that. I think it should be either way.

Cecil Louis has noted about Native rodeo, 'It is something that we can relate to; Indians have always been close to animals. At the Indian Rodeos you see another Indian competing with an animal or working with an animal. So, in a way it is special. It is a mixture too, of different tribes communicating and exchanging different ideas, learning about each other – the way each lives' (WIREA n.d.).

Conclusion

Many communities continue to have at least one rodeo a year, often combined with an Indian Days celebration or a pow-wow. Families still camp out during the celebrations, though fewer people set up tipis; most travel in recreational vehicles and use modern tents. In many places, such as the Calgary Stampede, Crow Fair, the Pendleton Rodeo, and the Omak Stampede, descendants of the original families still carry on the annual tradition. Mounted parades and grand entries into the rodeo arena continue to be very much a part of the opening events in both small and large community rodeos and fairs. People line the streets to see the parades with Native people dressed in traditional clothing.

In the rodeo profession many changes have taken place since the end of the nineteenth century. Between 1956 and 1976 Native people organized their communities to create a viable rodeo industry. Today their rodeo associations organize competitions, rodeo schools, clinics, and youth activities. This sport, in which talent, skill, and months of training are focused into just a few seconds of competition, continues to be popular both on reserves and in larger centres. Behind the chutes and in the stands are the 'rodeo family' – that group of people who travel together, care for each other, and follow the standards of excellence set by their role models and heroes.

Native veterans leading the Crow Fair parade at Crow Agency, Montana, 1994. Veterans are often asked to lead parades and pow-wow grand entries.

Dan Old Elk and Dexter Falls Down, Absalooka, from Crow Agency, Montana, 1994, waiting to be judged for their involvement in the Crow Fair parade. Note the eagle feathers and stone medicine adorning the horses. This horse medicine is intended to give the animals endurance so that they can step proudly in the parade. The rock necklace medicine on the horse in the foreground was passed down to Old Elk from his greatgrandfather, who was one of General Custer's scouts. Their horse medicine obviously works, as both men won some day money.

Some of the elaborately decorated Absalooka horse equipment used in the Crow Fair parade, Montana, 1994, has been passed down from generation to generation. This saddle blanket decoration is approximately 100 years old, as can be seen from the old spoons.

The following pages offer myths and images, reminiscences and poetry about the sport of rodeo and the enjoyment people found in Treaty Days and Indian Days celebrations. 'The Gambler's Son and Star Man' tells how a special horse saves a family's pride and fortune. An historical account of a Wild West show in Australia and a contemporary account of one in Paris suggest that though the times have changed much remains the same. Cowboy poetry has been around for over 100 years but only within the last ten have cowboy poetry gatherings become popular. Early poetry of Aboriginal cowboys is rare, though old-timers remember people reciting their own material. Today fewer than a dozen Native cowboy poets are known on the northern Plains and Plateau, two of them represented here. The cowboy and country music industry has produced some very talented Native musicians, songwriters, and singers. Some of their work appears here also. Finally, an article by Lakota cowboy Phil Baird records some of the names and stories of rodeo cowboys from the Dakotas. Throughout the section photographs show Native cowboys participating in the different rodeo events and explain the rules.

'Rodeo and Other Entertainment' is the final component of *Legends of Our Times*, yet it is only a beginning. There is a need to record the largely unknown history of Native rodeo participants, whether they are riding, roping, judging, or organizing the events. A large industry surrounds this economic activity, and Native people have made important contributions. As future generations of the rodeo family look back, they should know how it all started.

THE GAMBLER'S SON AND STAR MAN

Collected by James A. Teit

Horse racing and betting were an important part of Native gatherings. This
Secwepemc legend tells of a supernatural being who transforms himself into a horse to
help a man regain the wealth his father has gambled away.

A wealthy man gambled and raced horses with the chief of a neighbouring
tribe until he lost his dogs, horses, and everything he had. His wife and
son were much grieved because they had come to be so poor. The lad, in a fit
of shame and discontent, left home and wandered over the country.

One day, as he was crossing a plain, he saw a star fall down ahead of
him, and soon afterwards he saw a man walking towards him from the spot.
When the man met him, he said, 'I know you are downcast, and I pity you.
I have come to advise and help you. If you go to the far side of yonder hill,
you will see a horse that will speak to you.' The lad obeyed, and found the
horse, which looked very thin and miserable. Now, this horse was none
other than the Star Man, who had disappeared, and transformed himself
into a horse, which told the lad to mount, and said, 'I will take you to the
land of the chief who won your father's wealth and there you will race me
against his horses, and win back all your father's property.'

The lad did as requested, and was carried to the hostile chief, whom he
challenged to a race. The lad staked his clothes, horse, and all he had,
against one of the chief's horses. The latter laughed at the idea of such a
poor-looking animal winning a race: so he ran his worst horse against him.
The lad won the race, and now put up the horse he had won against
another of the chief's horses. The chief selected a better horse this time;
but the lad won again. Then he staked the two horses, and continued
enlarging his bet and winning races until he had won more than the value
of what his father had lost. In the last race the chief was much nettled, and
ran his very best horse. The lad's horse gave him a quirt and said to him,
'If the chief's horse gets ahead of me, then whip me.' When he whipped
him, his steed ran like the wind, passed the other horse, reached the goal,
and then met the chief's racehorse, and ran around him. The lad brought
his horse in dancing. The chief then wanted to buy the horse, but the lad
declined to sell it. He offered all his wealth for it; but the lad refused his
offer. Then the lad returned with all the horses, dogs, and property he had
won. When near home, his friend said, 'Now I will leave you,' and resumed
the shape of a man. He bade the lad good-by, and ascended to the sky as if

blown upward. When he got some distance away, the lad could only see a star, which finally reached the sky, and disappeared among the others. The lad reached home, and his parents were very glad to have their wealth restored to them.

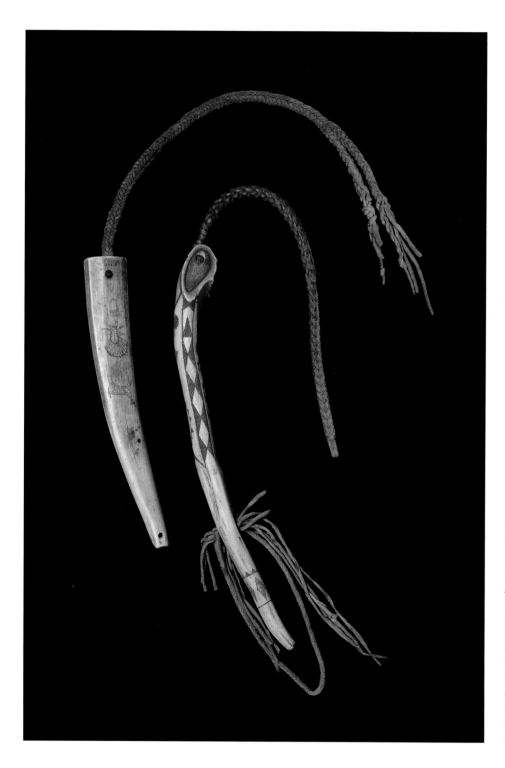

Quirt (left), 41.0 cm long, 39.0 cm lash, elk antler, rawhide, metal, skin, and ochre; quirt (right), 30.0 cm long, elk horn, skin, and ink. These horse quirts from the Plains (left) and Plateau (right) are two examples of the often elaborately carved, beaded, and incised whips used by both women and men. The handle of the quirt on the left is incised with blackened lines and dots. On one side are two bear claws and on the other are deer, a bear claw, and a fan. The import of these designs is unclear.

Bronco Busters, Basket Makers, and a Brass Band

Leslie Tepper

Since the late nineteenth century Native people have been part of Wild West shows and circuses and participated in the rodeo circuit. In 1911 a group from the BC Interior found employment in the entertainment industry by going to Australia.

On 25 February 1911 the *Victoria Daily Times* ran the headline 'Red Men Leave on Tour of Antipodes, Sail on Zealandia to give Exhibition in Australia – Wearing Ancient Costumes.' The story beneath the headline described the departure of the Native people:

> Taking a full passenger list and a large cargo of general freight loaded at Vancouver, the Canadian Australian liner *Zealandia*, [under] Capt J.D. Phillips left the outer dock last evening for the Antipodes ...
>
> Travelling in steerage on the vessel was a party of Canadian Indians who are being taken on a tour for exhibition purposes by a company formed in Australia. Capitalized at $25,000 and at the head of which is Lieut-Col Stacey, who passed through here some time ago on route to the Interior to make arrangements with the Aborigines to make the trip. There was mild excitement amongst the Indians at Lytton concerning the project. A large number of them were favourably impressed with the idea and agreed to leave on the *Zealandia* last night.
>
> The picturesquely clad throng of bronco-busters, Klootchman basket makers, [and] papooses in Native carrying baskets numbered amongst them a genuine Indian princess from Lillooet decked out in feathers, beads and skins. They took with them canoes, totem poles, old-time war implements, primitive looking utensils and numerous relics from the days of savagery, though blending modernism in the shape of a brass band. The tour should be a great success as the people in the Antipodes have never seen the Canadian red man garbed in his ancient costumes. The Company is under obligation to the Dominion Government to return the Natives to their home in British Columbia.

A month earlier the same Victoria newspaper reported that another seventeen people, also recruited by a Colonel Stacey – variously referred to as Colonel or Lieutenant Colonel – had sailed for Australia on the ship *Makura*. This group was probably from a northwest coast community, most likely from Cape Mudge on Quadra Island. They, too, took with them dance masks, small totem poles, canoes and 'other belongings of the Indians, including their blankets, head pieces of feathers, moccasins and tomahawks.'

While documentation for other groups of Native performers with Wild West shows, such as Buffalo Bill Cody's or Ranch 101, is fairly extensive,

Circular Quay.

Circular Quay, Sydney, New
South Wales, c 1911. This scene of
Sydney Harbor would have been
one of the first views that the
Native performers from British
Columbia saw as they arrived in
Australia.

very little is known about the people from the BC Plateau who joined them. From newspaper reports and passenger lists, however, it is possible to piece together something of the experience of this particular group of performers.

Colonel Stacey was an American entrepreneur who had emigrated to Australia. After a number of unsuccessful business ventures he established A.A. Amusements Company. Hoping to profit from the enthusiasm for Wild West shows and ethnic performances he set sail for British Columbia to recruit a troupe of 'Red Indians' for show purposes in Australia (Hise 1991).

When the Native performers disembarked at Sydney they had arrived at one of the largest cities in the world, with a population of almost half a million (Fitzgerald 1992). A dozen or more ships from around the world arrived and departed from its harbour each day. The newspapers of the day advertised a variety of film theatres, live stage performances, vaudeville acts, piano recitals, and concerts. Among the attractions was a steady appearance of ethnic performers. A Maori village had been established at Manly, a popular neighbouring beach with regular performances of songs and dances, skits and demonstrations, except of course on Sunday. A group calling itself the Royal Hawaiians was also advertised in the Sydney papers, along with the visit of an Indian fakir who had temporarily joined the ongoing vaudeville show.

The high point of the year for the entertainment business was the Royal Easter Show, an annual agricultural fair and exhibition. The already large consumer market in Sydney swelled with an influx of rural consumers. The judging of animal and vegetable products and equestrian competitions took place surrounded by sideshows, circuses, and travelling theatre groups. At various times from the early 1860s to the 1960s, when Canadian actor Lorne Green brought a troupe, Wild West shows performed at the Royal Easter Show (St Leon 1992). Colonel Stacey clearly hoped to share in this well-established entertainment market.

Advertisements for entertainment for the Royal Easter Show had been appearing in the newspaper for several weeks leading up to the opening of the exhibition on 11 April. The first announcement for the A.A. Amusement Company's Red Indian Troupe appeared on 7 April in the *Sydney Morning Herald*:

> Sydney Sports Ground – Next Wednesday, April 12 at 8 p.m. The Real Thing. Red Indians and Cowboys. The Indian Village will be true to life in every particular. Redskin Chiefs, Squaws, Papooses and Medicine Men. The Redskin in Peace and War. Whirlwind Riding, Expert Lassoing, War Dances, Indian Attack on and Burning of a Settler's Home and Gallant Rescue by a Band of Cowboys. The Wild West in Australia. What you have read of, dreamt of and previously seen only in pictures you may now see in real life. The Indian Village will be open for inspection Monday to Friday Afternoons. Location Sydney Sports Ground Moore Park. Direction: A.A. Amusements Ltd.

The following day the *Sydney Morning Herald* ran an advertisement for A.A. Amusements that announced, 'The Real Thing. Redskins in Sydney, Sioux,

Apaches, Iroquois, Blackfeet, Delawares. 31 Genuine Red Indians, members of the above tribes arrived in Sydney last night by S.S. *Gabo* from Brisbane and S.S. *Zealandia* from Vancouver and were driven to Sydney Sports Grounds.' There they set up a village of wigwams and tipis 'in which they will live as they do upon their native prairies.'

Even before the show opened A.A. Amusements had joined Skuthorp's Buckjumpers, an Australian rodeo troupe, in a combined cowboys-and-Indians performance. As the reviewers phrased it, 'A great entertainment of riding outlaws, bucking bullocks and mules will be varied by scenes showing Indian methods of warfare, village life, shooting, peace and war dances with a dramatic representation of an Indian attack on a pioneer's home, its destruction by fire, and a rescue by cowboys. Evening performance on Good Friday' (*Sydney Morning Herald*, 12 April 1911).

The 1911 fair was well attended. The final day had a recorded 20,000 visitors, an increase of 1,000 over the year before. Photographs in the annual report show people packed around the show rings and filling the pathways. The reviews were enthusiastic: 'An immense concourse of people responded last night to the attraction of Redskin Indians and Cowboys from America.' The Native performers, dressed in their outfits, marched around the cycle track of the Sydney Sports Ground to 'the delight of the huge audience, and throughout the evening paused at various points of it to execute their dance and give their melancholy war-whoops.' 'Races by the Indians round the field, skillful lassoing by the cowboys and the peace and war dances ... constituted the incidental "trimmings" to the main entertainment' of bronc riding. The final event of the evening was a dramatic attack by Natives on a 'farm-house.' They stealthily and very slowly advanced from the cycle track to the distant hut, the farm 'blazed right cheerily, the cowboys galloped up to effect a rescue, and the audience dispersed.'

The adventure of these Native people from British Columbia ended badly. A.A. Amusements went bankrupt very soon after the troupe's performances. Stacey is reported to have supported the Native people out of his own funds, but he too was deeply in debt. Nevertheless Stacey's company had made a bond with the Canadian government and guaranteed that the actors would be returned home. The company sold all their office furniture and the artifacts. The totem poles, masks, and costumes eventually ended up in the collection of the Australian Museum. They were recently returned to a Native community on the northwest coast after being repatriated in 1993 by the Canadian Museum of Civilization. In the absence of any documentation found to date, one can only hope that the sale provided sufficient funds to bring the Native people home to British Columbia.

THE MENACE OF THE WILD WEST SHOW

Chauncey Yellow Robe

Chauncey Yellow Robe, from Rapid City, South Dakota, was one of the first Dakota/ Lakota to receive a postsecondary education. He was greatly opposed to Native involvement in the Wild West shows that were springing up like wildfire around the United States, directing his protests against their historical inaccuracies. In the following speech, delivered at the 1914 annual conference of the Society of American Indians in Madison, Wisconsin, Yellow Robe refers to the massacre at Wounded Knee, which occurred four days after Christmas in 1890.

Some time ago, Judge Sells, the United States Commissioner of Indian Affairs, said: 'Let us save the American Indian from the curse of whiskey.' I believe these words hold the key to the Indian problem of today, but how can we save the American Indian if the Indian Bureau is permitting special privileges in favor of the wild-west Indian shows, moving-picture concerns, and fair associations for commercializing the Indian? This is the greatest hinderance, injustice, and detriment to the present progress of the American Indian toward civilization. The Indians should be protected from the curse of the wild west show schemes, wherein the Indians have been led to the white man's poison cup and have become drunkards.

Loren Cuny, Oglala Lakota, is from South Dakota. A professional rodeo cowboy and stuntman, in 1996 Cuny qualified for the Indian National Finals Rodeo in Saskatoon, Saskatchewan. He has worked as a stuntman on several films, and describes the experience here.

All I had to do was chase buffalo. Now that was something I always wanted to do. We got out there and they put us in this draw, and they had over 1,800 head of buffalo coming over this hill. I mean it sounded like a freight train coming. I'm sitting down below that hill and I looked up and saw all these buffalo, and I was thinking, 'I am gonna die for 450 bucks!! What am I doing here?' Those buffalo are coming over and the ground is shaking! They're pushing those buffalo with pick-up trucks and helicopters and my horse, he just went to kind of bucking around there and I just held him up. I tell you, the first day! You know, we're supposed to shoot rubber arrows into those buffalo! And I tell you, I was going haa, haa, haa – get back, get back!! You know, I didn't want to get run over! Those buffalo can run faster than a horse and spin on a dime. The first day it was scary for every one of us, you know. But after that we all loosened up and talked about it, and I mean we all had fun.

In some of the celebrations, conventions, and county fairs in Rapid City and other reservation border towns, in order to make the attraction a success, they think they cannot do without wild-west Indian shows, [and] consequently certain citizens have the Indian show craze. In fact, the South

Dakota State Fairs always have largely consisted of these shows. We can see from this state of affairs that the white man is persistently perpetuating the tribal habits and customs. We see that the showman is manufacturing the Indian plays intended to amuse and instruct young children, and is teaching them that the Indian is only a savage being. We hear now and then of a boy or girl who is hurt or killed by playing savage. These are the direct consequences of the wild-west Indian shows and moving pictures that depict lawlessness and hatred.

Before the closing history of the nineteenth century an awful crime was committed in this great Christian nation. It was only a few days after the civilized nations of the world had celebrated the message of the heavenly host [at Christmas] saying, 'Fear not, for behold I bring you good tidings of great joy which shall be to all people:' and 'Glory to God in the highest and on earth peace, good will toward men.' A band of Sioux Indians, including women and children, unarmed, were massacred. The wounded were left on the field to die without care at Wounded Knee by the United States troops just because they had founded a new religion called 'The Indian Messiah.' This was a cowardly and criminal act without diplomacy. Twenty-three years afterward, on the same field of Wounded Knee, the tragedy was reproduced for 'historical preservation' in moving-picture films and called *The Last Great Battle of the Sioux*. The whole production of the field was misrepresented and yet approved by the Government. This is a disgrace and injustice to the Indian race.

I am not speaking here from selfish and sensitive motives, but from my own point of view, for cleaner civilization, education, and citizenship for my race. We have arrived at the point where the great demands must be met. 'To the American Indian let there be given equal opportunities, equal responsibilities, equal education.'

REMEMBERING HEROES

David Pratt

David Pratt says of his subject matter here, 'Your heroes can be anybody. You pattern yourself after people you respect, not what they are. You become what they show you, and hopefully that's good.' Although both Will Rogers and Roy Rogers were of Native ancestry, 'Remembering Heroes' is not about race but about cowboy heroes.

I was a kid in the '50s and '60s.
I learned as I'd play.
I grew up with cowboy heroes,
I was Roy Rogers for a day.

I'd get up every mornin' – throw on a hat,
    strap on cap guns,
'Cause Roy and the bad guys were goin' to bat.
Well, those bad guys better find some place to hide
'Cause me and Trigger are ready to ride.

I'd go to sleep at night and Casey Tibbs would be waitin' for me in my
    dreams
I could ride the rankest broncs as handy as him, it seems.
All the cowboy tunes I'd sing while sittin' in a tree,
I'd daydream of bein' back in the saddle with Gene Autry.

Will Rogers found something good in everyone he met,
It didn't matter how deep he had to look,
You couldn't change him 'cause his mind was set.
He taught how to respect each and every man,
And no matter who you met they're greeted with an open hand.

John Wayne taught me how to be headstrong and always do what's right
And how to stand my ground if ever in a fight.
To think before I speak. Even though I fear,
Never show I'm weak.

Turk Grenaugh could spur the broncs and never give up try
And live with the pain 'cause cowboys never cry.

Above: Grant Fosberry, Okanagan, has just finished calf roping at the Quilchena Rodeo, 1993. Barb Stewart, Secwepemc, who took this photograph, has spent her life around the rodeo arena. She grew up in a ranching and rodeo family and is a champion barrel racer. In recent years, Stewart has worked for the Secwepemc Band and Tribal Councils and in her spare time has discovered new talents as a photographer and museum consultant. Her images convey the romance and excitement associated with rodeo life.

Right: Dakota/Nehiyaw cowboy poet David Pratt from Gordon's Reserve, Saskatchewan, has performed at the internationally known Cowboy Poetry Gathering in Elko, Nevada, and at the Canadian Cowboy Festival in Calgary, Alberta.

Each of my heroes were like fathers, they raised me since a child.
They taught me right from wrong and kept me from turning too wild.
They gave me lessons in strength to get me through when life is gettin' me down
I think about what they would do if they were still around.
And tried to make them proud of me as I've become a man
Their lessons are remembered, it's made me what I am.

Since I've grown, more heroes have come and gone,
What they've left behind gets me through this trek I'm on.

Since that fateful day in Cheyenne when Lane Frost hit the dirt,
It sort of makes me thankful that I really never got hurt
As he stood up and tried to walk and then regain
He waved Tuff over, then he fell again,
And there beside him until his life's end
Was a man like a brother, a true friend.

He taught us how to be our best at everything we do
And how to help others to be their very best too.
He showed how a smile could go so very far
When he stopped to greet the fans at the 87 NFR

He never thought of himself, it was others he'd try to please
A gift from above and he did it with such ease.

The man upstairs is smilin' at each of them for a job well done
They all had a hand in what I've become
They taught me values, morals, and much more
Without them, growin' up would have been a much heavier chore.

Now somewhere in my deepest thoughts they seem to cross my mind
And just when I need them the most they're with me just a step behind.
They've each left their legacy and we're really never apart
'Cause they live within me deep inside my heart.

*Shane Fisher, a Nehiyaw/
Anishnaabe cowboy from
Moose Jaw, Saskatchewan,
getting ready for his eight-
second bareback ride at the
oldest continuous rodeo in
Canada, the Wood Mountain
Rodeo, Saskatchewan.*

Buffy Sainte-Marie is a Métis/Nehiyaw singer and songwriter.

There was a time in the early '70s when I got pretty heartsick at doing city concerts where the audience knew nothing about the pride and joy and beauty and fun, only the pain. I felt like every night they were coming just to see the little Indian girl cry. The songs I'd written like, 'Now That the Buffalo's Gone' and 'My Country 'Tis of Thy People You're Dying,' were absolutely true; but in the Native community there were plenty of reasons to feel great, and whenever I was there I sure did. Just about every-body I knew made me smile and feel real proud.

'He's an Indian Cowboy in the Rodeo' is one of the 'brag about the people' songs I wrote in consequence of all that. I'd begun to tour with a band and do lots of concerts in the middle of nowhere we like to call Indian country, including lots of pow-wows and rodeos, and this is one of the songs I wrote to celebrate the beauty of Indian reality.

HE'S AN INDIAN COWBOY IN THE RODEO

Buffy Sainte-Marie

Buffy Sainte-Marie is a Métis/Nehiyaw born on a reserve outside Regina, Saskatchewan, and adopted and raised in Maine. Though she is a published author, an artist and illustrator, a poet and clothing designer, she is probably best known for her music. Her hit song 'He's an Indian Cowboy in the Rodeo' came out in 1971. Sainte-Marie says of the subject of her song, 'Yes ... he was a real guy. And a real cowboy. Cree. Gorgeous. Died in a fight before I ever really got to know him. I'll always be grateful he inspired me with such a happy song.'

Sun is up
Day is on
Look for me
I'll be gone
'Cause today's the day
I'm gonna see him again

He's an Indian cowboy in the rodeo
And I'm just another little girl
Who loves him so
He's an Indian cowboy in the rodeo
And I'm just another little girl
Who loves him so

Once he stopped
And talked to me
I found out
How dreams can be
With a big wide smile
And a big white hat

He's an Indian cowboy in the rodeo
And I'm just another little girl
Who loves him so
He's an Indian cowboy in the rodeo
And I'm just another little girl
Who loves him so

Bob Gottfriedson on Cottonwood, Kamloops, 1968. His family remembers that 'even from a young age Bob Gottfriedson had the desire, the strength, the will, and most importantly, the heart to be a cowboy.'

ON THE CHAMP OF '63

Garry Gottfriedson
for my brother, Bob

Heroes and legends are an important part of rodeo life. Bob 'Tonto' Gottfriedson is remembered as a phenomenal athlete and had many championship rodeo rides, starting in 1959 and through the numerous wins that qualified him year after year for the Canadian Finals, the National Finals, and the Indian National Finals. His bronc riding win at the Calgary Stampede in 1977 was the first by a Native person since the 1912 Stampede.

The year 1963 saw many championships for Bob as he travelled to rodeos from Baton Rouge, Louisiana, to Madison Square Garden, New York, and to the National Finals. The horses Come Apart, owned by the Gottfriedson family, and Moonrocket, one of the string owned by neighbour David Perry, were among the best of the bucking stock. 'Tonto' Gottfriedson died in 1991 at the age of fifty-two, and is remembered here by his brother Garry.

saddle bronc champ of '63
they tell me

I was too young to know
cowboys
but I knew him

he walked
the same dusty roads I do

men envied him
women wanted him

he was spirit
dressed in wranglers
gold and silver buckles

he was trickster
that beckoned respect

he fed Granny Faustine
& old Uncle Mitch full
of rodeo stories

el paso was behind the moon
shiprock was at the bottom of the ocean
but they knew Moonrocket and Come Apart

I never paid attention to stories
he was my mountain to climb
my big brother swooped me
into his muscular arms
& whisker rubbed me until
I was laughter weak

he rocked me to sleep
singing 'momma don't let your babies grow up to be cowboys'

he tucked me in safely
into Mom's home-made quilts
on Friday nights
& I dreamed I was him

strapped in an old rosined Hamley
on a chute fighting bronc
measuring my buck rein
& climbing aboard
until morning

when Mom clanked frying pans
scrambled eggs
peeled spuds
& brewed cowboy coffee
for him & Dad

at a pine table, they sat
exchanging stories
telling manly jokes
& planning trips

he always kept in touch
but I knew he would leave
like my repeating dreams

Alvin 'Dutch' Lunak, Amoskapi Piikunii, is a rancher and movie stuntman from Valier, Montana.

I have been riding horses since I was three years old. I got started in rodeo, though, by working for McCowan Rodeo, a Canadian stock contractor out of Lethbridge, Alberta. I didn't make much of a living riding bucking horses but I lived for riding bucking horses. In 1986 a bronc fell on me and broke my knee, and when I was thirty-two I gave up bronc riding altogether. When you get my age work is really limited.

I got a job doubling Kevin Dillon on a film called *War Party* for four months. I figured I would go into stunt work. I do a lot of stunts like horse falls, foot falls, and saddle falls. The training is pretty much natural. I try to keep my body in pretty good shape. I hit the heavy bag, run, swim, lift weights. A lot is in your mind. You need that self-esteem. Rodeo was a great training ground for me for the acting business. You've got to feel good about yourself. Doing stunt work you want a job that makes you look good.

Indian Rodeo Cowboys of the Dakotas

Phil Baird

Phil Baird, Sicangu (Brulé) Lakota, is an enrolled member of South Dakota's Rosebud Tribe. He competed as a saddle bronc rider before turning to his present roles of rodeo announcer, historian, and president of the North Dakota Cowboy Hall of Fame. Now living in Mandan, North Dakota, Baird was named North Dakota's Rodeo Man of the Year in 1990. Here he discusses renowned rodeo cowboys from the Dakotas, but the same could be done for any part of the northern Plains and Plateau. Photographs illustrate the various rodeo events mentioned.

American Indian rodeo organizations were not established in the United States until the 1950s, but Indian cowboys have always had a place within American western history, and many of them have come from the Dakotas. In many respects the Native cowboy was not very different from his non-Native counterpart. The American cowboy, collectively speaking, evolved as a response to ranch work with the early Spanish rancheros and later with the Texas cattle drives. Cowboys came from many ethnic backgrounds, including Indigenous tribes.

When rodeo was first exhibited through Wild West shows in the 1880s, Native people were recruited for staged reenactments of the so-called Indian Wars. Feathered warriors on horseback, wagons swerving recklessly in the arena at full speed, and crackling gunfire thrilled many a crowd. While most Native participants were engaged to act in the western dramas, a few developed their riding skills through special exhibitions such as the 'bucking bronco contest,' as Joan Morrison points out in an article in the *Lakota Times*, 16 January 1990. Rodeo turned into a sports extravaganza when towns such as Cheyenne, Wyoming, and Pendleton, Oregon, began organizing large cowboy competitions with world championship titles and lucrative prize monies. By the early 1900s Native cowboys specializing in rodeo contests were making names for themselves.

Early Native Bronc Riders
In the Dakotas several Native rodeo cowboys became noted for their riding skills in the early twentieth century. George Defender (1891-1933), born on the Standing Rock Reservation along the border of North and South Dakota, was acclaimed as one of the top bronc riders in the northern Great Plains. According to one source his most spectacular rides never got into the record books (Longbrake 1996). Chester Armstrong Four Bear, grandson of the

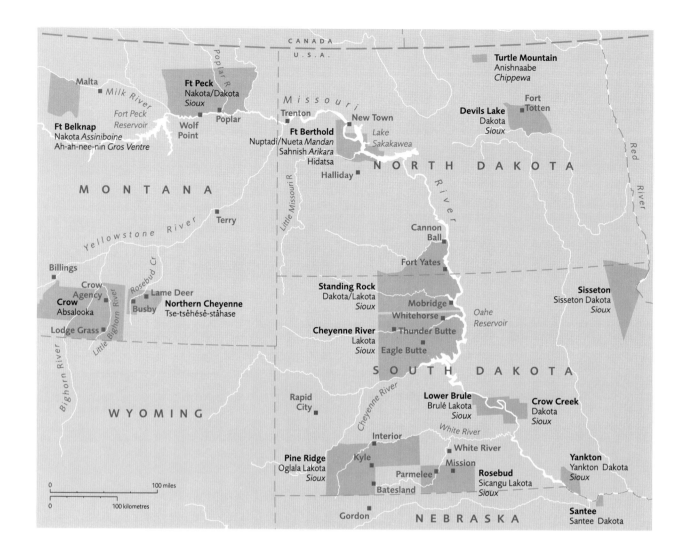

The Dakotas

leader of the Two Kettle band of Lakota people, was a South Dakota cowboy with considerable talents. Born in 1889, he polished his skills – bronc riding, rope spinning, and tap dancing – at rodeos and Wild West shows. Along with his cowboy exploits he also earned military honours when he was cited for bravery during action in France with the US army. An Oglala Lakota cowboy, Jake Herman (1890-1969) used his arena skills and special humour as a professional rodeo clown between 1910 and the mid-1950s. He was also a contestant, trick rider, animal trainer, fancy roper, and rodeo announcer during his arena career. After he retired Herman became an artist and wrote western articles for various magazines and newspapers (*Indian Country Today* 1994, 8). Born and raised near Thunder Butte on South Dakota's Cheyenne River Reservation, Chauncey Mandan competed in rodeos for over thirty-five years. He was described as a classy bronc rider who also entered the bareback riding and wild horse race events. In the 1940s he travelled throughout the midwestern United States with Johnny Iron Lightning and Wilmer Dupris on Eddy Bachman's Wild West Show. Mandan entered 'old timers' rodeos in 1980, when he was sixty-two (Longbrake 1996). Another South Dakota cowboy, Percy Kirk from the Sisseton-Wahpeton Reservation, travelled with Chauncey Mandan. Kirk competed successfully in professional rodeo under the name Eddie Collins (Kirk 1977). As the story goes, discrimination was responsible for some Native cowboys using different names. Rules were changed or scoring discrepancies occurred when Native cowboys competed, and it was a real test of fortitude for them to ride or rope against cultural bias.

Many Native cowboys began to compete on the rodeo trail in the first part of the twentieth century. From the Rosebud Reservation the Boneshirt brothers competed in big and small rodeos alike (Baird 1996). Other Rosebud cowboys riding about this time included Eddie Arcoren, Jess Leonard (Leneaugh), Adam Marshall, Paul Thin Elk, Robert Small Bear, Homer Stands, Guy Lambert, Ellie Swallow, Charlie Fallis, Steve Janis, and Willard Andrews, to name just a few (C. Colombe 1996). Cowboys from the Pine Ridge Reservation travelled to rodeos in towns such as White River, Interior, Gordon, and Rapid City. Some of the top bronc riders were Acorn Adams, Eddie Iron Cloud, Ray McGaa, Jake Little Thunder, Tom Tibbets, and John 'Buddy' White Eyes. Early French patriarch Baptiste 'Bat' Pourier left as his legacy many mixed-blood descendants who are ranchers and rodeo cowboys on the Pine Ridge Reservation (Iverson 1994, 193).

With federal policy encouraging land allotments and tribal agriculture at the turn of the century, the Fort Berthold Reservation of North Dakota also produced some talented rodeo cowboys from among its ranchers: Paige Baker Sr, Martin Cross, Hans Walker Sr, Philip Baker, Crosby Beaks, Burr Crows Breast, Lee and Glen Fox, Calvin Drags Wolf, and George Charging. Some of the Fort Berthold rodeo hands who competed in both amateur and professional ranks after the Second World War were Emanuel and Emerson Chase, Duane, Kenny, and Arnie Charging, Jim and Roy Crows Heart, Johnny Rabbithead, Tony Perkins, Milton Baker, Maurice and Solly Danks, and 'Gunny Sack Pete' Coffey Sr (Whitman 1954, 9-10; Charging 1996).

In the early reservation years the Standing Rock tribe saw a few of its cowboys testing their rodeo skills as well: Harry Fast Horse, or Swift Horse, Wally Kelly, Gene Four, Louis Gipp, Pete Claymore, and Ben Defender Sr. During the same era two old rodeo hands, John Loans Arrow and George Dunn Sr, of Fort Yates, raised bucking horses for local reservation rodeos (Chase 1996).

In later years several Fort Yates cowboys rode to prominence. Joe Harrison, now a rancher and part-time stock contractor, once held a national record when he posted the highest bronc riding score ever at the 1966 national high school finals rodeo at Wetumka, Oklahoma (Gipp 1996). Rodeo competitors from the same reservation included Colonel Harrison, Ambrose Dog Eagle, Bernie and Tony Two Bears, and members of the Butch Luger family – Sandy, Bruz, Kurt, Lisa, and Jody.

Above: The Gordon Crowchild team from Tsuu T'ina Nation, Alberta, at the Calgary Stampede wild horse race, 1993. Crowchild is the anchor man, who holds the rope to restrain the horse. Big Snake, hugging the horse's neck, is the mugger, whose job is to calm the horse down long enough for the rider to get his saddle on. This is usually done by biting the horse's ear. Once Billy Dodging Horse gets mounted he has to ride across the finish line.

Right: Dallas Ostrander from Lillooet, British Columbia, competing in the bareback event at the Calgary Stampede, 1993. In this event the rider has one hand in the riggin' and the other free. It is illegal for him to touch the horse or any part of his body or equipment with his free hand during the ride. Safety equipment such as the mouth guard, safety vests, and neck braces are finding their way into the rodeo arena today.

Landing a rope perfectly over a horse's head or a steer's horns is a skill unique to cowboy life. Hours are spent practising on objects that will stand still, such as a fence post or a bale of hay, before trying to rope a moving animal from the back of a running horse. Trick roping as a form of entertainment developed from these ranching skills, sometimes performed informally, as in the turn-of-the-century photograph here, and sometimes as part of a Wild West show. Trick roping is still practised, and the contemporary sequence here shows Cleveland LaFranier, from Lame Deer, Montana, in 1996. LaFranier is a grandson of George Highwalker Sr, Tsetsėhėsė-stähase, 1936 World Champion Trick Roper. When he was two years old LaFranier started roping everything in sight, including his favourite cat.

One well-known rodeo personality of the 1940-50s era was Maynard Tuske of the Standing Rock Indian Reservation. Known as the 'Prairie Kid,' he travelled with his father, Charles Tuske, and successfully competed in the bucking horse events. His career highlights included winning both the amateur bareback and saddle bronc riding at the Mandan 4th of July rodeo not once but several times. But perhaps Tuske's most remarkable achievement was simply competing in rodeo at all. As Wilbur Pleets put it in his memorial tribute to Tuske in *Indian Country Today*, 2 November 1995, 'knowing how to rodeo requires intense motivation, dedication, talent, and timing ... It is the genuine willingness to extend yourself. The Prairie Kid did all this and never did hear any applause or verbal comments for his accomplishments. For you see, Maynard Tuske, the Prairie Kid, was deaf. Now he enjoys all the applause in the Spirit World.

Native Cowboys as Rodeo Champions

Professional rodeo in the United States was organized into the Rodeo Cowboys Association (RCA) in 1945, a development that led to the formation of other organizations for high school, college, amateur, and Native rodeo. Native cowboys were soon visible as contestants, as organizational leaders, and as rodeo champions. State rodeo associations also started taking shape in order to standardize the rules and to co-ordinate rodeo schedules during the season. Native cowboys were soon earning top honours in rodeos sanctioned by these organizations.

At the first National High School Rodeo Association finals, in 1949 in Halletsville, Texas, Jack Runnels from Batesland, South Dakota, may well have been the first American Indian contestant (Runnels 1996). Runnels qualified for the nationals by winning the bull riding title at the first state high school finals in Rapid City. Among those helping him get started in rodeo was his greatuncle, well-known Pine Ridge Reservation bronc rider Jess Siers.

A Fort Berthold cowboy, Joe Chase of Halliday, North Dakota, became one of the early national champions after college rodeo was organized in the late 1940s. Chase earned two national intercollegiate bronc riding titles – in 1952 and 1953 – and later made a reputation in professional rodeo competing against the likes of Casey Tibbs, Alvin Nelson, Jim and Tom Tescher, Marty Wood, Duane Howard, Winston Bruce, Guy Weeks, and Deb Copenhaver (*Rodeo Sports News*, 15 January 1953, 4; 15 June 1953, 8).

Chase's younger cousin, Pete Fredericks, made his mark in both high school and intercollegiate rodeo. Fredericks won the national high school bareback title in 1953 and emerged a double winner in 1955 as the national all-around cowboy and saddle bronc champion. In 1957 he took first in the saddle bronc average and all-around honours at the national college finals in Colorado Springs (*Rodeo Sports News*, 15 August 1953, 5; Cullen 1955; *The Western Horseman*, September 1957, 37, 73).

Ted Nuce, Amoskapi Piikunii, bull riding at the Calgary Stampede, 1993. In 1992, Nuce was the first Native cowboy to win the top prize in bull riding at the Calgary Stampede. Although every sport in rodeo is potentially dangerous, bull riding is probably the most dangerous as bulls are known to attack the rider following his dismount. Holding only a rope, the rider has eight seconds to make his ride. A bell attached to the rope excites the bull and acts as a weight to help detach the rope from the bull once the rider has released his grip. The bull rider is not required to spur the animal, although spurring will award him more points.

Right: Nehiyaw rodeo bull fighter Herb Chisan, from Saddle Lake Reserve, Alberta, getting himself ready to save lives. If a bull rider gets into trouble the bull fighter's job is to come to the rescue, often putting his own life at risk.

Below: Jason Rabbit, Williams Lake Stampede, British Columbia, 1996, competing in the saddle bronc event. In saddle bronc riding the rider sits in a regulation saddle, which has no horn. The cowboy has only a bronc rein attached to a halter with which to stay secure in the saddle. The rider keeps time with the horse by synchronizing his spurring action with the horse's movement.

Bull riding, Quilchena Rodeo,
British Columbia, 1996. Small,
local rodeos are still held on
many reserves and in small towns
throughout the West. Attracting
mostly people from the local
community, these 'bullaramas,'
and 'jack-pot' rodeos reflect the
original intent of the community
coming together for some fun.
Sometimes the rodeos act as quali-
fying rounds for the Indian
National Finals Rodeo, and also
provide an opportunity for local
craftspeople to sell their stock.
The rodeo shown here was part
of a small business weekend
workshop. Other rodeos are
organized in memory of someone
in the family who has died, or as
part of a wider community
activity such as an elder's gathering.

Both Chase and Fredericks eventually became top professional competitors in the Rodeo Cowboys Association. They both qualified several times
for the RCA National Finals Rodeo, established in 1959, and were the only
Native contestants from the Dakotas to compete at the NFR during the
1960s. Native cowboys were abundant when the North Dakota Rodeo
Association (NDRA) was founded in 1953, and Fredericks and Chase were
named among the first North Dakota champions (Baird 1993, 73-5). During
the next ten years more Fort Berthold cowboys earned state championships: Almit Breuer, Milton Baker, Buddine Fredericks, Mervel Hall, Buzz
Fredericks, Dale Little Soldier, Gainus Little Soldier, and Esley Thorton Sr.

One of the better known NDRA rodeo champions was Angus Fox of
New Town. After being named the national high school saddle bronc runner-
up champion in 1955, he won his first NDRA bronc riding title the following
year (Cullen 1955, 3). Fox, who competed on North Dakota's first college
rodeo team, claimed his tenth and last North Dakota bronc riding championship in 1973.

The Three Affiliated Tribes in North Dakota boast a string of NDRA
champions after 1970. The record books show Ed Hall, Neil Karlson, J.D.
Youngbird, Arby Little Soldier, Ron Brugh, Esley Thorton Sr, Darren Holeman,
Collette 'Coco' Hall, and Frank White Calf as successful rodeo champions
from the Fort Berthold Reservation. From the Standing Rock Reservation,
Clayton Hagel and Bruz Luger earned NDRA championship honours more
than once. One of the top female rodeo contestants in the Dakotas was four-
time state barrel racing champion Peggy Ward of Fort Yates.

The counterpart to the NDRA, the South Dakota Rodeo Association
(SDRA), was formed by 1960. This organization saw several cowboys of

Right: Bull fighter Dicky Bear, Nehiyaw, 1997. There are often several people dressed as clowns in a rodeo arena. Although all are there to assist the cowboy who finds himself in trouble with a bull, only one or two are actually bull fighters and the others entertain the crowd.

Below: Break-away roping, Tsuu T'ina Nation Rodeo, Bragg Creek, Alberta, 1994. A growing number of Native women are taking part in break-away roping, in which the contestant ropes her calf and then releases the rope. There is no need to dally-up and tie the calf, as is done in the calf roping event.

*Bull rope, 1974, 341.5 x 6.6 cm;
miniature bull rope hat band,
1974, 2.1 x 23.5 cm. Rope and
leather, by Tony Little Mustache.
Rodeo bull riders have very little
to hang on to during their riding
event – just a rope. Little
Mustache, an Apatohsi Piikunii
from Brocket, Alberta, has been
braiding bull ropes for cowboys
in Alberta for years.*

Native descent win SDRA rodeo championships early in its first decade: Bud Annis and Red Traversie of Eagle Butte; Pete Longbrake of Cherry Creek; Dugan LeBeau from Pine Ridge; and Louis 'Salty' Twiss from Buffalo Gap. A top SDRA all-around cowboy during this time had family roots on the Rosebud Reservation. Beginning in 1964 Keith Whipple worked all three men's timed events and gathered fifteen SDRA championship saddles during his active contesting years. In 1974 alone he won the all-around, calf roping, bulldogging, and team roping titles. He claimed several team roping championships with his cousin, Stan Whipple of Rosebud, who in turn travelled with roping partner Harold Knox of Parmelee. Since the early 1970s Cheyenne River Reservation contestants have also been listed as year-end SDRA champions: Roger and Justin Lawrence, Vicki Birkeland, Jess Knight Jr, Tater Ward, Jim Reeves, Todd Ward, Gumbo Lamb, and JoBeth Reeves. From the Pine Ridge Reservation area, past SDRA champions include Howard Hunter, Paul 'Flip' Wilson, Tim Jacobs, and Frank Hunter.

Nehiyaw cowboy Marcel Saulteaux from Mameo Beach, Alberta, making his start in the calf roping event at Tsuu T'ina Rodeo in Bragg Creek, Alberta, 1994. The calf roper must allow the calf lead time before the horse can leave its box. Failing to do so brings a time penalty. Lead time is measured in feet and varies with the length of the arena and the depth of the box from which the horse starts.

Native Rodeo Organizations of the Dakotas

As increasing numbers of Native cowboys and cowgirls emerged in the 1950s efforts were made to organize all-Native rodeos in the American Northwest and Southwest. The All-Indian Rodeo Cowboy Association (AIRCA), one of the first, was established on the Navajo Reservation in 1958 (Jackson 1968, 64, 66). (This was a specifically Navajo association, not to be confused with the pan-Canadian AIRCA.) Through such organizations world Native rodeo champions soon became recognized in the eyes of Aboriginal people and the American public.

C.L. Johnson, Minneconjou Lakota, is a bull rider from the Cheyenne River Reservation in South Dakota who has qualified for the Indian National Finals on more than one occasion. For the past seven years or so he has been involved with the film industry, primarily as a stuntman.

Doing stunts there's some acting involved. When you're doing a major header [block-buster movie] you've got a major adrenaline rush and you're not even thinking of the cameras. I'd rather do stunt work than acting. It's a rush. It's like getting on a bull. It's controlled fear and anything can happen. You plan it all out and hope for the best. You have to have your head on right, then it's rock 'n' roll.

This is a tough business. Native Americans have been doubled by Caucasians for a long time. Now some of the coordinators are starting to use us. Everyone talks about prejudice. I usually snuff it out before it gets out of hand. I've been a world traveller and swing a pretty big loop. As much as I hear other people talk about it, I haven't experienced it too much. I don't know if I have an air about me or an arrogance. I don't know.

In the mid-1960s an Absalooka cowboy, Delmar Eastman, helped start the All-American Indian Activities Association (AAIAA) in the northern Great Plains (Condon 1996). Eastman, a Bureau of Indian Affairs police officer in Fort Yates, envisioned an organization to promote all-Indian competitions and recognize Native champions. After several organizational meetings he was successful in securing the support of different tribes in Montana, North Dakota, and South Dakota. Representatives from various reservations were identified to serve on a governing board. Eastman was selected as the first president.

Initial discussions focused on sanctioning a variety of tribally sponsored events such as pow-wows, rodeos, softball games, and basketball tournaments, but the first AAIAA group stayed focused on the promotion of Native rodeo. And with good reason. Up until this time few all-Indian rodeos were held anywhere in the country. Much work was done by early leaders to try to establish Native rodeos in the northern Plains. One of the first tasks was gaining approval by the RCA for professional Native rodeo cowboys. Through the efforts of cowboys Pete Fredericks and Joe Chase, Amoskapi Piikunii rodeo announcer Jay Harwood, and others, the RCA agreed that Native cowboys who were RCA cardholders would not be penalized for competing in AAIAA rodeos (Fredericks 1995).

After the association was up and running intertribal contests were promoted among Indian reservations in Montana, North Dakota, and South Dakota. AAIAA rodeos were scheduled at Lower Brule, Pine Ridge, and Rosebud in South Dakota; Fort Totten, New Town, and Fort Yates in North Dakota; and at Wolf Point and Crow Agency in Montana. For the next few years the number of AAIAA-sanctioned rodeos depended mostly on local efforts in these reservation communities (Condon 1996). Though official records are not available it is believed that the first AAIAA rodeo champions were named in 1967. Professional Klamath/Modoc barrel racer Vi James remembers that she received an AAIAA championship buckle in her event in that year and that Clinton Small of Lame Deer, Montana, won a trophy buckle at the same time (V. Colombe 1996).

Organizational changes began to emerge when new leadership took over in 1970. Rosebud Reservation rodeo stock contractor Joe 'Bad' Waln of Parmelee, South Dakota, became AAIAA president, and Standing Rock rancher Bob Sherwood served for the next few years as secretary treasurer (Waln 1996). One of the first developments was a year-end championship finale. After an aborted attempt the previous year at Malta, Montana, the

---

George Saddleman, Okanagan, from Quilchena, British Columbia, enjoys every aspect of the sport of rodeo from helping to organize events in his role as president of the Western Indian Rodeo Association to driving his children to rodeos on the circuit and encouraging their participation in the sport. He often works as a rodeo announcer.

It can be real exciting because you've got the front row seat to all the rodeo actions. You know who is coming out in the rough stock events or the timed events. You're right in working with the stock contractor so that you can describe how old the horse is, and what he does, where he has been, and how many he's bucked off, and who's won money on him, and this sort of thing. And you work with the judges as well so you can describe their play by play of what's actually happening with the rodeo and keep people informed that way. And same with the contestants, you get to know them because you've been travelling with them. Or you talk to them before the rodeo, or before the next rodeo you run in to them. Rodeo people get together and that's all they talk about is rodeo. The world could be falling apart, you know, and that's all people talk about.

It can be hectic too because even though you have a program sitting in front of you, things do happen. You know, a horse might get out of the arena, or a team roper would get a rope burn. A contestant might get hurt, so you may have to fill in while the first aid people come and tend to him or take him out. You are trying to keep the sponsors happy 'cause they want the blurb twenty times during the rodeo, and if you don't do that then there's a little note coming: 'Where's my name?' Then there's a change of program, so I got to listen to the chute boss, listen for the judges, listen for the committee chairman, listen to the timers. So you got about a good eight people talking all the same time. You have to have that ability to sort of put them waiting in line and just announce it as you think of it.

A lot of community rodeos, because you're right in with the people, you get a lot of interruptions. But at the big show like Calgary, the announcers are way up, and he just does the program, and he's not worried about some lost little boy, or some elder lost her upper teeth somewhere, you know, 'cause it's amazing all the things. I get to be a lost and found because there's nowhere else.

first AAIAA Finals Rodeo was held in 1971 at Mandan, North Dakota. Gary Not Afraid was recognized champion for all-around and calf roping, Clyde Colliflower for bareback riding, Ed Hall for saddle bronc, Bob Bement for bull riding, Arby Little Soldier for steer wrestling, Marcie Sherwood for barrel racing, and Junior Small for team roping (Sherwood and Sherwood 1996). Another development was the incorporation of the organization in 1972 in South Dakota. With this action the name of the association was changed to the Indian Activities Association (IAA) (South Dakota 1972). A revised structure of governance was adopted, with state vice-president positions established for Montana, North Dakota, and South Dakota. Those who served first in these posts were George Colombe of Mission, South Dakota, Guy Madison of Poplar, Montana, and Al Two Bears of Cannon Ball, North Dakota (McLaughlin 1973, 9).

By 1974 the association was considering a major organizational shift to focus exclusively on Native rodeos. According to Roger Condon, the IAA vice-president, a meeting was held to discuss a resolution to establish a new Native rodeo association. After some debate the IAA was reorganized into the Great Plains Indian Rodeo Association (GPIRA) (South Dakota 1974). Condon, a Standing Rock native and federal health program administrator, served for a year as the first president. Bob Sherwood, whose daughters

Nehiyaw cowboys Dean Louis and Leon Moutour from Samson Reserve, Alberta, team roping at the Crow Fair Rodeo, 1994. The header ropes the steer by the horns; the heeler ropes the steer's hind legs. Roping only one hind leg results in a five-second penalty.

*Team roping, Quilchena Rodeo,
British Columbia, 1996.*

*Two of the three generations of a
Secwepemc barrel racing family
from Kamloops, British Columbia. Joan Perry, shown here, won
the BC Barrel Racing Championship and many saddles and buckles in her fifteen years of racing.
Her daughter, Barb Stewart,
took up racing as a young girl,
eventually competing against
her mother and winning the BC
Barrel Racing Championship in
1963. Barb's young daughter,
Karly, has started early in the
family tradition by competing in
the stick horse barrel race.*

Bobbi, Leslie, and Marcie dominated the IAA and GPIRA barrel racing event for five years, continued his role as secretary treasurer with diligent help from Donna Sherwood.

The first GPIRA Finals Rodeo was held in 1974 at Bismarck, North Dakota. Emerging as the champions were Howard Hunter Sr of Kyle, South Dakota, for all-around, bareback, and saddle bronc; Cliff Glade of Terry, Montana, for bull riding; Gary Not Afraid of Lodge Grass, Montana, for calf roping; Bruz Luger of Fort Yates for steer wrestling; Leslie Sherwood of Mobridge, South Dakota, for barrel racing; and Esley Thorton Sr of New Town, for team roping.

The following year the GPIRA leadership reins were handed over to Warren Means, who was then executive director of the United Tribes Employment Training Center in Bismarck, North Dakota (Means 1996). The UTETC campus was the site for the IAA and GPIRA Finals from 1973 to 1975. Native rodeo business activities in the region were anchored in North Dakota during this time.

From GPIRA to World Indian Champions

In 1975 an Indian National Finals Rodeo was established in the United States. A group of RCA Native cowboys, including Jay Harwood and Pete Fredericks, incorporated the INFR Commission and began planning a professional event similar to the RCA National Finals Rodeo. The Native event, like that of the RCA, would showcase international rodeo competition by including cowboys from the United States and Canada.

With its large Native population, the Southwest was chosen to unveil the first world Indian rodeo championships. Because INFR contestants were to qualify through Native rodeo organizations, the GPIRA became the regional association for Native cowboys and cowgirls in the Dakotas and eastern Montana. The first finals were held at Albuquerque, New Mexico, in 1976. When it was over Gary Not Afraid, an exceptional roper in anybody's arena, became the first cowboy from the northern Plains to win a Native world calf roping championship.

Since then many Native world champions have come through the ranks of the GPIRA. Eight-time North Dakota rodeo champion Frank White Calf was named the world's best Native bulldogger at the 1977 final in Salt Lake City. The following year, according to the INFR finals program, Chuck Jacobs of Pine Ridge Reservation won the world bareback championship. Jim Jacobs followed in his older brother's footsteps to win six world Indian bareback titles over eleven years. The former high school all-around champion from Pine Ridge also enjoyed success in professional rodeo, winning the PRCA Badlands Circuit bareback championship in 1986. Other INFR champions to have come through the GPIRA are North Dakotans Ron Brugh, Terry Fischer, and Pam Hall, a two-time world Indian barrel racing champion. From South Dakota outstanding arena performances have been turned in by C.L. Johnson, Billy Ward, Reuben 'Boy' Clifford, Merle Temple, Troy Ward, and Marty Hebb.

One of the great INFR competitors, and another GPIRA member, has been Jerry Small of Busby, Montana. Raised in a rodeo family, he worked the men's timed events and eventually garnered seven Native world championships, including five all-around titles from 1977 to 1987. The Tse-tsêhêsê-stâhase cowboy still competes today in professional and Indian rodeo associations. Perhaps one of the best-known Native cowboys is Howard Hunter Sr. Early fame came to this Oglala Lakota cowboy from Kyle when he won high school team trophies by himself while competing in three rough stock events: bareback, saddle bronc, and bull riding (Hunter 1996). In 1971, travelling for a year on the SDRA circuit, he was named the top South Dakota saddle bronc rider. Hunter moved on to professional rodeo after being introduced to the reigning RCA world saddle bronc champion, Shawn Davis (Witte 1975, 2). Clearly impressed, Davis guided Hunter on the RCA circuit. In a short time Hunter was winning prestigious rodeo events such as Cheyenne Frontier Days. His talents eventually led him to qualify three times – in 1976, 1979, and 1980 – for the National Finals Rodeo in Oklahoma City. But Howard's greatest career achievements came in the world of Native rodeo. A perennial GPIRA champion, he rode to four world Indian bronc riding titles from 1980 to 1990, the most anyone has ever won in that event. Because of his many accomplishments in rodeo arenas throughout the United States and Canada, he is one of the most recognized contemporary Native cowboys.

The Indian National Finals Rodeo has also been instrumental in recognizing Native cowboys for their contributions to the sport of rodeo. One of the first to be acknowledged was INFR co-founder Pete Fredericks, who received the first Indian Rodeo Man of the Year award. Another recipient was Harlan Gunville of White Horse, South Dakota. In the 1970s he became the first Native stock contractor member in the Professional Rodeo Cowboys Association (PRCA). Gunville and his extended family from the Cheyenne River Reservation provided considerable support to and leadership in the GPIRA as well as producing PRCA rodeos in the Dakotas.

Contemporary Native Rodeo Cowboys

Although some tribal elders lament the dwindling number of children raised 'with their relatives of the Horse Nation,' Native cowboys, young and old, are still to be found among the Nations of North and South Dakota. Some continue to make the presence of the American Indian cowboy felt in the sport of rodeo.

At the PRCA level Native cowboys Tom Reeves, Marty Jandreau, and Bud Longbrake are following the professional rodeo trail. College rodeo has

Bruce Labelle, Nakoda, from Morley, Alberta, steer wrestling at the Calgary Stampede, 1997. The rider on the left, the hazer, rides along the steer to help the animal run straight ahead. These horses are trained not to overrun the steer. The 'wrestler' must jump off his horse at full gallop, onto a steer that is also running at full speed, grab the animal by the horns, bring it to a stop and flip the animal onto its side so that all four feet of the steer are extended. The cowboy who can perform this feat in the quickest time wins, provided he has no penalties.

Robert Young Pine, from Stand Off, Alberta, 1993, trying to do his job in the steer wrestling event. It looks as if the steer has Kainai cowboy Young Pine pinned down. It isn't supposed to happen this way, but sometimes the animal wins this event.

continued to see Native contestants over the past three decades. A few years ago Melvin Sierra of Pine Ridge finished as the national college runner-up bull riding champion while competing for South Dakota State University, and he also won the world Indian bull riding championship at the 1996 INFR in Saskatoon, Saskatchewan.

The establishment of regional Native rodeo associations and of the Indian National Finals Rodeo has done much to promote Native cowboys and cowgirls in the rodeo world. These efforts also led to the creation of reservation organizations such as the Standing Rock Rodeo Association and the short-lived Oglala Sioux Rodeo Association. All-Indian rodeos have provided opportunities for Native competitors to ride or rope among their tribal people and perhaps to earn a world championship title along the way.

Native rodeo cowboys from the Dakotas who competed successfully at different levels of rodeo and never won a championship are too many to mention, and we also cannot forget those who participated as stock contractors, rodeo clowns and bullfighters, pick-up men, and rodeo announcers. In their own way they made their people and communities proud over the years. Their involvement in rodeo deserves its own chapter, to be written some day soon. Native cowboys have always had a unique presence in America's western heritage. Some of the greatest Native rodeo cowboys came riding, and are still riding, from the prairies and badlands of the Dakotas.

Down the Road ...

The Aboriginal people of North America have a long tradition of adaptation and change, and the people of the Plains and Plateau are no exception. Over more than 120 years, Plains and Plateau people went from life as hunters and gatherers, when horses, buffalo, and deer roamed their territories in abundance, to the brink of starvation in the late nineteenth century. Their livelihood, ceremonies, feasts, dances, and songs were almost destroyed, as were the buffalo and the massive herds of horses. Fortunately, people were strong and continued to pass down the stories of their relationship with these sacred beings. The legends continued; songs were sung and ceremonies carried out in secret. People adapted to their new environments, their reserve boundaries, new diet, new non-Native neighbours, and new way of existence.

Native people continue to adapt. Today sacred beings – particularly the horse, dog, buffalo, and deer – continue to be a part of everyday life. Stories about the coyote and dog are told with new voices in a new context. The religious ceremonies that honour these animals are no longer illegal and continue to be practised in many communities. Ranching life is difficult, but people persevere in carrying out this life style and tradition. The buffalo herds have returned to many communities in both Canada and the United States. Reserves are continuously changing with new land claim negotiations and issues of self-government. Non-Native neighbours continue to live alongside reserves, sharing new technology, religious beliefs, and culture.

This book has challenged the stereotypes about 'cowboys and Indians.' Native people have been presented in their roles as cowboys, ranchers, artists, artisans, western clothing designers, photographers, stock contractors, poets, and musicians. We have looked at the relationship between Native people and the sacred beings associated with ranching and rodeo. We have also presented some of the Native contributions to ranching and rodeo life in Canada and the United States, honouring the men and women who have lived in harmony with their Native heritage while adapting to a cowboy way of life.

References

Acres Western. 1971. *The Upper Nicola Indian Band Development Plan*. Vancouver: Acres Western

Alcorn, Rowena L., and Gordon D. Alcorn. 1966. Indian legend on horseback. *Frontier Times*, n.s. 40, 2: 22-3

—. 1983. Jackson Sundown, Nez Percé horseman. *Montana: The Magazine of Western History* 33, 4: 48-51

Allison, Mrs. n.d. Reminiscences from Mrs Allison, Hope, BC. British Columbia Provincial Archives ref. no. A1636

Baird, Phil. 1993. *Forty Years of North Dakota Rodeo*. Garrison, ND: Garrison

Baird, Ray. 1996. Interview by Phil Baird. Mission, SD, July

Belanger, Art. 1983. *Chuck Wagon Racing – Calgary Stampede's Half Mile of Hell!* Surrey: Heritage House

Brown, Joseph Epes. 1992. *Animals of the Soul*. Rockport, MA: Element Press

Brown, Judge William C. 1914. Okanogan, Old Fort, and the Okanogan Trail. *Oregon Historical Society Quarterly* 15: 1-38

Brown, Mandy. 1995. Interview by Leslie Tepper. Lytton, BC

Buckley, Helen. 1992. *From Wooden Ploughs to Welfare*. Montreal: McGill-Queen's University Press

Canada. 1966. *Copy of Treaty and Supplementary Treaty No. 7, Made 22nd Sept., and 4th Dec., 1877, between Her Majesty the Queen and the Blackfeet and Other Indian Tribes at the Blackfoot Crossing of Bow River and Fort MacLeod*. 1877. Reprint, Ottawa: Queen's Printer and Controller of Stationery

Carstens, Peter. 1991 *The Queen's People: A Study of Hegemony, Coercion, and Accommodation among the Okanagan of Canada*. Toronto: University of Toronto Press

Carter, Sarah. 1993. *Lost Harvests: Prairie Indian Reserve Farmers and Government Policy*. Montreal: McGill-Queen's University Press

Charging Sr, Arnold. 1996. Interview by Phil Baird. White Shield, ND, January

Chase, Jack. 1996. Interview by Phil Baird. Bismarck, ND, September

Colombe, Charles. 1996. Interview by Phil Baird. Mission, SD, May

Colombe, Vi (James). 1996. Interview by Phil Baird. Mission, SD, May

Condon, Roger. 1996. Interview by Phil Baird. Fort Yates, ND, March and June

Cullen, Pearl. 1955. *North Dakota Rodeo Association Newsletter*. August

Department of Indian and Northern Development. 1974. *Interim Policy and Guidelines for Agriculture*. Ottawa: Government Publications

Duncan, Kate C. 1991. Beadwork on the Plateau. In *A Time of Gathering: Native Heritage in Washington State*. Edited by Robin K. Wright, 189-96. Seattle: University of Washington Press

Evans, Dr. Wayne. 1996. Interview by Phil Baird. Vermillion, SD, September

Ewers, John C. 1985. *The Horse in Blackfoot Indian Culture*. Washington: Smithsonian Institution Press and Bureau of American Ethnology

—. 1986. *Plains Indian Sculpture*. Washington: Smithsonian Institution Press

Farnum, Allen L. 1992. *Pawnee Bill's Historic Wild West, A Photo Documentary of the 1900-1905 Show Tours*. West Chester, PA: Schiffer

Fitzgerald, Shirley. 1992. Interview with Sydney City Historian by Leslie Tepper. Sydney, Australia, May

Fredericks, Pete. 1995. Interview by Phil Baird. Bismarck, ND, December

Fugleberg, Paul. 1991. *Buffalo Savers: The Story of the Allard-Pablo Bison Herd*. Polson, MT: Treasure State Publishing

Geist, Valerius. 1991. *Buffalo Nation*. Calgary: Fifth House

Gipp, Robert. 1996. Interview by Phil Baird. Fort Yates, ND, May

Goodstriker, Rufus. 1993. Interview by Morgan Baillargeon. February

Graham, William. 1991. *Treaty Days: Reflections of an Indian Commissioner*. Calgary: Glenbow Museum

Grandidier, C.J. 1875. Letter to the editor of the *Victoria Standard*, from Okanagan Mission, 28 August 1874. In *Papers Connected with the Indian Land Question, 1850-1875*, 145-8. Victoria, BC: Government Printing Office

Guichon, Lawrence P. 1959. Interview in *Free Press Weekly Prairie Farmer*, 18 February. Nicola Valley Archives Association, Merritt, BC

Haines, Francis. 1995. *The Buffalo: The Story of American Bison and Their Hunters from Prehistoric Times to the Present*. Norman: University of Oklahoma Press

Haines, Roberta. 1991. Eastern Washington Native peoples: A personal introduction. In *A Time of Gathering: Native Heritage in Washington State*. Edited by Robin K. Wright, 155-63. Seattle: University of Washington Press

Harris, Cole. 1997. *The Resettlement of British Columbia: Essays on Colonialism and Geographical Change*. Vancouver: UBC Press

Hise, Beth. 1991. *Report on Cape Mudge Collection in Australian Museum*. Ottawa: Canadian Museum of Civilization

Hunter, Annie (Pourier). 1996. Interview by Phil Baird. Kyle, SD, May

Indian Country Today. 1994. Indian Rodeo: Past, Present, and Future, special edition, January

Iverson, Peter. 1994. *When Indians Became Cowboys: Native Peoples and Cattle Ranching in the American West*. Norman: University of Oklahoma Press

—. 1995. The road to reappearance: Indian and cattle ranching in the American West. *Tribal College Journal of American Education* 7, 2: 23-6

Jackson, Dean. 1968. *The Western Horseman*. Indian Rodeo Association Colorado Springs, July

Joe, Mable. 1996. Dog travels to the sun. In *Our Tellings: Interior Salish Stories of the Nlha7kápmx People*. Edited by Darwin Hanna and Mamie Henry, 89-94. Vancouver: UBC Press

Kelly, L.V. 1980. *The Range Men*. Toronto: Coles

Kirk, Betty Jo. 1977. Interview by Phil Baird. Pierre, SD, July

Little Mustache, Butch. 1992. Interview by Morgan Baillargeon. Tsuu T'ina Reserve, Bragg Creek, AB, July

Knight, Rolf. 1996. *Indians at Work: An Informal History of Native Labour in British Columbia, 1848-1930*. Vancouver: New Star Books

Loeb, Barbara. 1991. Dress me in color: Transmontane beading. In *A Time of Gathering: Native Heritage in Washington State*. Edited by Robin K. Wright, 197-201. Seattle: University of Washington Press

Longbrake, Faye. 1996. Interview by Phil Baird. Dupree, SD, May

Louis, Garry. 1995, 1996. Interview by Morgan Baillargeon. Montana Reserve, Hobbema, AB

—. 1997. Interview by Morgan Baillargeon. Ottawa, ON, and Hobbema, AB

Louis, Ned. 1995. Interview by Leslie Tepper. Vernon, BC

MacEwan, Grant. 1995. *Buffalo: Sacred and Sacrificed*. Edmonton, AB: Alberta Sport, Recreation, Parks and Wildlife Foundation

McLaughlin, Charlotte. 1973. IAA Rodeo. *Standing Rock Star*. Fort Yates, Standing Rock Reservation, ND, July

Marriott, Alice, and Carol K. Rachlin. 1968. *American Indian Mythology*. New York and Scarborough: New American Library

Means, Warren. 1996. Interview by Phil Baird. Billings, MT, April

Medicine Shield, Joe. 1992. Interview by Morgan Baillargeon. Video recording. Calgary, July

Mellows, Carol Abernathy. 1990. The clash of cultures 1800-1858. In *Okanagon Sources*, edited by Jean Webber and the En'owkin Centre, 91-117. Penticton, BC: Theytus Books

Neihardt, John. 1972. *Black Elk Speaks*. 1932. Reprint, New York: Pocket Books

O'Reilly, P. 1875. Mr. O'Reilly to the Chief Commissioner of Lands and Works, Yale, 29th August 1868. In *Papers Connected with the Indian Land Question, 1850-1875*, 50-1. Victoria, BC: Government Printing Office

Parker, Patricia. 1990. *The Feather and the Drum: The History of Banff Indian Days 1889-1978*. Calgary: Consolidated Communications

Pickering, Robert B. 1997. *Seeing the White Buffalo*. Denver: Denver Museum of Natural History

Potts, Melvin. 1993, 1995. Interviews with Morgan Baillargeon. Montana Reserve, Hobbema, AB

Powell, J.W. 1873. Superintendent of Indian Affairs Report. 11 January. Typescript. Ottawa: Department of Indian and Northern Affairs

Provost, Pat. 1992. Interview by Morgan Baillargeon. Tsuu T'ina Reserve, Bragg Creek, AB, July

Ray, Verne F. 1978. *Cultural Relations in the Plateau of Northwestern America*. 1939. Reprint, New York: AMS Press

Roe, Frank Gilbert. 1951. *The Indian and the Horse*. Norman: University of Oklahoma Press

Rosa, Joseph G., and Robin May. 1989. *Buffalo Bill and His Wild West: A Pictorial Biography*. Lawrence: University of Kansas

Ross, Alexander. 1855. *The Fur Hunters of the Far West*. 2 vols. London: Smith Elder

Runnels, Jack. 1996. Interview by Phil Baird. Batesland, SD, April

Saddleman, George. 1996. Interview by Leslie Tepper. Quilchena, BC, August

St Leon, Mark. 1992. Interview by Leslie Tepper. Sydney, Australia, May

Sandoz, Mari. 1954. *The Buffalo Hunters*. New York: Hastings House

Sapp, Allen. 1986, 1994. Interviews by Bob Boyer. Regina, SK

—. 1989. Press release, Allen Sapp Gallery, North Battleford, SK

Schlick, Mary Dodds. 1994. *Columbia River Basketry: Gift of the Ancestors, Gift of the Earth*. Seattle: University of Washington Press

Sherwood, Robert, and Donna Sherwood. 1996. Interview by Phil Baird. Mobridge, SD, May

Signalness, Manfred. 1990. *Fifty Years in the Saddle. Vol. 3*. Watford City, ND: Fifty Years in the Saddle

Slatta, Richard W. 1990. *Cowboys of the Americas*. New Haven: Yale University Press

South Dakota. 1972. Secretary of State. Corporate Division office. Document. Pierre, SD, 1 December

—. 1974. Secretary of State. Corporate Division office. Document. Pierre, SD, 16 May

Spinks, Nathan. 1997. Interview by Leslie Tepper. Lytton, BC, September

Standing Alone, Peter. 1993. Interview by Morgan Baillargeon. February

Teit, James A. 1900. The Thompson Indians. *American Museum of Natural History Memoir* 2, 4: 163-390

—. 1912. Mythology of the Thompson Indians. *American Museum of Natural History Memoir* 8, 2: 203-416

—. 1917. Coyote and Deer. In *Folk-Tales of the Salishan and Sahaptin Tribes*. Edited by Franz Boas, 40-1, 82-3. New York: American Folklore Society

—. 1930. The Salishan Tribes of the Western Plateaus. *Forty-fifth Annual Report for Bureau of American Ethnology, 1927-1929*, 23-396. Washington: Bureau of American Ethnology

Tylor, Ron. 1976. *The Cowboy*. New York: A Ridge Press

Waln, Joe 'Bad.' 1996. Interview by Phil Baird. Parmelee, SD, March

Walton Ann T., John Ewers, and Royal B. Hassrick. 1985. *After the Buffalo Were Gone*. St Paul, MN: Northwest Area Foundation

Whitman, Carl. 1954. Ken Charging Rodeo. *Bar North*. Bismark, ND, July

WIREA. n.d. *What Is W.I.R.E.A.?* Kamloops: Western Indian Rodeo and Exhibition Association

Wissler, Clark, and D.C. Duvall. 1995. *Mythology of the Blackfoot Indians*. Lincoln: University of Nebraska Press

Witte, Randy. 1975. Howard Hunter, Indian Bronc Rider. *Rodeo Sports News*. Denver, CO

Yellowbird, Marvin. 1997. Interview by Morgan Baillargeon. Samson Reserve, Hobbema, AB, September

Yellow Face, Willard. 1993. Interview by Morgan Baillargeon. North Peigan Reserve, Brocket, AB, August

CREDITS

An honest attempt has been made to secure permission to reproduce all material used, and if there are errors or omissions these are wholly unintentional and the publisher will be grateful to learn of them.

Illustrations

Allen Sapp Gallery, North Battleford, SK: p. 117, from the collection of the Allen Sapp Gallery, City of North Battleford

BC Archives, Victoria, BC: p. 101 bottom, A005277; p. 102 top, H-07132; p. 104, B-05677; p. 175, G-04373; p. 177, F-03511

Buffalo Bill Historical Center, Cody, WY: p. 157, P.69.109, photograph by Elliott and Fry; p. 160, P.69.1014

Canadian Museum of Civilization, Hull, QC:
Photographs by Morgan Baillargeon: p. 39, neg. CMC S93-8592; p. 47, neg. CMC K97-1433; p. 94, neg. CMC 94-396; p. 95, neg. CMC K96-1347; p. 111 top, neg. CMC K94-1853; p. 111 bottom, neg. CMC K95-618; p. 145, neg. CMC 96-1057; p. 146, neg. CMC 93-1043; p. 150 bottom, neg. CMC K95-2118; p. 162, neg. CMC K96-952; p. 185 top, neg. CMC K95-1157; p. 185 bottom and detail p. 151, neg. CMC 97-353; p. 186, neg. CMC 96-1090; p. 197, neg. CMC K95-710; p. 199, neg. CMC 96-946; p. 202, neg. CMC K94-1718; p. 203 top, neg. CMC K94-1778; p. 203 bottom, neg. CMC K94-1671; p. 216, neg. CMC K96-1227; p. 224, neg. CMC S93-8478; p. 226 bottom, neg. CMC 96-700, 701, 703; p. 229 top, neg. CMC K96-2125; p. 231 bottom, neg. CMC 94-592; p. 233, neg. CMC 94-586; p. 236, neg. CMC 94-739; p. 241, neg. CMC K93-3896
Photograph by Steve Darby: p. 214 bottom, neg. CMC K97-345
Photographs by Harry Foster: p. 8, CMC II-B-14, neg. CMC S97-17812; p. 20, CMC V-B-436, neg. CMC S97-17828; p. 21, CMC II-C-918, neg. CMC S97-17808; p. 26, CMC V-E-281, neg. CMC S98-0001; p. 27, CMC II-C-182, neg. CMC S97-17814; p. 30, CMC II-A-45, neg. CMC S97-17818; p. 31, CMC II-A-3, neg. CMC S97-17819; p. 35 top, CMC V-E-321, neg. CMC S98-0002; p. 35 bottom, CMC V-X-76, CMC V-C-118, CMC V-L-15, CMC V-B-107, CMC V-C-108, CMC V-L-16, CMC V-D-106, CMC II-A-141, neg. CMC S97-17845; p. 38, CMC V-Z-8.1 and 2, CMC V-X-202 a,b, CMC V-X-131, CMC I-A-1, neg. CMC S97-17831; p. 42, CMC V-D-91 a,b, neg. CMC S97-17842; p. 43, CMC V-B-441, neg. CMC S97-17843; p. 46, CMC II-C-588, neg. CMC S94-36771; p. 50, CMC V-H-23, neg. CMC S98-0004; p. 54, CMC II-A-40, neg. CMC S97-17815; p. 56, CMC V-E-295, neg. CMC S98-0003; p. 60, CMC V-A-640, courtesy George Littlechild, neg. CMC S97-17856; p. 64, CMC V-B-333, neg. CMC S97-17844; p. 65, CMC II-C-916 and CMC II-C-917, neg. CMC S97-17823; p. 88, CMC II-C-910 and CMC II-C-901, neg. CMC S97-17806; p. 89, CMC V-E-353 a-b, neg. CMC S97-17846; p. 96, CMC II-C-581, neg. CMC S97-17810; p. 112, CMC II-B-65, neg. CMC S97-17807; p. 120, CMC V-E-454, neg. CMC S97-17840; p. 121, CMC II-C-899, neg. CMC S97-17809; p. 123, CMC V-E-434, neg. CMC S97-17834; p. 124, CMC II-C-908, neg. CMC S97-17816; p. 136, CMC V-A-641 a,b, neg. CMC S97-17825; p. 137, CMC V-Z-99, neg. CMC S97-17835; p. 140, CMC II-C-209, neg. CMC S97-17811; p. 141, CMC II-A-167, neg. CMC S97-17817; p. 143, CMC II-B-36, neg. CMC S97-17821; p. 144, CMC II-Z-1 a,b, neg. CMC S97-17838; p. 147, CMC V-E-431, 432, 435, 436.1,2, neg. CMC S97-17833; p. 148, CMC V-A-579, 578, 581, neg. CMC S97-17827; p. 149, CMC V-B-699, 700, 593, neg. CMC S97-17830; p. 150 top, CMC V-B-594, neg. CMC S97-18022; p. 155, Wood Mountain Museum 997.02.01, courtesy Travis Ogle, neg. CMC S97-17826; p. 158 top, CMC II-A-95, neg. CMC S97-17851; p. 158 bottom, CMC II-B-66, neg. CMC S97-17854; p. 159, CMC II-A-168, neg. CMC S97-17852; p. 166, CMC V-E-345, neg. CMC S97-17841; p. 171, CMC II-C-909, neg. CMC S97-17850; p. 193, courtesy of Thain White, Thain White Collection, neg. CMC S97-17849; p. 206, CMC II-X-21 and CMC V-X-394, neg. CMC S97-17820; p. 232, CMC V-B-597, 599, neg. CMC S97-17836
Photograph by Jim Goodstriker: p. 178 bottom, neg. CMC K97-546
Photograph by Elliot Tepper: p. 196, neg. CMC S97-17863
Photographs by Leslie Tepper: p. 109 top, neg. CMC K97-1640; p. 109 bottom, neg. CMC K97-1647; p. 113 bottom, neg. CMC K97-1654; p. 142, neg. CMC S97-17862; p. 178 top, neg. CMC K97-1835; p. 188 bottom, neg. CMC S97-17864; p. 189 top, neg. CMC K97-1856; p. 189 middle, neg. CMC K97-1890; p. 189 bottom, neg. CMC K97-1885; p. 230, neg. CMC K97-1826; p. 237 top, neg. CMC K97-1661

Mike Copeman, Fort Saskatchewan, AB: p. 225, #10-26; p. 228, #36-22a

Andrew Czink, New Westminster, BC: pp. 229 bottom, 240

Glenbow Archives, Calgary, Canada: p. 7, NA-239-20; p. 23 top, NA-395-8; p. 79, NA-659-11; p. 169, NA-274-2; p. 182, NA 16-421; p. 183, NA 3213-3, photograph A.P.K. Co.; p. 190, NA 689-1

Hardin Photo Service, Hardin, MT: p. 194, #138

Fred Kobsted Photography, Calgary, AB: p. 218, Fred Kobsted Photo, courtesy Joan Perry

George Littlechild, Vancouver, BC: pp. 34, 60, courtesy George Littlchild

Colin Low, Montreal, QC: p. 173, photograph by Colin Low

Midwest Jesuit Archives, St Louis, MO: p. 72, De Smetiana Collection, Jesuit Missouri Province Archives, St Louis, Missouri IX-C9-18; p. 76, IX-C9-59; p. 97, IX-C9-106

Milwaukee Public Museum, Milwaukee, WI: p. 29 and detail p. 17, no. 43757, photograph by Sumner W. Matteson Jr, SWM-1-F-600; p. 154, no. 43717, photograph by Sumner W. Matteson Jr

Stanley Munro and Nathan Spinks, Lytton, BC: p. 70. Courtesy of Stanley Munro and Nathan Spinks

National Archives of Canada, Ottawa, ON: p. 5, C-006288; p. 23 bottom, C-088931, photograph by charles Gentile; p. 68, C-012940; p. 85, PA-188556, photograph by Ronny Duke; p. 134, PA-186251, photograph by Gladys Thomas; p. 161, C-005810; p. 163, C-013040

Courtesy of the Nicola Tribal Association, Merritt, BC: p. 179, photograph by Troy Hunter

Courtesy of the Nicola Valley Museum Archives Association, Merritt, BC: p. 86 top, PR 96; p. 101 top, PN 129; p. 105 top, PR 205; p. 105 bottom, PR 204; p. 107 bottom, PR 244; p. 114 and detail p. 1, PN 80, photograph by H. Priest; p. 170, PE 1608

Courtesy of the Okanogan County Historical Society, Riverside, WA: p. 188 top, neg 265. Photographs by Frank Matsura: p. 86 bottom and detail p. 81; p. 99 and detail p. ii; p. 181 bottom; p. 226 top

O'Keefe Ranch and Interior Heritage Society, Vernon, BC: p. 33, F30-18; p. 83, F20-15; p. 102 bottom, F7-12; p. 107 top, F45-9

Courtesy of the Oklahoma Historical Society, Oklahoma City, OK: p. 167, no. 3901, photograph by H.J. Stevenson, El Reno, OT

Leanne J. Perrin, Ochapowace, SK: p. 231 top, photograph by Leanne J. Perrin

Provincial Archives of Alberta, Edmonton, AB: p. 84, PA 1433/3

Provincial Archives of Manitoba, Winnipeg, MB: p. 3, Edmund Morris 571 (N19180); p. 44, Edmund Morris 132 (N16269)

Royal British Columbia Museum, Victoria, BC: p. 24, PN 6708, photograph by J.A. Teit

Keith and Lorna Shuter, Merritt, BC: p. 113 top, photograph by Troy Hunter, courtesy of Keith and Lorna Shuter

Barb Stewart, Kamloops, BC: pp. 181 top, 198, 214 top, photographs by Barb Stewart; p. 237, middle and bottom, courtesy of Barb Stewart

Thain White Collection, Dayton, MT: pp. 192, 193, courtesy of Thain White, Thain White Collection

University of Oklahoma, Norman, OK: p. 153, Western History Collections, University of Oklahoma Libraries no. 1973, photograph by Walter S. Campbell

Wood Mountain Historical Society, Wood Mountain, SK: p. 127, #1253; p. 130, #249, used with permission

Wood Mountain Post Provincial Historic Park Collection: p. 128, WMP 79.7.1, courtesy of the estate of William Lethbridge

Texts

Parts of the introductory text to Ranching Life are from 'Native Cowboys on the Canadian Plains: A Photo Essay,' by Morgan Baillargeon. © 1995 by Agricultural History. Reprinted from *Agricultural History*, Vol. 69, No. 4, by permission.

The following people kindly gave permission for parts of their interviews to be produced here: Virginia Baptiste, Sarah Boensch, Mike Bruised Head, Todd Buffalo, Kim Colliflower, Loren Cuny, Clara Spotted Elk, Dennis Fraser, Troy Hunter, C.L. Johnson, Garry Louis, Jay Louis, Alvin (Dutch) Lunak, Joan Perry, Tyrone Potts, Brian Pratt, Victor H. Runnels, George Saddleman, Buffy Sainte-Marie, Muriel Saskamoose, Pamela Word, Winston Wuttunee, Carter Yellowbird.

The following sources kindly gave permission for their texts to be produced here:
'The First Horses,' *Medicine Boy and Other Cree Tales*, by Eleanor Brass. Calgary: Glenbow-Alberta Institute 1979. Reprinted with permission.
'Painted Pony' and 'on the champ of '63' by Garry Gottfriedson reproduced with the permission of the author.
'Âyahkwêw's Lodge' from *Native Canadiana* by Gregory Scofield published by Polestar Books Ltd., 1011 Commercial Drive, Vancouver, BC V5L 3X1
'Buffalo Woman Leads the Buffalo out of the Earth.' Copyright © 1954 by Mari Sandoz. Copyright renewed © 1982 by Caroline Pifer. Reprinted by permission of McIntosh and Otis, Inc.
'Coyote and Buffalo' from *Our Tellings: Interior Salish Stories of the Nlha7kápmx People*, compiled and edited by Darwin Hanna and Mamie Henry. © In trust, Snk'y'peplxw (Coyote House) Language and Culture Society and Mamie Henry. Vancouver: UBC Press 1996. Reprinted with permission from Herb Manuel.
'The End of the World: The Buffalo Go,' from *American Indian Mythology* by Alice Marriott and Carol K. Rachlin. Copyright © 1968 by Alice Marriott and Carol K. Rachlin. Reprinted by permission of HarperCollins Publishers Inc.
James A. Teit, 'The Deer.' From the Upper Thompson and Lytton, in *Folk-Tales of the Salishan and Sahaptin Tribes*, edited by Franz Boas. Reproduced by permission from American Folklore Society from *Memoirs of the American Folklore Society*, Volume XI, 1917. Not for further reproduction.
James A. Teit, 'Coyote and wood-tick.' AMNH Memoirs 8(2), The Jesup North Pacific Expedition, 1912, p. 211, 212. Courtesy of The American Museum of Natural History.
James A. Teit, 'Coyote.' From 'Old-One,' in *Folk-Tales of the Salishan and Sahaptin Tribes*, edited by Franz Boas. Reproduced by permission from American Folklore Society from *Memoirs of the American Folklore Society*, Volume XI, 1917. Not for further reproduction.
'Dog Chief,' from *Mythology of the Blackfoot Indians*, compiled and translated by Clark Wissler and D.C. Duvall, 1908. Lincoln: University of Nebraska Press 1995
'Man's Best Friend' and 'Remembering Heroes' by David Pratt produced with the permission of the author.

'Lonely Cowboy' and 'Tried, True, and Tested' by Tim Ryan
reproduced with the permission of the author. © Mission
Valley Music 1994, Preshus Child Music 1994

'Allen Sapp' by Bob Boyer produced with the permission of the
author.

'At Wood Mountain We Are Still Lakota' is produced with the
permission of the Lakota Project Committee, Wood
Mountain Historical Society. Information contained therein
was taken from interviews with elders Elizabeth Ogle and
William Lethbridge and other members of the Lakota community presently living at Wood Mountain. Historical information was collected from the National Archives of Canada,
Record Group 10 and Record Group 18 as well as the
Saskatchewan Archives and the Moose Jaw Library Archives.

James A. Teit, 'The gambler and star man.' AMNH Memoirs
2(7), The Jesup North Pacific Expedition, 1912, pp. 726-727.
Courtesy of The American Museum of Natural History.

'The Menace of the Wild West Show,' speech was delivered by
Chauncey Yellow Robe, of Rapid City, S. Dakota at the fourth
annual conference of the Society of American Indians, held at
Madison, WI, 6-11 October 1914. As recorded in Arthur
Parker, ed. *Quarterly Journal of the Society of American Indians* 2, 3
(1914): 224-5

'Indian Rodeo Cowboys of the Dakotas' by Phil Baird produced
with the permission of the author. Some of the individuals
and events described are based on oral history kindly shared
by different people. This article is a humble attempt at capturing some of this history before it is lost. Because of space
limitations, not all Indian rodeo cowboys and cowgirls could
be mentioned. No one individual, organization, or Indian
reservation was intentionally omitted.

'He's an Indian Cowboy in the Rodeo,' copyright Buffy Sainte-
Marie, Gypsy Boy Music. Used by permission

INDEX